Paths to
Educational Reform

Paths to Educational Reform

Wm. Clark Trow

Professor Emeritus — Education and Psychology
University of Michigan

●

EDUCATIONAL TECHNOLOGY PUBLICATIONS
ENGLEWOOD CLIFFS, NEW JERSEY 07632

Printed in the United States of America.

Library of Congress Catalog Card Number: 71-122810.

International Standard Book Number: 0-87778-002-1.

First Printing.

Foreword

Educational reform is a vital topic of current and widespread interest. The subject is of increasing concern as students, teachers, parents and taxpayers question educational processes and results.

American society has changed dramatically even within the past decade. Our pattern of education, which is based primarily upon an agrarian way of life, no longer serves the purposes and problems of our society. Since over 70 percent of our population live in cities, the problems of the megalopolis and the correspondingly large schools and school districts are of crucial significance.

Today's school calendar, developed in an agrarian culture, allows for an extended seasonal vacation at planting and harvest time when children were needed on the farm. Today's short school day and the beginning of public schooling at age five reflect the life in which mothers stayed home and had not joined the labor force.

Technology has made possible unimaginable frontiers of change in our society. It has revolutionized the American working life, and education must reflect the influence of technology in this area. Today many people are employed in jobs that did not exist ten years ago. The process of skill obsolescence increases at a frightening pace. It is estimated that three-quarters of the jobs which will exist in the year 2000 do not exist today. Thus, educators must teach today's generation of students to be adaptable. Adult education must continue to be part of this effort. Gone are the days when the 3 R's fully prepared a student to meet the challenge of his environment.

Through the mass media, technology has also increased our awareness which, in turn, has changed the quality of American life. The complexities of this modern age demand more and more education for succeeding generations, and the challenges which face the institutions which prepare teachers. There seems to be no single pattern by which every undergraduate can become a skilled and motivated teacher. It is not achieved solely by a required number of specific university credits, or by specific university courses, or by possession of a teacher's certificate. All these requirements and credentials are only a temporary passport enabling a prospective teacher to be welcomed into the complex and changing world of the classroom.

Professor Trow has contributed a life-long study of educational reform in the present volume. He discusses its many different facets. He shows how simple and yet how complex the problem of educational reform is in a dynamic society.

I like Professor Trow's formulation of the central problem we face. In the beginning of Chapter 8, dealing with "Assumptions Are Not Axioms," he states:

> We still try to fit pupils into the school instead of adapting the school to the needs of the pupils. And this is quite contrary to the most basic of educational principles—to teach pupils where they are in their development.

Professor Trow is critical of credits, accreditation and certification. In Chapter 14, "The Credentials Mill in a Technological Age," he summarizes his view:

> In the case of educational accreditation, the basis for such belief and trust is often unsound, and the trust is misplaced, otherwise there would not be so many incompetent teachers. Furthermore, there is rarely any evidence that the work required to obtain such credentials will increase an individual's competence. In short, it is a patchwork, mechanical system that has expanded over the years for administrative purposes and has been applied wholesale with little or no regard for the individuals most concerned, the student, the prospective employer and the children to be taught.

There are a number of other comments and suggestions which should be useful to those who are interested in changes in education.

Professor Trow is critical of the "chopped-up instructional program" which he says "needs to be overhauled." He observes that "It is an impressive monument to administrative convenience."

The chapters dealing with Technology and Educational Reform are especially pertinent to current problems. The recent report of the Commission on Instructional Technology (March, 1970) which I appointed in April, 1968 can well be read in conjunction with Professor Trow's chapters, which were written before the Commission's Report was published.

The problems involved in educational reform are difficult and pervasive, and their solutions are urgent. Professor Trow's insights and comments should be helpful in the continuing struggle to make educational processes and practices more relevant to the needs of a rapidly changing society.

Wilbur J. Cohen, Dean
School of Education
The University of Michigan
Secretary of
Health, Education, and Welfare, 1968

Preface

The story is told of a motorist driving to Bangor, Maine, who was disturbed at finding a signpost with the inscription "To Bangor" pointing in the direction from which he had just come. He inquired about it from a farmer who happened to be working in a near-by field.

"Oh yes," the farmer said. "The fellow who put up that sign found a rock ledge on the right-hand side of the road and couldn't set the post in it. So he put the sign on the other side of the road."

"But doesn't it confuse people," the traveler inquired, "when they see the sign pointing in the wrong direction?"

"No, I reckon not," said the farmer. "You see, everybody knows where Bangor is."

Similarly, it would seem that everybody knows the path that leads to the needed reforms in education. But, in this case, unfortunately, there are many different paths—leading in different directions. An advocate for any one of them, whether student, professor, board member, parent or taxpayer, may seem stupid, obtuse, or downright malevolent to some of the others. He may be none of these, however, only ignorant. Though he may be well-informed in some branches of knowledge, and conscientious in his desire to do good, he is still likely to be ignorant of the educational past, and of the possibly justifiable claims of those who recommend other paths.

Education is seemingly unique in that, unlike other areas of knowledge, it is not taught in schools and colleges except to those who wish to embark on it as a career. The student and future citizen may learn about government, business, science, art, music, and even religion. But unless he specializes in education, all he will know about it will be what he found out by being subjected to it. His experience is "from the under side," like that of Don Marquis's famous typing cockroach. This is enough to enable him to agree with the experts that something should be done, but not enough to decide what. He has little or no idea of the complexity of the educational process or of the diversity of needs to be satisfied, or of the possible choices of content and method. Even the professionals are not in agreement either on basic philosophy or on technical details, swayed as they often are by very human and often conflicting interests.

I have had occasion for a good many years to observe what has been going on, and more recently have been concerned about the effectiveness of many traditional procedures, and also about the narrowness of the views of some who advocate change. I have therefore sought to clarify the situation somewhat in articles written during the decade of the sixties, some of which have appeared in professional journals. These, together with a half dozen or so others, I have brought together in this volume.

My aim has been not only to advocate what seem to me to be essential educational reforms, but also to paint in a little of the background so that these recommendations, and others as well, may be seen in proper perspective. Many of the problems are complex, and several of the solutions recommended, while not new as recommendations, would produce startling changes if introduced into the programs of most schools.

The findings of educational research, the manufacture of teaching machines, and the designs of technologists can be of value only as they are reflected in educational practice. And this will occur only as the general public recognizes the need for them. Education takes place not among theorists or inventors, but in the interaction of students with teachers and teaching materials; and its possibilities can be realized only when they and the members of school boards, parents, and other informed citizens join with professional people in creating a demand. This they are not likely to do unless they also realize how inadequate many educational practices are, and unless they find out what can be done to improve them.

Information about educational matters is now receiving more attention than ever before, but the coverage is spotty. Dramatic events such as protest marches, sit-ins, confrontations and teacher strikes, as well as expensive crash programs, make the headlines, whereas some of the customary procedures that people take for granted are what need attention; it is at these points, more often than not, that reforms must come.

Both the conditions and the recommended changes the reader will find repeated like the musical themes of a symphony or opera. He may even feel that the writer is less like a composer than he is like a fundamentalist preacher repeatedly urging the desirability of personal salvation. True, many of our schools are not as bad as they might be, just as many sinners are not without hope. But we are all too content with mediocrity, with the second or third best, or worse. We must learn to recognize the shortcomings and some of the possibilities, and act accordingly. We owe it to ourselves and to the children and young people in our schools and colleges.

Wm. Clark Trow

Acknowledgements

I am indebted to the editors of the following journals for permission to reprint in whole or in part the portions of this volume which have appeared in their pages:

The School Review, The University of Michigan School of Education Bulletin, Psychology in the Schools, The Kappa Delta Pi Record, Occasional Papers of the Oakland Schools, Pontiac, Michigan, *The Journal of Teacher Education, Educational Leadership, The High School Journal, The Educational Record, The Phi Delta Kappan, Educational Technology,* and *The Journal of School Psychology.*

By the Same Author

The Psychology of Confidence, 1923.

Scientific Method in Education, 1925.

The Religious Development of Adolescence (Translation from the German of Oskar Kupky), 1928.

Educational Psychology, 1931. Revised edition, 1950.

Character Education in Soviet Russia (Ed. Translation by Paul D. Kalachov from Russian writers), 1934.

Introduction to Educational Psychology, 1937.

The Junior Citizen Series (with others, six pamphlets), 1940. Revised edition, 1951.

Human Values in Elementary School (with Warren A. Ketcham), 1952.

The Learning Process, 1954.

Psychology in Teaching and Learning, 1960.

Teacher and Technology—New Designs for Learning, 1963.

Contents

Part IV
Toward an Educational Technology

Part V
Technology and Educational Reform

Paths to
Educational Reform

Part I
Education or Catastrophe

1. EDUCATIONAL CRITICS—PRO AND CON
   People have long been critical of educational methods and curricula.

2. PATHS PREVIOUSLY TAKEN
   If the race for survival is to be won, criticism must be informed concerning earlier institutions and practices that influence education today.

3. TEACHING THE THREE R'S
   Those who advocate reforms will want to know about some of the current purposes and practices in teaching the familiar school subjects.

4. HOW SHALL WE TEACH ETHICS?
   They will also want to know about the broader objectives of desirable social behavior.

5. CONFLICTS AND VALUES
   And it will also be important to know about the divergent life values and ways of reconciling them.

1.
Educational Critics – Pro and Con

The American people believe in education. In the United States of America, more children and young people are getting more education than anywhere else in the world, and more than at any time in history.

VOTE OF CONFIDENCE

The strong vote of confidence of the American people in their schools is strengthened by the fact that it comes from all groups and classes. Teachers and administrators gather in local, state and national conferences and conventions to discuss their problems and work out ways of meeting them more effectively. Boards of education devote long hours to the labor of keeping the schools running and making them something of which the communities can be proud. Research workers conduct thousands of studies to find out specifically how learning takes place in an educational setting. Scientists help to adapt school programs to the new knowledge that is rapidly accumulating. Farmers vote for the consolidation of school districts in order to provide educational opportunity for their children equal to that in the suburbs. Labor organizations have a long history of vigorous support of educational programs for all the children. Businessmen and industrialists look to the schools as the source of supply for the employees they need. And industries not only pay out large tax sums, but also provide fellowships for technical training, while legislatures vote heavy appropriations, and private donors contribute generously to educational institutions.

SOME VOTE NO

Schools are institutions, and institutions are made up of people. People being what they are, it could hardly be expected that the vote of confidence would be unanimous. The most critical are the educators themselves. They know about many of the weaknesses of our educational system; they have been trained to deal with them, and they devote their professional lives to the task.

Representatives of a number of lay groups have been quite vocal in their criticisms, among them the "taxpayers." We are all taxpayers, but here I refer to the individuals and organizations that are congenitally opposed to all taxes, particularly those that affect *them.* While they perform a useful service, they are likely to be short-sighted, preferring a cheap building now to reduced upkeep later, and crying out not only against building "educational palaces," but also against supporting school services aimed at furthering differing educational objectives.

There are also a few college professors among the critics—sometimes referring to themselves as scholars and scientists. Since a college professor has been defined as "a man who thinks otherwise," it is perhaps surprising that their opposition vote is not larger than it is. For the most part, the objectors decry what they refer to as the anti-intellectualism of the schools, by which they usually mean that their specialization, be it in the sciences or the humanities, in their opinion, is not given the attention it should have.

Some religious leaders likewise find themselves among the dissidents, either with the epithet "Godless schools" on their lips, or the argument that little or no attention is paid to moral and spiritual values.

A few journalists are also to be found on the roster, some with signed articles, some anonymously revealing the slant of their editors or owners in the selection of news stories, as well as in what is actually written. But all prefer to report dramatic incidents, knowing that many of their prospective readers are more interested in a strike or a riot than in proposed reforms. The education writers tend to become political reporters; City Hall, not the Board of Education, becomes their "beat" to cover.

WHAT HAS BEEN GOING ON?

Be it said to their credit, some critics are aware of what has been going on during the last half century or so; the industrialization, the destruction of European imperialism, the Russian and Chinese revolutions, two world wars, a depression, military intervention in South Asia, a changed concept of federal government, instantaneous aural and visual communication and near instantaneous transportation, the smashing of the atom, and the beginning of the exploration of outer space. This is surely no time for ignorance, no time for nostalgic sentimentality, and certainly no time for false leadership.

One group of critics that lives in the present and looks to the future is nevertheless the sorriest of all. It includes a small number of brilliant men who hold prestigious positions in other fields, but whose appraisals of education have been as ill-informed and seemingly as ill-intentioned as those of the lesser gentry.

THE MESSAGE OF THE LAY CRITICS

What are we told by this rather odd assortment of men (and a few women) who take pen in hand to excoriate American education, whatever their motives may be? We are told that this enterprise to which so many are devoting their lives, and which is supported by such an overwhelming vote of confidence by the American people, is about as effective as a blown fuse. We are told that we are squandering our money on useless gadgetry and wasting the pupils' time on silly games. A few paranoid individuals assert that the management of education is in the hands of a gigantic conspiracy of power-hungry vested interests, and it is high time the scholars and scientists seized control. We are told that morons are graduating from high school instead of being put to work, and students at each level of schooling have learned practically nothing at the level below.

THE GOOD OLD DAYS

Nearly all the lay critics of education have one peculiarity. They look backward. They point, somewhat vaguely, to a time of enlightenment before the degenerate days set in, a time when education was more like what they think it ought to be now. The time varies with the speaker. Some locate it in the classical period, but it could not have been in ancient Greece, for Plato and Aristotle, Pericles and Sophocles never got as far as trigonometry, had few great books to read, and spoke and wrote the vernacular without any study of Latin to train their minds. Others seem to place it during the Middle Ages or the Renaissance, when some had this latter advantage, but not many. The Victorians among them are partial to the nineteenth century, when Britannia ruled the waves, and English schoolboys wrote Latin verses to prepare for the responsibilities of imperialism.

But most of the lay critics are a bit hazy about the more distant past. They turn the calendar back to the "little red schoolhouse," the shrine of the "three R's," the intellectual cradle of those who made America great. Or they settle for a date close to their own school days, which they nostalgically recall.

THE PAY-OFF

As a consequence, what happens? Parents wonder whether their children are being adequately prepared for college or for the hazards of the competitive world. Taxpayers doubt if they are getting their money's worth. "Disgruntled Parent" and "Taxpayer" write letters to the editor of the local paper. The bond issue is coming up for vote, absolutely essential for the needed renovation in plant and program, to say nothing of additional staff members to take care of the increase in the numbers of pupils and educational innovations and reforms. But people are doubtful. Where there's smoke, there must be some fire. School officials drop their regular duties and enlist the support of influential lay groups. Tempers rise; battle lines are drawn; the school fight is on. Perhaps the superintendent will stay, and perhaps not. But the bond issue is out the window. And the lay critics can feel well pleased. They have aired their prejudices, helped maintain the circulation of some magazine or other, and aroused public interest in education. Why should they worry if what they have written is a tissue of lies and half-truths? Why should they bother about reading up on education, doing their own homework? But the rest of us can well do so, if only to avoid being taken in by the biased distortions of those who write only to misinform.

People in a democracy have a right to know about their schools and to criticize them if they want to. Furthermore, schools and other institutions are all the better, due to intelligent interest and criticism. But criticism that springs from ignorance or that artfully conceals facts is not only wasteful but positively injurious to the best interests of the children and of the wider community.

PATENT MEDICINE OR PRESCRIPTION

The well-intentioned but uninformed critic is apt to see only the symptoms, and conclude that the patient is in terrible shape. But the matters that really need attention, the causes, are not so obvious; and they are usually not to be cured with the bottle of tonic he has for sale, whether it be more grammar, more Latin, more religion, more "great books," or less football, less home and family living, less vocational work, or less John Dewey.

One cannot demonstrate the falsity of his diagnosis or the ineffectiveness of his remedy in a few well-turned phrases. The matter is too complex. Meanwhile his medicineman sales talk sounds so plausible that the hearers step right up and buy their bottles. The cure is often worse than the disease.

A little more knowledge is a helpful thing, but it is often hard to come by. Information about education is to be found in many volumes—textbooks, monographs, yearbooks, reports, manuals, journals, and other documents. But most of this is specialized knowledge. Moreover, it is written for professional people, and so presupposes a professional background on the part of the reader. The intelligent layman scarcely knows where to turn to obtain any clear idea of what the schools are doing, or why they are doing it, or what their real problems are.

The need for more knowledge about educational matters is everywhere evident. An intelligent grocer of my acquaintance noted that in a film he saw, taken at Moscow University, the students stood when the professor entered the lecture hall. He felt that American students could well show similar respect to their professors, which in itself was gratifying. But he did not know that this is traditional European procedure, and actually revealed about as much *real* respect as an army salute!

Another example: one magazine article described in glowing terms the excellence of the Boston Latin Grammar School, but made little mention of the important fact that it can *select* its students, which the regular public high school cannot do. And it quoted the head of the school in such a way as to make it appear that it took inspiration from an early alumnus, Benjamin Franklin. Those familiar with Franklin's autobiography know that he attended the Boston Latin Grammar School for one year only, when he was eight years old, and during the year he was promoted three times. Few would insist that these fumbling efforts at placement account for Franklin's genius, or that the eight-year-old Franklin succeeded during this one year in leaving his stamp on the policies of the school with such clarity that it lasted down to the present day. In fact, as educators know, in his mature years he did much to get a quite different type of school started.

COMPLEXITIES AND DIFFERENCES

What even the well-intentioned lay critics do not fully realize is the enormous complexity of the American educational system. They sometimes speak of "the other side" of a question as if it were a coin with but two sides. Instead, it is more like a polyhedron. Innumerable factors affect the answer to the basic question: What is best for the children? And then we must go further and ask "which children?" for there are wide differences among them, and what is good for some may not be good for others.

We are committed to the policy of universal, free, compulsory education for all. This includes not only the academically talented, but also the mentally retarded who are trainable, the disadvantaged, and those with physical and emotional handicaps, the disturbed and the delinquent.

And what shall they be taught? It is easy to say that the purpose of education is to transmit the cultural heritage, and this is true in part. But a glance at the row of volumes of an encyclopedia is enough to make us realize that all of this heritage cannot be transmitted to everybody. Selections must be made, and what is selected must be adapted to differing ages and abilities.

CURRICULUM AND OBJECTIVES

In the elementary school, most attention is given to the tools of learning, the verbal and numerical symbols used in the transmission of the cultural heritage, with a gradual broadening out in the high school to include the knowledge of the world and of man, classified for convenience into different subjects with their related concepts and means of inquiry.

But people must not only know, they must also think and do, and what they think and do must somehow contribute positively to their own well-being and to that of the society in which they live; otherwise the taxes of the state would be used for its downfall. Western culture has within it the seeds of its own destruction, not the hydrogen bomb alone, but its reliance on force, its gangster ethics, and the moral degeneracy that have wrecked more than one proud nation. There are many elements in our culture that should not be transmitted to future generations, and the school is one of the agencies of society set up to combat them.

The democratic ideal is an unstable equilibrium of individual initiative and creativity, of competition and aggression, and of cooperation and rationality. How will young people learn to make sensible decisions, to exert wise leadership, and to make intelligent choices among values, and so maintain the equilibrium?

From this wider point of view, the curriculum becomes more than subjects or disciplines, important as these are. And progress toward the goals sought must be assessed so that we may know whether or not what we are doing is leading toward our objectives. New measurement devices are being created for this purpose, and it may well be that the traditional report card will eventually become as extinct as the slate and the quill pen.

METHOD AND ORGANIZATION

The cultural heritage may be symbolically recorded in a shelf of encyclopedias or great books, of scientific reports and mathematical formulas, but it cannot be transmitted in this form. It must pass through the living tissues of human beings, be re-enacted in their behavior through their nerves and muscles, and be reflected in their attitudes and emotions. Children in school are not rows of brains into which learning is to be injected with a hypodermic needle. They bring their bodies with them. They are people, with varying abilities, interests, aptitudes and needs. If they are to be taught to think and do what is needful, the methods of teaching are important. Some methods are effective, and some are not only ineffective, but harmful. Teachers, too, are people, with varying degrees of skill, but their skill can be improved. They must be trained not only in the knowledge and skills their pupils will be expected to acquire (the task of the liberal arts colleges) but also in the ways of learning and teaching, the function of departments and schools of education, which also have the task of preparing supervisors, administrators and other educational workers.

The success that accrues is closely related to the larger organization for which the citizens of the community and state are responsible, the facilities they provide, the salaries they pay, their choice of board of education members, and the general support they give to the whole educational enterprise.

THE SCHOOL'S RESPONSIBILITY

Those in charge of the schools of America have undertaken a tremendous responsibility, perhaps more than they should have undertaken. But it has literally been thrust upon them. It is nothing less than to help each child and youth in the land *to become all that he is capable of becoming.* The people who are responsible for this work must have faith, not only in education, but also faith in the children and youth who crowd into their classrooms, and faith that the American people will not let the students down. And we cannot afford to let these young people down, for they are ourselves to be. They will run our machines, occupy our offices and laboratories, sit at our desks, and stand at our benches, our counters and our lecterns. They will be America tomorrow and in the years to come.

These years will be different from the years we have known. We do not yet comprehend the explosive changes that have occurred during the last half century, not in America alone, but in the rest of the world as well. And man-machine systems, cybernetics and atomic power are still in their infancy. Education must somehow keep pace with the changes. We cannot afford to let ignorance or nostalgic sentiments throw us back educationally to the nineteenth century. On the other hand, we cannot afford indiscriminately to take on everything that is new merely because it is new. To plan for the well-being of our children and our children's children, the intelligent cooperation of educational and of well-informed lay groups is essential. The school, perhaps more than any other institution, is the crystallization of the thought and ideals of an age. It is the agency which enables the individual to take his place with others as a participating member of the society in which he lives. It is the chief instrumentality by means of which a culture remains alive and able to adapt itself to the needs of the future.

American ideas and ideals, as they are embodied in the schools and other institutions, have many sources. Some are derived from a European heritage, while others seem to be indigenous to our soil, the product of the American frontier. Many have been filtered through the research laboratories, where much sludge has been thrown out, though much still remains. But the story should be told as of today. Those who know the story will not be misled by uninformed critics or crackpots masquerading in authoritative garb. They will be able to evaluate the criticism, as well as its source. They can formulate their own educational ideas, participate in educational councils, understand educational needs, and criticize and suggest in ways that will be a help and not a hindrance to better learning, better teaching, and new and better schools, for the new world that is now in the making.

2.
Paths Previously Taken

Families were the first teachers. They still are, and will continue to be in the foreseeable future, in spite of the efforts of various communal enterprises to take over. In the family, from mother, father, brothers, sisters, from the earliest days, children have learned the accepted ways of eating, drinking and eliminating body wastes. They have learned to play games and get around, and they have learned to talk and to understand the talk of others. In primitive tribes the boys learned to hunt and fish; among pastoral peoples they learned to take care of sheep and goats, camels, cows or horses. In agricultural regions they learned to plow, plant and harvest; and in commercial cultures they learned a trade. The girls learned how to get their men and how to take care of the cave, the hut, the cabin, the house and the small children. All this learning was very practical and was a home industry.

The tribal magic, traditions and ceremonies were taught by the elders, or by a priesthood, if there was any, often in connection with the pubertal rites which betokened coming of age. Where a written language developed, the priests were sometimes the ones who taught its mysteries, as in Egypt, Palestine, and in medieval Europe. In other countries, as in ancient China, Greece and Rome, secular teachers were employed, and the priests (and priestesses) gave their time to their oracles or auguries, or other ceremonial activities, or to the training of neophytes for their priestly duties. Retired military men were called upon to induct the young bloods into the art of war, whether it involved the use of spears and swords, bows and arrows, chariots, or elephants.

CURRICULUM DIFFERED

In any case, learning was different in different cultures, and it still is. Early education in China required the young to memorize the Chinese literary classics, whereas the recent emphasis has been on Mao's dogma. The ancient Persians, according to Herodotus, taught their young men to ride, to draw the bow, and to speak the truth, whereas modern Persians emphasize, among other things, memorizing the Koran in the original Arabic. The classical Greek curriculum consisted of music, poetry and athletic sports, a curriculum which modern classicists would probably deplore as being anti-intellectual. However, Hellenic literature and scholarship taught the Romans and the Arabs, and through its revival centuries later, the Europeans and colonial Americans. Medieval European learning, beginning in about the fifth century, consisted of instruction in the seven liberal arts—grammar, rhetoric and dialectic (or logic), called the *trivium*, and arithmetic, geometry, music and astronomy, the *quadrivium.*

The scholars of the medieval period of Western civilization were fortunate in one respect at least. Though their library resources were meager, largely limited to theological works, they all used the same language, Latin. So from whatever part of Europe a student came, he could understand the language of the university he attended. But gradually the Roman tongue was corrupted by the local dialects and became the Romance languages in the south—Italian, Spanish, French, Portuguese and Rumanian—while to the north, it was supplemented by Germanic and other sources to produce English. From the resulting European polyglot, national languages and literatures developed in which, especially after the invention of printing from the movable type by Gutenberg in the fifteenth century, books became available, both scholarly and otherwise. So the need for a knowledge of Latin in order to have anything to read gradually disappeared.

The Renaissance brought the wealth of long-buried Greek literature and scholarship to light, which stimulated a renewed interest in the classical heritage; and the new learning found a place in the schools and colleges. This was followed somewhat later by the scientific and technological developments that were rapidly changing the world. And still later, the social or behavioral sciences made their demands on the curriculum.

If any conclusion can be drawn from history, it is that the youth in any human society are taught what is considered important and necessary for survival in *that* society. Of the many other things that were formerly important and necessary, but have outlived their usefulness, some have been dropped, but others continue to be taught. The tendency for vestigial forms to remain in the curriculum has perhaps nowhere been so delightfully caricatured as by the late Harold Benjamin in his story of The Saber-Tooth Curriculum, in which the primitive art of fish-grabbing was abandoned elsewhere in favor of nets and fishhooks.

IN AMERICA, CHILDREN ALSO LEARNED

The instruction of the American frontier followed the early family pattern. The children learned at home to plant and harvest, cook and sew, buy and sell, to plan and execute, and to work together for common ends. Schoolmasters, and a few school mistresses, taught the written language.

When they left school, some of the boys were apprenticed to master workmen to learn a trade. Others hired out to storekeepers and went into business for themselves, or worked in a lawyer's office, or in that of the local doctor, and accompanied him on his rounds. If a boy was intellectually ambitious, and his parents had enough money, he might go to a private Latin grammar school, where he could start learning the languages of ancient Greece and Rome. The literature of the ancient Hebrews he was taught in translation at home and at the local church.

The rural district school, in its day, was a noteworthy contribution to the American scene. Largely through the efforts of the sturdy men and women who established it, this country, unlike many in South America, Eastern Europe, Asia and Africa, had no plague of illiteracy to be stamped out. True, the successive demands for cheap labor brought millions of illiterates to our shores; but their children received better educational treatment than they had been able to obtain back home. But today, the one-room "little red schoolhouse," even with a coat of different-colored paint, is an anachronism, with its poorly-prepared teachers and meager intellectual fare.

THE GOOD OLD DAYS

And yet some people look back to it, often with nostalgic longing. The old-timer, who may even have attended one, gazing through a rose-colored haze, no longer sees the harsh outlines of things as they were. The sharp edges of his childhood experiences are forgotten, for they were but the tools or the lathe that turned out a rugged but estimable character. The treatment he received made him what he is today, and he is satisfied. He is like the old deacon who objected to the preacher's reading from a revised version of the Bible: "The St. James version was good enough for St. Paul," he said, "and it is good enough for me!" He feels that others should have the experiences he has had; and his solution for the world's ills is to go back to the good old days—if not to the little red schoolhouse, at least to the days when he was a boy.

To the old-timers in our midst, with their nostalgic recollections of the past, to which they think we should return, we can properly answer that the world does not move backwards. Even though there were many pleasant things about the life of a generation ago, we cannot recapture them. We cannot return to the past if we would, and we would not if we could.

A little more than a half century ago, we had finished a "war to end all wars," one that was to "make the world safe for democracy." Japan was beginning to gather "the world under one umbrella," and India was still the brightest jewel in the British crown. The Russian Revolution had begun, and "the ten days that shook the world" had given this country its first bad attack of Communist jitters. We were all set to return to "normalcy," but were actually headed for the greatest depression in our history. We listened to radio programs through cystal-set earphones, and silent movies were running vaudeville out of business. Airplanes were one-man crates, and the "struggle buggy" had already begun to make the isolation of rural America a thing of the past.

The world hasn't stood still during the last half century, and neither have the schools. A generation ago, most school buildings were fire traps (many are still in use), with narrow stairways and corridors, poor lighting, often poorly ventilated and unsanitary. Many of the teachers had not progressed beyond high school, punitive "discipline" was the chief means of control, and the curriculum encouraged the great majority of the pupils to leave school even before they finished the elementary grades.

EARLY SCHOOLS WERE FOR THE FEW

The world has changed tremendously, even in the memory of those now living; and changes are still going on. But we do not have to depend on our memories for past events. Our recollections may be far from typical, and they do not give us the depth of perspective that a little knowledge of history provides. What was American education like, not a generation ago, but a century, even two centuries ago? What is the tradition that still holds back educational reform?

The early American schools were copied from European models. In Europe, education followed an aristocratic plan. Children of upper-class families—the nobility and the wealthy—went to one set of schools that led to the university. Lower-class children, from poor families, if they got any education at all, went to a different set of schools that stopped at the end of four or five years; and then they were apprenticed to learn a trade, or went into some kind of unskilled labor, worked on the family acres, or on the estate of some nobleman, joined the army, or went to sea. Teachers of these children attended special training schools that did not lead to the university at all.

In colonial America only a very few young men, and no women, went to college. A diary entry of a Harvard student, however, shows that boys were boys even in the year 1758:

> Came to college, began Logick,
> Fit with sophomores,
> Mowed President's grass,
> Did not go to prayers,
> President sick, wherefore much deviltry carried
> on in college.[1]

President Dunster had made the infant Harvard College as close a copy as he could of his alma mater, Magdelen College, Oxford. This sophomore-fighting grass-mower and his classmates, to be admitted, had to "understand Tully (Cicero) or such like classicall Latine Author extempore, and make and speake true Latine in Verse and Prose . . . ;

and decline perfectly the Paradigims of Nounes and Verbes in the Greek tongue."[2] To be admitted to Yale in 1745, a student must "be found able Extempore to Read, Construe, and Parce Tully, Vergil, and the Greek Testament, and to write True Latin in Prose and to understand the Rules of Prosodia, and Common Arithmetic, . . . "[3] After the student was admitted, he continued with the study of Latin, Greek, Hebrew, the Bible, ethics, logic, rhetoric, composition, a little mathematics and history. The pattern of the English-type college, derived from the 15th century *trivium* and *quadrivium* (with music and astronomy forgotten), not only provided the traditional education of the privileged classes, but also became the model for democratic America.

Thanks to our imported aristocratic school system, the majority of children had no chance to progress beyond the very meager offerings of local "dame schools," or the "reading and writing schools." Thomas Jefferson thought something should be done about this situation. So in 1799 he introduced a plan for the State of Virginia that would permit a few poor children to go to college. In his day, such a plan was quite radical. In fact, it was not approved:

" . . . A visitor is annually to chuse the boy, the best genius in the school, of those whose parents are too poor to give them further education, and to send him forward to one of the (proposed twenty) grammar schools . . . for teaching Greek, Latin, geography, and the higher branches of numerical arithmetic . . . By this means twenty of the best geniuses will be raked from the rubbish annually, and be instructed, at public expense, so far as the grammar schools go. At the end of six years' instruction . . . one half . . . are to be sent and continued three years . . . at William and Mary college."[4]

With its reference to the rest of the children as "rubbish," the quotation shows the force of the aristocratic tradition, even in the mind of Jefferson. And, of the subjects mentioned, Greek has now fallen by the wayside, geography and arithmetic continue, and Latin still has status appeal, associated as it is with the aristocratic tradition.

WHEN WE WERE COLONIES

But the process of change was a slow one, and many different kinds of schools came and went. In general, these were the choices, though they were not always available:

Colonial Period 1650 - 1800
A Selective Class School System

Elementary
>   tutors, for the well-to-do
>   apprenticeship, for those in meager circumstances
>   charity or pauper schools, for the poor
>   school of the 3 R's, gradually took shape, combining
>   > the dame school
>   > writing school
>   > secular Sunday school

Secondary
>   Latin grammar school
>   English grammar school
>   Franklin's Academy

Higher
>   English-type college

The children of the well-to-do were taught by private tutors who prepared them to enter grammar school. Girls usually proceeded no farther, except to be instructed in the polite accomplishments of the fair sex, which included fancy sewing and perhaps dancing, playing the spinnet, or reading French.

The parents of middle-class children combined forces to hire a woman to teach reading, usually in a room in her own home (the dame school), and sometimes also a writing master. These arts, as well as number work, in some cities were taught in the secular Sunday school to children who worked in the factories during the week. The dame school, the writing school, and the Sunday school were gradually combined to form what came to be known as the school of the three R's—Reading, 'Riting, and 'Rithmetic. This was the institution that became enshrined in the "little red schoolhouse" and in the thousands of rural district schools throughout the land. When they finished this school, the boys were either apprenticed to learn a trade, tilled the family acres, or opened up new homesteads in the West. The girls needed no further education. They married the boys.

The costs of instruction in the three R's were prorated to the parents—the more children in the family, the greater the cost. Many parents were not financially able to pay the "rate bill" and thus to take advantage of the system. Moreover, the schools were few in number; and, as a consequence, a good many colonials and their children signed their legal documents with an X. Charitable people back in England became disturbed about the meager educational opportunities, and collections were taken up to provide elementary schooling for the poor children in the American colonies by the English Society for the Propagation of the Gospel in Foreign Parts. However, there was a certain stigma attached to attendance at the charity or pauper schools, as they were called, some of which were supported by public funds. The idea was not quite in harmony with the ideals of equality taking shape in the nation to be. But it took many a long and bitter fight to get rid of them, and to provide for public education for all.

TRANSITION

The nineteenth century was the period of transition. A universal, nonsectarian and free school system gradually came into being through the devoted efforts of many people. Among them was Horace Mann, who resigned his position as president of the Massachusetts Senate to become secretary of the Massachusetts Board of Education (in 1837), and Henry Bernard, who held a similar position in Connecticut. In general, these were the variations:

Transitional Period 1800 - 1900
Increases in Free Schooling

Elementary
    infant school
    primary school
    free school
    monitorial school
    reading and writing school
    district school, three R's
    intermediate school

Secondary
>   Latin and English grammar schools
>   Franklin's academy
>   female seminary
>   private college-preparatory school
>   manual training school
>   high school

Higher
>   liberal arts college
>   women's college
>   normal school, for training elementary teachers
>   state university, including professional schools of
>   theology, law, medicine, engineering and agriculture

An interesting *entr'acte* was the short-lived monitorial system of Lancaster and Bell, which at first looked like a great bargain. Only one schoolmaster had to be hired for one or two hundred children. They were organized into squads of a dozen or so members with a bright pupil as leader of each. The bright pupils, who were instructed by the master, in turn taught and drilled the pupils in their squads. The schoolmaster served as the top sergeant and kept the whole thing going. At least it was a bright idea, and it served for a time in some cities to bridge the gap for a number of pupils between some schooling and none at all.

The revolt against the narrow, classical curriculum imported from England gradually gained in strength. Many years after the eight-year-old Benjamin Franklin spent his year at the Boston Latin Grammar School, he was instrumental in founding a new type of school called the academy (1749). During the next fifty years the movement spread to all parts of the country.

It is interesting to compare the curriculum of the academy with that of the schools that prepared for Harvard and Yale. It included arithmetic, algebra, geometry, geography, astronomy, rhetoric, litera- ture, natural and moral philosophy and Roman antiquities. Surveying and navigation in some institutions revealed important vocational interests. Other subjects were sometimes added: botany, chemistry, general history, declamations, and debating. The female seminary, the feminine counterpart of the academy, developed partly as a finishing school, and as colleges began to open their doors to women, partly as a preparatory school.

The academy represented the protest movement against the traditional classical curriculum. In his "Sketch of an English School— For the Consideration of the Trustees of the Philadelphia Academy," Franklin[5] wrote:

"Thus instructed, youth will come out of this school fitted for learning any business, calling, or profession, except such wherein languages are required: and though unacquainted with any ancient foreign tongue, they will be masters of their own, which is of more immediate and general use, and withal, will have attained many other valuable accomplishments; the time usually spent in acquiring those languages, often without success, being here employed in laying such a foundation of knowledge and ability, as properly improved, may qualify them to pass through and execute the several offices of civil life, with advantage and reputation to themselves and country."

In view of the continued emphasis on Latin in the secondary schools, it is interesting that the English Philosopher John Locke,[6] over fifty years earlier (1693), had written:

"Can there be any thing more ridiculous, than that a Father should waste his own Money and his Son's Time in setting him to learn the *Roman Languages* when at the same time he designs him a Trade, wherein he having no use for *Latin* fails not to forget that little which he brought from school? . . . Could it be believed, unless we had everywhere amongst us Examples of it, that a Child should be forced to learn the Rudiments of a Language which he is never to use? . . . If you ask them why they do this they think it as strange a Question as if you should ask them, Why they go to Church. Custom serves for reason."

"WHAT KNOWLEDGE IS OF MOST WORTH?"

And customs change slowly, for the question was still a live one in 1859 when Herbert Spencer[7] published his famous essay with the title, "What Knowledge Is of Most Worth?" In it he argued that an educational program should be judged according to whether or not it prepares for "complete living." The first step, therefore, in judging or modifying such a program would be to decide on the leading activities and needs of life, and second, to see how well the instruction prepares young people for them. In listing the activities and needs of life in the order of their importance, as he saw it, he virtually set the prevailing curriculum on its head:

> Those ministering directly to self-preservation.
> Those which secure for one the necessities of life.
> Those which help in the rearing and disciplining of offspring.
> Those involved in maintaining one's political and social relations.
> Those which fill the leisure part of life and gratify tastes and
>   feelings.

If we translate these into their present-day equivalents, they would read: health, vocation, home and family living, citizenship, and humanities (or leisure-time activities). A weakness in Spencer's contention that the arts and humanities should come last in order in education, since they are the last in order of necessity, perhaps is that traditionally many of the other matters had been taken care of in the family, and the schools had been set up primarily for the fifth. But with the increasing knowledge that scientific inquiry was supplying, and with the onset of the industrial age, the family was handling the job in a manner that was somewhat less than satisfactory. And the state, for its own advantage, needed to see to it that it was done better. It is hardly worthwhile to argue over the order of importance of the items, since they are all now generally recognized as important. The questions are now more detailed—*What* knowledge within each of the areas he listed is of most worth? *How* should it be taught? *To whom*? and *When*? Spencer's emphasis on the importance of science was undoubtedly influential in stimulating school and college authorities to give a more important place to scientific and technological subjects, and his utilitarian approach brought the problem of educational objectives to the fore, and in general prepared the way for the modern period.

In America, the academies and other tuition boarding schools gradually gave way to the state-supported high school, though many private schools have survived either as remnants of the aristocratic tradition of the English public (private) schools, as the only representatives of adequate education in backward and undeveloped regions, or as institutions offering special educational programs. Church-connected private schools appeared as preparatory schools for denominational colleges and theological seminaries, or as parochial schools in which instruction in sectarian doctrine was provided. The secular parts of their program have tended to develop along with the public schools.

In Europe, the rapidly burgeoning body of the sciences found a place in separate institutions paralleling the slowly dwindling classical schools. Pupils had to make choices between the classics and science, or take long, written qualifying examinations when they finished their primary or elementary grades. And they still do. In America, however, the common school system became more composite in character, and choices in curricula were being made gradually as pupils proceeded through the high school and on into college. What was sought was a balanced program of study of arts and sciences for all the students, either through an elective system or modified by "majors" and "minors," which tended to group a student's courses along the lines of his interests and abilities.

Thus, by the turn of the century the educational ladder had been constructed—a unique achievement of American educational enterprise. Based on the principle of universal, free, compulsory education in the elementary and high schools, it permitted all who had the ability and the means, and who sought the manifest advantages of this single route, to climb upward to the university, its crowning glory.

AND NOW—EDUCATIONAL OPPORTUNITY FOR ALL

The creation of the educational ladder was a remarkable achievement. In general, the plan was this:

Modern Period, 1900 -
Consolidation and Extension Upward

Elementary
>nursery school, one or two years
>kindergarten, one year
>elementary school, six years
>special schools for the handicapped

Secondary
> junior high school, three years
> senior high school, three years
>> terminal and preparatory—college entrance,
>> general, commercial, industrial, agricultural

Higher
> Junior or community college, two years
> liberal arts college, four years
> teachers college
> land grant college
> state university, added professional schools—
>> graduate school, theology, education, dentistry,
>> forestry, agriculture, business, architecture,
>> pharmacy, public health, etc.

But remarkable as was the erection of the American educational ladder, it soon became evident that there was something the matter with it. It was a dangerous piece of apparatus, since out of each hundred children who started to climb it, only one or two ever got to the top. The others, now referred to as "dropouts," fell off or were pushed off at one rung or another in the ascent, resulting in what is sometimes picturesquely called "pupil mortality." Most of the children dropped out during the upper elementary school years at grades seven and eight; that is, at the end of the years of compulsory schooling.

In fact, the wholesale exodus of children from the schools as soon as they were old enough to climb the barriers of the attendance law constituted a clear vote of no confidence in the school program. What was the reason for this lack of holding power of the schools?

The cause was not far to seek. Grades seven and eight were a kind of review and coaching period to prepare the pupils for entrance to high school. The high school program was narrow and unappetizing to many, with its classical tradition and its objective to prepare pupils for college. The college program, which fitted well enough the needs of some, was of little or no interest to the great mass of the pupils. It contained what passed for learning once, but now there were other things to learn and do. Why should children work hard to prepare to go where they weren't going anyway? It didn't make sense. If the schools were to be of value to the majority of the children, the first thing to do was to break the stranglehold of the traditional college requirements on the curriculum of the lower schools.

THE JUNIOR HIGH SCHOOL

Support for this move came as a consequence of quite irrelevant developments, namely the rapid growth in population following the turn of the century. Not only was the birth rate increasing, but American industry was expanding by leaps and bounds, so rapidly, indeed, that great numbers of European families were induced to come to this country by the glowing offers of wages that to them seemed out of this world. As a consequence, school buildings were jammed, and to take care of the overflow it seemed quite practical to build new buildings for the seventh, eighth and ninth grades, thus relieving the pressure on elementary and high school buildings alike. And so the junior high school, in some places called the intermediate or middle school, came into being.

Here, then, in this new institution, was the opportunity to introduce the changes that were so badly needed to make up for the deficiencies of the old, single-track educational ladder. In Europe, the upper classes attended classical secondary schools that led to the universities. The lower class children attended lower schools with terminal programs providing some kind of trade training. But the American junior high school was different. It was a transitional school for *all* the children. It paralleled the onset of adolescence, the time when life choices are beginning to be made. And so it provided:

1. A gradual transition from the elementary school, self-contained classroom where the pupil was taught everything in the same room, and (perhaps except for music) by the same teacher, to departmentalized instruction where he began to go to different rooms and teachers for different subjects and activities.

2. The beginning of differentiated courses of study. These were to lead to separate programs in the senior high school. The academic program leading to college would continue; and, in addition, industrial and commercial programs were offered, and one in general education for those who would not go on to college. Arrangements were made, however, for transition from one program to another.

3. The beginning of a guidance program. This was at first largely limited to vocational guidance, to help pupils decide which program they should follow.

4. An enriched curriculum, one better adapted to the interests, abilities, aptitudes and needs of all the children. As a consequence, there was greater emphasis on music and the visual arts, recreation and vocational experiences; and the effort was made to relate the regular subjects to the lives of the pupils and to their probable future needs.

The junior high school was a radical innovation in its day; but, like so many innovations, it is now taken for granted, as are the educational changes that came with it. While the ideal of equal educational opportunity for all is not yet fully realized, the educational ferment of the first quarter of the century, as embodied in this institution, was responsible for remarkable gains.

THE NEW EDUCATIONAL LADDER

The nursery school for children of three and four years of age made a tentative appearance, chiefly as a private arrangement of working mothers, or connected with a university as a place for the scientific study of small children. It is rarely a part of any tax-supported public school system.

The one-year kindergarten preceding the first grade, however, has become a well-established American institution. The kindergarten idea grew out of the teaching and experience of Friedrich Wilhelm Froebel (1782-1852), German philosopher and mystic, and was amalgamated with the private kindergartens stimulated by the work of Maria Montessori in Rome in the early nineteen hundreds. The chief idea of the kindergarten now is to provide for the break from home to the larger social group, through opportunities for children to play together, and so acquire the rudiments of social living; and also to provide pre-reading experiences through contacts with the world of nature and the spoken word.

The regular six-year elementary school, as commonly found, is supplemented by a number of special schools for children who are physically or mentally handicapped. Its chief function is to provide the needed nurture for the best development of the children, particularly in the systems of words and numbers that are basic to our civilization.

The secondary school period is now usually separated into the junior and senior divisions, three years being given to each, though a two-year junior high school with a four-year senior high is not uncommon. Variations are apt to be the consequence of the numbers that can be accommodated in available buildings, rather than of any educational theory. Some have argued for a four-year junior school and a four-year senior school that includes the first two college years, but this idea has not received any wide acceptance.

The high school program has diversified in various ways, the industrial, commercial and agricultural curricula being the most common supplements to the general terminal curriculum and the preparatory course. But with the gradual liberalization of the college entrance requirements, the differentiation between the high school curricula becomes somewhat less sharp, often with one or more subjects like English and history in common.

In many states, a number of junior colleges have grown up, usually as a part of a city school system. They are torn between supplying the first two years of the liberal arts college, and a terminal program catering to the vocational interests of the local population.

The first normal school was founded at Lexington, Mass., in 1839, as a consequence of the efforts of Horace Mann. These schools followed the French model in preparing elementary school teachers, in the absence of any effective interest on the part of the colleges. At first they provided a two-year program which gradually increased to four years, with a curriculum scarcely distinguishable from that of a liberal arts college.

Many of the land-grant colleges, established by the Morrill Act (1862), set up following an original grant of public lands for training in agriculture and the mechanic arts, have become universities with liberal arts, teacher training, and other schools and colleges. These, and the original schools and colleges in the state and a few private universities, have developed graduate departments in the arts and sciences and in various areas of professional training. Professional schools have wholly or in part broken away from the parent graduate school stem, including education, dentistry, public health, pharmacy, business, forestry, and others. Now it is no longer necessary, as it was earlier, for anyone to go abroad for advanced study. The balance is more even, and in some areas has tended to incline in the other direction.

FROM YESTERDAY TO TOMORROW

This, in bare outline, is the story of the development of education in America. No effort has been made to recount the laborious steps taken to move nearer to the goal sought, to enable each child to become all that he is capable of becoming. Old-timers, "taxpayers," vested interests, outraged parents and citizens, and general inertia brought the struggle down to the local level time and time again—to the city, the school district, the parish or village. But the victories have been more numerous than the defeats, and the uneven front has been pushed steadily ahead, thanks to the good sense and determination of the majority of American citizens.

Certainly, the schools today are not the way the old-timer remembers them. *They probably never were.* Nor are they as good as they should be. The struggles are not over. But they are a reasonable facsimile of the mid-twentieth century. It is not the world of yesterday in which our children will live, but the world of today and tomorrow.

3.
Teaching the Three R's

"Reading and 'Riting and 'Rithmetic
Taught to the tune of the hick'ry stick."

The illiterate alliteration, reading, 'riting and 'rithmetic, has had a continuing appeal, and the 3 R's have come to symbolize what are referred to as the fundamental processes. A little enlargement on the story of the 3 R's is appropriate as representative of school learning, not only because of the large number of persons concerned, but also because it contains at least two widely controversial issues—phonics and grammar.

The "school of the three R's" came as a result of a gradual consolidation of the colonial dame school, writing school (later reading and writing school), and secular Sunday school. It provided the pattern for the thousands of district schools across the country as the "school ma'am" displaced the schoolmaster of the early settlements. In the early days it provided the "book l'arnin'." The fare was meager, but it was supplemented by the rich educational experiences provided on the farm and in the rural homestead. The district school handed on the instruction in the three R's to the twentieth-century elementary school, where the majority of the children find little to supplement their formal education in the tenements, flats, apartments, or even in the ranch-type houses in which they live. Objectives have, therefore, been broadened and offerings increased to meet the varied needs of the greatly expanded school population.

There are some who feel that the wide variety of subject matter that has been introduced has resulted in a loss of emphasis on the study and mastery of the three R's, the verbal symbols of communication. Jokers have had a field day drawing cartoons of children playing games, engaging in other group activities, and generally having a nice time, but seemingly not learning anything. Uncertain parents have wryly repeated the one about the child who asked, "Do we have to do whatever we want to today, or can we study some more arithmetic?" High school teachers have worried about the unexpected incompetencies in their classes, and college professors have culled the more ludicrous literary efforts of their students, and deplored the kind of instruction that has produced such atrocities. These aspersions and misgivings are understandable, and serve to emphasize the fact that it is not easy to make everybody even passably literate.

The wide range of pupils' abilities and their adjustment problems present a number of difficulties in instruction and administration. Heavy increases in enrollment have brought poorly trained teachers into the schools, and in many places resulted in undesirably large classes. Mounting salary scales and construction costs have forced some communities to put some of their pupils not only in temporary buildings but also on half-day shifts.

We Teach Them Better Now. In spite of all this, the task of teaching the communication skills, and the language of numbers is taken very seriously in the schools. Countless studies have been made of the effectiveness of different methods of instruction, and probably a major part of every elementary school day is devoted to them. Why, then, are the schools not doing a better job? The answer is that they *are* doing a better job, better than at any time in the past, as revealed by comparisons that have been made of the test performance of children "then and now."

It may be that the objections are based fundamentally on the belief that the secondary school, and the college as well, should use a higher cutting point, that unless young people are able to develop such and such abilities, they should not be allowed to continue past certain positions on the educational ladder. This is a tenable position, and one that can be debated intelligently. It is possible that those with higher ability would profit if teachers did not have to spend class time coaching those of lesser ability. And it is also possible that those with lesser ability should be excluded for their own best interest and sent to a different kind of institution, or retained in a special coaching class until they have been drilled to read, write, spell and compute at some accepted level of competence.

Such a procedure is certainly rational, and it would probably have been adopted long ago if children were inanimate objects instead of people. If such a plan were followed, the first difficulty would be to establish a satisfactory cutting point, which would be an agreed-on score in each subject, or an average of several scores. The second difficulty would be to establish satisfactory instruction for those below the cutting point. These, of course, are not insuperable difficulties.

The English have long employed such a system at home and in their colonies. On finishing the elementary school at the age of eleven, or shortly thereafter, children are given a set of examinations, the results of which determine their educational and hence to a large extent their vocational future. This examination system has been under fire for a number of years, and national commissions have been set up to study it. Complaints have emphasized the traumatic nature of the experience, the emotional involvement of parents in the success or failure of their children, and the unsatisfactoriness of a single examination for eleven-year-olds to determine their future careers. More important are the known facts concerning the irregular nature of human growth, since some children develop more slowly at first and then show unexpected spurts, sometimes outdistancing those who had earlier surpassed them, and later attaining considerable academic success and even scholarly renown. The "eleven plus" examination does a manifest injustice to such children and is on the way out.

In contrast with this selective pattern of secondary education, the American idea of the comprehensive high school presents different problems. It is perhaps less logical than one which sorts the children into different categories and sends them to different types of schools accordingly. But it seems to be closer to what we know about human nature, allowing as it does for the important life decisions to be made more gradually as the evidence accumulates, and meanwhile permitting the children to continue in the communities of their friends and develop in a more normal fashion. Whether a young person belongs or does not belong in high school (or in college) is a matter of opinion and should be recognized as such. And opinions will differ. The problem is to find the situation in which he can learn best, and so become what he is capable of becoming. The problem has not been solved for all children. We are not interested in producing an educational elite, cut off from the masses. But we are concerned about developing leaders competent in various fields of endeavor. In doing this we do not want to relegate those of less promise to the rubbish heap, as we used to do. Nor do we wish to sort them out arbitrarily, and perhaps prematurely, in order to fit a preconceived idea of what a school should be.

READING

People can learn to understand others, to talk and to think more or less effectively by merely growing up at home, on the farm, in the village, or city; but they cannot learn to read and write in this way. The written symbols require special instruction, to which the leaders in countries where illiteracy is a social and political problem can testify. The American schools have taught an increasing number of people to read and write, but it is a time-consuming and costly task. Probably more research studies have been conducted on the process of learning to read than on any other single educational problem, as a consequence of which a great deal is definitely known about it. In spite of this fact, many people who have given the matter little thought feel quite competent to instruct the experts. While the failures of a few children are still baffling, one thing that is known is that reading is a more complex process than many realize, and that reading difficulties, like diseases, cannot all be cured by the same medicine. A number of different factors are involved.

One important factor is the level of mental ability or intelligence. One college professor reports that he cannot remember when he could not read, and a young Ph.D. in history claims that he learned the letters from studying the headlines of the newspapers that were placed on the floor under his high chair. At the other extreme are the feeble-minded who are never able to do more than recognize a few simple words. Between these two extremes is the range of abilities of the pupils normally found in the elementary schools. Our society expects the schools to teach them all.

Another, though related, factor is the rate of individual growth. In most states children are required by law to enter school at the age of six, when they are enrolled in the first grade, though some may attend nursery school or kindergarten earlier. Many people seem to think the job of the first-grade teacher is to teach the children in the grade to read; that is, to recognize, pronounce and understand simple printed sentences. As a rule, however, we know that children cannot profit by instruction in reading until their mental age is at least six and a half years. Some children will not reach a mental age of six and a half until they are seven or eight years old.

Still another related factor is home background. If parents are functionally illiterate and lacking in intellectual interests, the words the children know will be few and their powers of conceptualization meager. Recent governmental efforts have produced such schemes for compensatory education as "Higher Horizons," "More Effective Schools," and "Head Start," but they have not been very successful.

There are many other instructional tasks in the first grade besides teaching reading, such as for example, getting children used to being away from their parents and playing together amicably. And there are many things children can do that will get them ready to begin to read. These are sometimes called pre-reading activities. They include looking at pictures, learning the names of things, telling little stories, listening to stories read to them, and so on. These activities build up a favorable attitude toward reading and develop their acquaintance with words, so that when they are "ready," that is, when they have matured enough, they will start in.

But there is no use trying to teach all children to read during their first year in school. It cannot be done. Sometimes they are kept in the first grade for another year. Many are promoted to the second grade where supposedly they start in where they left off the year before. The pre-reading "pool" is an ungraded three- or four-year group from which children move into the fourth grade as soon as they are sufficiently mature and have developed a certain degree of reading skill. This plan is still in the experimental stage. There are a few "bugs" in it that have to be removed before it can be generally adopted.

Physiological difficulties constitute another factor in teaching reading. Apart from eye and ear defects, a few children have been found to have other handicaps that may interfere with reading progress, such as, for example, a low basal metabolic rate. Or they may have difficulty in perceiving form and direction visually, perhaps because of brain injury. Such children can sometimes be taught by having them practice tracing enlarged letters with their fingers, which enables them to perceive their forms kinesthetically. Montessori included this exercise among the techniques used in her children's houses in Rome, and fine sandpaper letters were among the materials used in the Montessori kindergartens in this country.

Emotional difficulties seem to lie at the root of a number of reading failures. Frustrations, anxieties, or hostilities in the home or school environment may produce an antipathy to all school work; and hence no learning. Or negativism may develop against the reading situation itself. The resulting aversion may be neurotic in character, and thus be as impossible to control voluntarily as the aversion of the claustrophobic person to entering buildings. Force and punishment are obviously no solution for such cases, and should be replaced by a period of emotional rehabilitation.

The above factors relate to differences in pupils. Another set of problems have to do with the methods and principles of instruction to be employed with children who are normally intelligent and have no special disabilities.

One tried and true educational principle is to proceed from the simple to the more complex. This principle seems easy to apply in reading: teach the letters first, followed by syllables, little words, larger words, sentences and paragraphs. This is logical enough, though a bit dull and meaningless at the start. Also, some little words are rather difficult to understand, such as erg, state, god, snide, truth, wry, shrew and others. But of course these can be avoided, or only the simpler meanings introduced. The greatest trouble with this principle, however, is that it is sometimes at odds with another equally tried and true principle, to proceed from the familiar to the unfamiliar. Thus a child might be more ready to start with delicatessen or merchandise, or with hydrogen or television than with wry or shrew! A variation is to have them read what they have said.

Phonics or Words? Educational practice at one time or another has been caught on the horns of these two principles. Those who have supported the simple-to-complex principle have favored the old alphabet method, or what is known technically as the phonic method; those who have supported the familiar-unfamiliar principle have favored what has been called the word-recognition method. The truth, as usual, lies somewhere in between; in this case, in an intelligent use of both.

However, the phonics problem has been known to explode, and the fall-out has carried well beyond the boundaries of educational meetings, perhaps largely because a child's failure in learning to read seems to reflect on the intelligence of the parents. Phonetics is the science of speech sounds, but the term phonics is applied to certain elementary aspects of phonetics, particularly as they relate to methods of teaching children to pronounce words. Systems of phonic instruction have been devised consisting of long lists of letter combinations like da, de, di, do, du, or dab, def, did, dot, dus, and so on for pages and pages. The theory is that after weeks of drill on these syllables the children will be able to pronounce, and therefore to read, almost anything. Such systems were given a careful workout during the first quarter of the century, and have since been largely discarded.

The reasons for discarding them are fairly obvious. Drill on meaningless syllables stifles interest and reduces it to the vanishing point. Furthermore, English is not a phonetic language, like Italian, for example. The same letter has several different sounds, and therefore cannot be counted on to sound the same wherever one meets it; and sometimes it has no sound at all. While the consonants are fairly regular, hard and soft c and g being exceptions, the vowels and diphthongs follow few rules and signal many different sounds. Children are likely to run off the track in sounding out letters when trying to pronounce such words as bug and bugler; give, gist and gigantic; or anger, hanger, and danger, and on to bough, cough, through, though and enough! So how do you pronounce sough! Even when the learner succeeds in pronouncing the words correctly, there is no assurance that he knows what they mean, and if he does not know the meaning he isn't reading. In fact, successful pronunciation is likely to throw the teacher off the track, because the child gives the impression that he knows meanings when he pronounces words. The main purpose of the whole proceeding is likely to be lost in the pile of syllables.

The word-recognition method is not an invention of modern progressive education, as some uninformed critics seem to think, for it was urged by Horace Mann in the 1830's; but it has rarely, if ever, been used exclusively. It involves acquainting children with the appearance of familiar words and phrases which they recognize as wholes, just as people learn to recognize other objects as wholes, like houses and trees and faces, for example, without first being exposed to a seriatim presentation of the parts into which they can be analyzed. The method has been criticized on the ground that it does not take advantage of the letter system of the alphabet, but teaches words as if they were Chinese characters. Furthermore, an excessive use of this system has in the past resulted in difficulties in spelling, since pupils were not trained to notice individual letters. Then, too, it has been argued that children taught by this method are helpless when they meet a new word and have to have someone tell them what it is, because they have not been taught to sound out the letters and guess at the pronunciation. These are valid criticisms not of the word recognition method, but of its improper use.

On the other hand, it has two distinct advantages. One is that it enables pupils to start reading simple stories quite early. The words look different, and they can quickly learn to recognize those with which they are already familiar. To read little stories made up of these words creates the same feeling of progress that an older person gets when his beginning conversational phrases in a foreign language are understood. Such reading enlists the pupils' interest, without which learning is an unnecessarily unpleasant and laborious affair.

The other advantage is that it develops the ability to read rapidly. Instead of forming the habit of examining each letter and syllable separately, the pupils quickly learn to perceive whole words and groups of words at a glance. Emphasis on silent reading also helps in this respect. Thus children learn to use context and understand meanings.

However, letter sounds are also taught, not in long lists, but in connection with meaningful material. Children's dictionaries and readers provide opportunities for word study, including spelling, pronunciation, synonyms, antonyms, connotations, and the like, so that words and meanings are taught together.

Speed, Words and Meaning. How fast can we read? The older method of teaching reading was to have the pupils read aloud, so they were slowed down by the process of pronouncing. Those who learned this way usually found it hard to go any faster when they read silently. However, if pupils are also taught to read silently, they can read faster and still understand what they are reading. Of course, some things have to be read slowly to be understood, but stories can be read much faster, and with just as much or even more enjoyment. There is so much to read nowadays that it is hardly sensible to plod along at the oral rate. Most adults with practice can double their rate of reading ordinary prose. Sometimes, too, one merely wants to find out something, so he skims along until he comes to the information he is looking for. Thus there are at least three speeds of reading that pupils are helped to acquire at school—oral, silent, and skimming.

Which words should be taught? This question has been answered fairly satisfactorily by the prepared lists of words based on a word count of their frequency of use. In general, it is sensible to begin with words that are used most often; and so elementary school readers and other books are prepared which select from the 500, 1,000 or 2,000 most-used words. The word count reduces what is referred to as the "vocabulary load" to a reasonable size, though it does not mean that other words of current significance cannot be introduced.

How are word meanings taught? Phonic methods emphasize pronunciation, and if by these methods pupils can be taught to recognize words with which they are already familiar, all well and good. But there is a possibility that they will also learn to parrot words with little or no idea of what they are reading about. In one experiment[1] fifth-grade children were asked how big "huge" is, in the sentence in their reader which said:

"Iron ore is obtained from Red Mountain near Birmingham, Alabama. Try to imagine standing on this mountain in the evening watching the city brighten with the red glare from the huge furnaces in which ore taken from the very hill on which you stand is being made into steel."

Some thought that huge meant about a yard high, or as big as the filing cabinet in the office, while at the other extreme were some who thought it was as big as a new skyscraper in New York City. Visual aids are a great help here, but these have their dangers. A city child said she thought a cow was as big as a mouse, because the two were of equal size in the picture book she had looked at, and she had never seen a cow. Excursions are therefore planned so that children can see and hear and handle the things they talk and read about, and elementary school rooms are often cluttered with all kinds of collections of local minerals, flora and fauna, to the disgust, no doubt, of the custodians. The oral and written reports and evaluations of field trips and projects are largely for the purpose of familiarizing pupils with word meanings and language usage so that they will not only understand what they read, but will be able to use the language themselves more effectively.

Why learn to read? This is perhaps a silly question, though reading had little value for most people before the invention of the printing press. It is certainly true that many of the things formerly to be learned only by reading are now described and illustrated on radio and television. However, there still seems to be plenty of need for an understanding of the written and printed word. In a way, reading can be said to be an end in itself, because of the enjoyment to be found in it. Improvement in any skill is satisfying, reading included, and it is still more satisfying to use the skill. But one also reads in order to find out something. For this reason, pupils are so instructed that they not only learn to read, but they also read to learn. This is more than just a verbal twist. For example, pupils look up words in dictionaries, encyclopedias, and, in developing projects, they read in order to find out about their part of the project. Thus they are getting practice in reading and at the same time using what they read for some purpose.

Speeches and Orations. When children come to school, they have already learned to talk. The earlier schools built on this skill not only by oral reading, but also by having children learn recitations and declamations. They came to school, or to the "opera house" where prize speaking contests were held, the girls in pretty white dresses, the boys almost unrecognizable in their Sunday suits and with their hair slicked down, and delivered themselves of "readings" and "orations" such as "Spartacus to the Gladiators" or "Curfew Shall Not Ring Tonight," with gusto before an admiring audience made up of parents and townspeople. Styles in public utterance have changed, however. Except, perhaps, for political platforms and church pulpits, the informal, conversational tone has largely displaced the florid welkin-ringing of an earlier day, and school practices have tended to follow along.

Children tell, discuss and report. Or they have panel discussions and model assemblies, mock radio programs, puppet shows, and informal plays. They hold committee and council meetings to decide and plan. Thus they get practice not in making speeches so much as in talking and expressing their ideas either from their chairs around a table, or on their feet in front of an audience of their peers. Since this is the kind of speaking that almost everyone engages in, if he can, it seems reasonable to provide practice in doing it effectively.

'RITING

Handwriting is a motor skill which receives less attention now than it did in the earlier days. There are several reasons for this. The writing school had its writing master, whose influence was considerable; and this was one of the schools that merged to form the school of the three R's which carried on the tradition. Its curriculum was meager, but with the addition of new subjects and the invention of the typewriter and dictaphone, the steel engraving model seemed less attractive. Even those who once had mastered the "Spencerian script" or the "Palmer method" became careless as they grew older, and their writing, though perhaps esthetically attractive, was often quite illegible. And then good handwriting lost out to spelling as a status symbol. *Why* it is difficult to say, unless it was because it was regarded as a mere skill, without intellectual overtones, and competitions lacked box-office appeal.

A good argument can be made for improved handwriting, in view of the size of the dead letter office, and the often costly errors in business communication, particularly in numbers of items and in prices. Perhaps the time taken deciphering the letters of friends is well spent, for it keeps them longer in mind, but at other times we run into petty annoyances, like the housewife who left a handwritten request to the milkman for two quarts of chocolate milk and the next morning found on her doorstep eight cartons of cottage cheese.

If there were a strong public demand, there is no doubt but that the schools could improve the handwriting of their graduates, although at the expense of some other instruction. As it is, esthetic standards are no longer insisted on, and a modicum of readability has become the objective.

In recent years, so-called manuscript writing has come into favor for beginners because it is more like the printed form that pupils see in their readers than is the running or cursive script; and so it can be learned more quickly. Since the cursive script is favored by adults, common practice is to shift over to it in the third or fourth grade. In some ways this is unfortunate, for manuscript writing is quite as rapid and, as a rule, more legible. But if pupils change to the cursive script, they are more ready gradually to be able to read the handwriting of their elders.

Spelling. The second "R" usually stands not only for handwriting, but also for the unruly orthography of the English language. For some reason or other there is little complaint nowadays about poor handwriting. But in spite of the spelling bees of yore, a similiar lack of enthusiasm used to be shown for regularity in spelling. This tolerance is revealed in the requirements for college entrance at Harvard and Yale in the preceding chapter, and even more dramatically in the Lewis and Clark journals.[2] For example, Thomas Jefferson's private secretary, Meriwether Lewis, of the famous Lewis and Clark exploration of the American Northwest, wrote in his journal of how he reached this

> ... most distant fountain of waters of the mighty Missouri in surch of which we have spent so many toilsome days and wristless nights. Judge ... the pleasure I felt in allying my thirst with this pure ice-cold water.

His companion, Lt. William Clark, not to be outdone, wrote:

> The [Sioux] warriers are Verry much deckerated with Paint Porcupine quils and feathers, Large leagins and mockersons all with buffalow roabs of Different Colours.

Such creative spelling on a freshman essay today would be sure proof that the professors of education are anti-intellectuals bent on destroying our democracy. We happen to live in an age that reveres correctness in spelling; and so the schools do try to teach children to spell, though they recognize there are other values in life which might on some occasions be more important. But the teaching of spelling would probably receive even more attention than it does if we knew less—or more—about it.

The experts have been baffled ever since J. M. Rice, in 1897, discovered by a series of tests of over 33,000 pupils that those who received ten minutes of instruction a day could spell as well as those who received fifty minutes. Some pupils, for no known reason, spell almost all words correctly with ease while others, often quite as bright otherwise, seem never to learn. Studies have shown that pupils spell words they have not been taught as well as those they have, though they may arrive at this competence somewhat later. And pupils are often unable to spell correctly words they have written out five, ten, twenty-five times. Such facts as these tend to make teachers throw up their hands and concentrate on the larger educational objectives!

For those parents and other citizens who believe that such an attitude is pure defeatism, that everyone can learn to spell and should be made to, the following list is inserted. To play fair, hand the book to someone else and write the list as he dictates the words to you: proceedings, principles (meaning rules), manual, believe, foreword, occasion, desirable, separate, causative, parallel, conceivable, questionnaire, proceed, repetition, prominent, existence, definite, aggression, resistance, perceive, privilege, comparative, procedure, supersede, comparison, equipped, liaison, precede, personnel, embarrassed, picnicking, sacrilege. If you score 100%, ask any elementary school teacher to allow you to teach the children in her grade how to spell, and your request will probably not be denied! However, before you accept the offer, remember that to be able to do something oneself is not the same as being able to teach others to do it.

If the public demands better spelling on the part of elementary or high school graduates, the schools will make every effort to oblige, though they will not be responsible for other consequences! But until it does, the pupils will probably spell no better, or worse, than the rest of us.

The King's English. Writing, of course, is more than handwriting and spelling, just as speaking is more than pronouncing words. The object of instruction is to enable the learner to express himself understandably in the acceptable forms of standard English. Standard English, like standard French or Spanish, or any other language, is the preferred dialect.

Many people still think that correct English is what the grammars say it is. But grammarians are recorders and cataloguers of language. Their rules and exceptions are not necessarily guides, but systematized tabulations of usage. Standard usage is the changing dialect as it is spoken and written by the leading group, formerly the king and his court, but more recently by those in the dominant political and economic circles. The spreading out of power through the processes of political democracy and of industrial ownership has tended to broaden accepted usage and to make alternate forms of expression "correct," particularly in the matter of pronunciation, while the development of the so-called mass media of communication—newspapers, radio and television—tend to exert a steadying influence.

Dialects may contain forms once accepted but no longer standard. Hence, many of the "mistakes" that teachers correct pupils for are either older forms that are no longer acceptable, like the double negative, forms from outlying regions that were never standard, or newer forms which may be coming into standard use. As the linguists, or students of language point out, there are, roughly speaking, three patterns of English: one for formal use, one for informal use, and one for the non-acceptable dialects.

For example: *Standard formal*: We definitely reject the idea of special privilege for the few. *Standard informal*: Nobody is going to tell me I'm not as good as the next man. *Non-standard dialect*: Ain't nobody going to tell me I ain't as good as you be.

America is a country of upward social mobility, as the sociological phrase goes. People can, if they wish, improve their social class status, and many wish to do so. There is, indeed considerable pressure, both psychological and social, to "keep up with the Joneses," not only in owning status symbols like houses, automobiles, swimming pools and color television sets, but in other ways as well. One of the identifying signs of social class is the dialect used, as Bernard Shaw demonstrated dramatically in his *Pygmalion*.

Why Teach Grammar? A question that is sometimes raised is whether grammar should be taught at all. Many are of the opinion that what they view as the inability of young people, particularly in the colleges, to write and speak "correct" English is due to the lack of instruction in grammar in the schools, and that we should therefore go back to teaching it. If they mean that the correct use of standard English in writing and speaking should be taught, there is certainly no objection, but this is not the same thing as teaching grammar. People who have been brought up in homes and neighborhoods where good English is used may know nothing about grammar, yet they write and speak correctly. There must, therefore, be other ways of learning proper usage.

If a child reads the sentence, "The boy hit the ball," he knows which hit and which got hit. Also, it is possible to teach him that "boy" is the subject and is in the nominative case, "hit" is a verb in the past tense and is the predicate of the sentence, and "ball" is a noun, the direct object, and is therefore in the objective case. But since he already knew the meaning, all the grammar seems unnecessary. The reason for this is that grammar is actually not a series of rules and definitions, but it is the device which a language uses to signal meanings. Illustrations could be multiplied to show that in English, grammatical knowledge is of little help either in understanding meanings or in using language. If it had been found to be useful, there would be no question about the desirability of using it. And to the extent that it is useful, it is and should be used.

Even in learning foreign languages, it has been found that the grammatical method of teaching can be overdone. Young people after a year of German can do little more than recite *der, die, das,* and with a year or two more can translate simple prose stumblingly, and converse little if at all. The direct methods of teaching are patterned after the way people learn their native language. They learn to understand and speak first. Reading and writing can come somewhat later, with such grammatical rules as are helpful. Those few who are to become students of language will of course make a study of grammar in their more advanced courses.

Naturally, the conventional grammatical nomenclature is convenient in talking about language forms. But making pupils memorize declensions, conjugations, parts of speech and rules of syntax turns out to be an ineffective way to try to teach them the use of the English language. Many who use the language ably were given this kind of instruction, but it does not follow that it was this instruction that was responsible for their competence. Their native intelligence, the kind of English spoken in their homes while they were growing up, the correcting they received from their parents, the numbers of books they read from childhood on, and their persistent talking far outweigh the influence of any grammar they were taught in school.

Those who believe that high school pupils should be taught to speak and write more nearly in accord with standard English usage have a good point. But they confuse the issue when they insist on the way it should be done; that is, by teaching more grammar.

'RITHMETIC–FIGURING AND THINKING

Since the annual arithmetic test in the form of the income tax was instituted, adults are perhaps less critical of children's mistakes in the third "R" than formerly. The same kind of study has gone into the problems of teaching pupils to manipulate numbers that has been given to reading. The effort has been made to teach pupils to add, subtract, multiply and divide before they were "ready," i.e., when they were too young to learn efficiently, and when they could see no sense in what they were trying to do. These are mechanical processes that can be performed on a machine. The important thing that the machine cannot do is think, and this aspect of arithmetic has tended to be neglected, as illustrated by the familiar question, "Do you multiply or divide?" If children first get used to ideas of more and less, greater than, and less than, twice as big, half as big, and so on, computation later consists merely in putting in numbers to represent the different amounts.

In present-day teaching, the thinking part of arithmetic is finally receiving the emphasis it deserves. It has also eliminated specialized information and processes that are rarely if ever used, except by a few technicians, like troy weight and cube root, and also the artificial problems like the one that stumped the poor scholar.[3] "If a 57-foot telephone pole falls across a cement highway so that 17-3/6 feet extend from one side and 14-9/17 feet from the other, how wide is the highway?"

"That seemed to me like an awfully silly way to get the width of a highway," the poor scholar commented. "I didn't even try to answer it because it didn't say whether the pole had fallen straight across or not."

To make arithmetic more meaningful and also more practical, the objective is to provide practice in the kind of arithmetic that most people use and are likely to need. For those with sufficient aptitude, further mathematical experience is desirable; and for the mathematically talented, trigonometry and higher algebra can be provided in high school, though this is not often done. But one thing we are sure of: no stated amount of mathematics should be required of everybody in high school. A few should have a great deal, and a few none at all.

The point of all this is that the "three R's" really are taught in the schools, and that they get a great deal of attention, more than most people realize. And further, that improvements in teaching materials and methods have been made as a result of experience and scientific studies, and that the average performance in these skills is better than it was earlier when relatively more time was given to them. Teaching them is a continuing responsibility, and as more is learned of the mental processes involved and of the difficulties of individual learners, the job will be done even more efficiently. It is in some ways the most important task of the elementary school. However, given adequate instruction, children learn at the rate they are growing; some slower than others, some faster, and no great amount of change may be expected.

4.
How Shall We Teach Ethics?

The problem of pupil conduct probably takes up more school time than anything else except the fundamental processes themselves—and causes more headaches. The schools have accepted the problem and are prepared to meet it with a rich arsenal of weaponry to discourage misconduct: in the earlier days, the birch rod and the hickory stick, and later, the ruler, the rubber hose, scolding and reprimand, staying after school, lowered marks, sitting in the hall, sending to the principal's office, isolation, suspension, and expulsion. The caning in the English public schools seems positively primitive by comparison. In addition, the psychoanalytic, psychiatric and mental hygiene movements have brought in specialists in guidance and counseling.

That they have not been successful, in spite of all this extra overhead, is evidenced by the sins of omission and commission among juveniles in the schools, and adults who have passed through them—the troublesome, deceitful, untrustworthy, the vandals, delinquents, and criminals. How should we teach ethics?

SPIRITUAL VALUES

Most of the answers seem to relate to one or the other of two words, "spiritual" and "moral." When the writer hears these words bandied about by critics of our public school system, he asks the speakers what they mean by the terms. This question usually reveals to the speakers either that they do not know what they are talking about, or that they have a very narrow, and sometimes a definitely sectarian, concept of the terms they are employing. As a matter of fact, each word has more than one correct meaning. It is an enlightening experience to read and ponder the several meanings of these two words as they are given in an unabridged dictionary.

For many, the term "spiritual" is definitely theological. It pertains to the ideas, beliefs, and faiths of religious and sectarian groups with respect to the Deity, the supernatural, life after death, etc. For them it is practically synonymous with the word "religious," and is supported by those who believe that Bible reading and other forms of religious worship should be included in the public school program. Such rites and ceremonies presumably become a means to some end. To the extent that this end is indoctrination in the beliefs of one or another religious group, we seem fairly well agreed that it has no proper place in the public schools. To the extent that this end is the improvement of the life adjustment of the pupils, it should be considered. What is the evidence to show that religious studies help in pupils' life adjustment?

Besides the dubious value of the testimonial, the evidence is difficult to find. Only slight correlation has been found between knowledge of the Bible and good conduct.[1] The percent of inmates in prisons and reformatories who were church members and who expressed church preferences has been found to be higher than that of people outside such institutions.[2] The correlation of moral conduct with church and Sunday school membership and attendance has been found to be low.[3] Total church membership has shown a low negative correlation with an index of the characteristics which make a city good to live in, and with an index involving certain qualities of intelligence, morality, and devotion to the home. Also, communities with the largest percentage of church members were below average in good reading, home ownership, and continuance in school, and had more than their share of illiterates and child labor. There was, however, a low negative correlation between church membership and homicide, deaths from venereal diseases, and illegitimate births. Church membership thus seems to be more related to certain phases of traditional morality than to the broader aspects of social values.[4] [5]

From such results as these, one can but conclude that spiritual values in the sense of religious instruction, as now carried on, have little, if any, relation to many aspects of desirable social adjustment.

MORAL VALUES

The word "moral" also has more than one meaning; but generally it is applied to conduct in harmony with the social standards of a particular group, especially when for one reason or another, such conduct is difficult to practice. The standards may be derived from religious or nonsectarian sources, or from both. Different religious, cultural, and class groups hold to differing standards, as is well known. However, in any one society there are large areas of agreement. How effective have been the educational schemes employed to improve the morality, sometimes referred to as the "character," of the school population?

Twenty years ago, the children in a certain community received an efficiency certificate in a junior high school citizenship program. The investigator found little or nothing in their subsequent careers to distinguish the winners from the non-winners.[6] Low correlation has been found between moral conduct and moral knowledge. There is, for example, no evidence that the study of biography or the length of time in school influences character. Children have been found to score higher in dishonesty the longer they had been participants in a once much-publicized character-education program.[7] [8]

From such studies as these, too, one can but conclude that moral values as commonly taught have little, if any, relation to desirable social adjustment. The implication is that among all the influences brought to bear on the life of a child, moral instruction of the kinds studied is not sufficient, by itself, to produce any discoverable effect.

Group Membership. It might be supposed from the studies reported briefly above, that moral behavior shows no pronounced correlation with any measurable factor. But such is by no means the case. On the negative side, various conditions have been found to produce undesirable conduct, among them over-emphasis on marks at school,[9] and at home, marital maladjustment[10] and parental overprotection or neglect.[11] On the positive side, measurable improvement in conduct has been found where child-teacher relations and classroom morale have improved, and where special emphasis is placed on both actual experience and on the discussion of the significance of an activity. [12] [13] While there is low correlation between the practices of honesty by best friends not in the same schoolroom, the correlation triples for best friends in the same room.[14] This finding demonstrates the fact of group priority. The standards of the group become internalized by the group members.

Group membership, then, with good morale or *esprit de corps,* particularly in cohesive groups, influences favorably the behavior of the individuals in the group. If this hypothesis is accepted, methods to produce such group cohesiveness and group spirit should be employed. This inference seems reasonable, but it is directly contrary to common practice, which aims to develop individual competition under authoritarian control and direction. And it is well known that an authoritarian group climate tends to produce aggression and intragroup antagonisms which result in conduct opposite to that desired.[15]

Frustration. Lastly, there is the frequently found correlation between moral conduct and intelligence.[16] Conversely, a higher number of problem tendencies are found among slowgrowing children.[17] It is difficult to accept any basic physiological reason for this, but social factors suggest themselves. Slow-growing children[18/20] are often subjected to greater pressures to "keep up with the class" and are faced with adjustment tasks more difficult for them, since they are slow growers. These conditions could be expected to induce more frustration behavior of an undesirable sort. An example of this might be evidenced by the fact that during the elementary school period, when boys grow more slowly than girls, boys are more often disciplinary problems in school, and more often appear in juvenile court.

Undesirable behavior, therefore, is connected with factors producing excessive frustration, such as low intelligence and slow growth, which tend to produce pressures and conflicts at home and at school. If this hypothesis is accepted, it follows that a way to produce desirable behavior is to structure the environment, so far as possible, in such a way that these pressures and conflicts are reduced. This inference seems reasonable, but it is directly contrary to commonly held views and current practice which lead, instead, through standardized curricular demands, the marking system, and punishment, to increased pressures and increased frustrations—and increased misconduct.

What inferences are to be drawn from these conclusions? They certainly do not imply any disparagement of spiritual and moral values, however defined. But they do at least suggest that the customary means employed to attain these values are not particularly effective.

Instead of talking about spiritual and moral values, then, let us seek to discover what our real objectives are, and then search out ways to attain them. What ends do those who wish to enhance spiritual and moral values in the public schools actually seek? What kinds of behavior do they wish to inculcate? It is my belief that, unless they mean the exploitation of the schools for their own sectarian purposes, the ends they seek may be stated as follows: *to provide for the pupils the conditions needed for their fullest development, conditions which tend to make the pupils integrated, well-adjusted participants in constructive social activity.*

It is unnecessary at this time to elaborate this statement of educational objectives. However, it will be noted that the first part emphasizes the individual development of the person and would include what are sometimes called life orientation, esthetic appreciations, and even a life philosophy. The second part eliminates neurotic and delinquent behavior and emphasizes social vs. anti-social conduct.

The program for spiritual and moral education cannot be limited to didactic materials and verbalizations about the virtues, but must be a part of every activity of the curriculum. It must recognize the values of our culture, and study the ways in which these can be incorporated in the school program. Nor will the way consist of scolding and punishing pupils for doing what they have virtually been forced to do. Instead, activities will be included which students have a part in planning. In carrying forward these activities, students will have instruction *and practice* in sharing responsibility and in dealing with tensions that arise. They will be treated as persons who are learning, and they will be rewarded, as is fitting in all learning, by the satisfactions of success in the enterprises they have undertaken.

Thus, our objective in elementary education includes more than proficiency in the fundamental processes. Indeed, for the whole school program it includes the teaching of ethics, by providing, under guidance, experiences which further the aims of those who emphasize the importance of spiritual and moral values and desirable conduct.

5.
Conflicts and Values

In a static society, little educational change is called for; but, in a dynamic society, continuing change is necessary. In the United States, population increases and the accompanying industrialization and cultural modifications have produced conflicting opinions and differing value systems which tend to slow down action and affect the direction of change.

CONFLICTING OPINIONS

Sharp differences of opinion are usually found in three areas—support, tradition and curricular differentiation. The great majority of Americans believe in education and give it strong support through taxes and private donations. But a good many people have fought the movement for free education for all, or they believe enough is enough, and have succeeded in keeping many schools in a state approaching penury. Teachers' salaries were meager until the law of supply and demand was pushed aside in favor of union affiliation with labor groups, which have taught teachers how to get attention. The penurious have objected to the building of schoolhouses they called educational palaces, and their ballots have kept in use buildings that are unsanitary fire traps, and have failed to provide the renovation needed not only in plant and equipment, but also in curriculum and method.

A second familiar area of conflict is the one between tradition and innovation. What has supposedly always been done is often considered right, and generations grow up who know no other way. This attitude came to the fore when, after World War I, the innovations of the junior high school were introduced. And more recently we have heard embattled parents and teachers say with feeling, "I don't want my child taught by a machine," or "After all, nothing can take the place of the live teacher in the classroom." Some teachers feel comfortable in the familiar surroundings, while innovations make them feel anxious and even frustrated. Others, however, tire of the old routines and the old failures, and prefer the new and the exciting. Often the two conflicts combine in objections to the new when it seems to be more expensive.

A third area of conflict is between those who would give priority to social demands—education to transmit the social heritage (in its totalitarian form, education for the state), and those who would consider first the needs of the children. The latter favor the child-centered school, adapting to pupil differences, and the goal of helping every child to become what he is capable of becoming. And it appears in such highly controversial programs as those for home and family living, and more recent inner-city efforts to educate the culturally deprived.

CONFLICTING VALUES

Such conflicts as these are usually based on differing values, and for this reason it seems appropriate to consider the nature of the value concept and its place in science and education.

Not long ago, I asked a graduate student in social psychology what his subject teaches about value judgments. Without hesitation he smilingly replied with the genotype of all value judgments: "They're bad!" Many social scientists have tried to follow the lead of the natural scientists in consigning value to the limbo of lost souls that never will be missed. And they have been aided and abetted by non-scientific scholars, both religious and secular, who have made pronouncements to the effect that science can tell 'how' to do things, but not 'what' to do. Even some who are willing to use science to discover the most efficient means to attain the ends about which there is general agreement, will not accept its services to determine what ends should be sought. This position is taken, for example, by Fiegel,[1] who states that: "It is one thing to describe by means of declarative statements what *is* the case, or to predict what will (probably) be the case if certain conditions are fulfilled; it is another thing to prescribe by means of overtly or covertly imperative sentences . . . what ought to be done."

TRADITIONAL DUALISM BETWEEN FACT AND VALUE

It does not lie within the scope of this chapter to formulate a reply to this point. Suffice it to say that the traditional dualism on the basis of which facts have been accepted as the proper realm of science, and values excluded, has in recent years been vigorously assailed by philosophers and social scientists alike.[2] The former, influenced to no small degree by Dewey,[3] are represented, among others, by Geiger,[4] who has stated his views as follows: "It is a little surprising then, that one of the most conspicuous (and mischievous) cultural hang-overs still plagues social science just as it haunts natural science and philosophy. I refer to the antique dualism between fact and value . . . What are the alternatives? What are the substitutes for scientific inquiry in the handling of human values? . . . The answers can be found in brute power or in mystical illumination, in retreat to the The Church (whichever one) or in esoteric obscurantism."

The psychiatrist Franz Alexander[5] has written: "The discussion of this topic appears to me as much outmoded as a controversy over whether machines heavier than air can rise up against the force of gravity and fly . . . The dichotomy between 'facts and values' is a pseudo-distinction, and the problem of whether values belong to a realm which is beyond the reach of scientific methods is a pseudo-problem."

The anthropologist Clyde Kluckhohn[6] believes that, "No tenet of intellectual folklore has been so damaging to our life and times as the cliché that 'science has nothing to do with values.' If the consideration of values is to be the exclusive property of religion and the humanities, a scientific understanding of human experience is impossible." And he quotes F.S.C. Northrup: "The norms for ethical conduct are to be discovered from the ascertainable knowledge of man's nature, just as the norms for building a bridge are to be derived from physics."

E.L. Thorndike,[7] in his presidential address before the American Association for the Advancement of Science in 1963, stated that,

"Judgments of value are simply one sort of judgments of fact, distinguished from the rest by two characteristics: They concern consequences. These are consequences to the wants of sentient beings. Values, positive and negative, reside in the satisfaction or annoyance felt by animals, persons, or deities."

VALUE PRESSURES ON THE SCHOOLS

In recent years, philosophers have given increasing attention to axiology, the study (or science) of values. A few psychologists have addressed themselves to problems of choice or preferential behavior in organisms of higher complexity than the white rat, and some have pondered the nature of the social values of psychologists. Anthropologists have observed and reported culturally defined and strongly-held beliefs, codes, and sanctions; and sociologists and economists have theorized about social and economic values, respectively. But educational psychologists have given scant attention directly to the problem of values and value judgments or seen that value theory, unformulated though it may be, permeates all educational interrelationships. This problem of values involves the study of the process by which individuals learn to make choices of means and ends, and of the interrelationships of these choices to each other in the life orientation of the individual.

The charge of churchmen that the schools do not teach "moral and spiritual values" was recently passed on up to the highest educational echelons, and at a conference of the Educational Policies Commission, certain members were unwilling to admit even that good health is a value, so great was the confusion on the subject. And the Commission as a whole could not agree on a statement regarding values freed from the sanctions of theocratic ideology. As a consequence, it was decided to issue a monograph[8] and to encourage workshops in which teachers would develop their own concepts of moral and spiritual values, though it was pointed out that when spiritual values are defined in terms of theological doctrine, they are properly not a part of the school program.*

*See, for example, John Dewey Society, Seventh Yearbook, J.S. Brubaker (ed.), *The Public Schools and Spiritual Values.* New York: Harper, 1944, and

The ultra-intellectuals of the literary humanistic persuasion have likewise added their voices to those of the ecclesiastical critics, contending that the function of the schools is to transmit the cultural heritage and give training in the "intellectual disciplines," usually with particular emphasis on their own academic specialization. Replies to these gentlemen[9] have had to point out, among other things, that there are likewise other values to be considered, inasmuch as their predilection for arbitarily determined academic standards for all pupils revealed an extremely narrow view even of what knowledge is of most worth.

VALUE CONCEPTS IN EDUCATION

However, the axiological naiveté of many educators, and of citizens generally, does not imply that problems of value are new to education. Scattered and uncoordinated efforts have here and there been successful in building value concepts into the structure of educational theory and practice. These efforts may be referred to briefly as intuitional, empirical, rational, and experimental.

Intuitional. The intuitional efforts are illustrated by the work of the great educational reformers, Rousseau, Pestalozzi and Froebel, who did much to shift the value orientation of the schools from an authoritarian, society-centered pattern to one emphasizing individual needs and development. The importance of many values that have been traditionally neglected was emphasized by the Progressive Education group of our own time, but still largely on an intuitional basis.

Empirical. Values have of necessity been handled empirically by school boards and superintendents, since they are subject to the pressures of public opinion. As a consequence, health values (and some others as well) were forced in, but they had to enter through the back door of afterschool, extra-curricular activities. Intellectual values have,

National Education Association, Department of Elementary School Principals, *Spiritual Values in the Elementary School.* Twenty-sixth Yearbook, 1947. Since the term "spiritual" has so many different meanings, it might be better if its use were forbidden in educational writings and speeches, or if authors were required to furnish a definition of their meaning. It might be going too far to demand an operational definition!

of course, always been in good repute, but they have suffered from the enthusiasm both of the instrumental-value, formal disciplinarians, and of the latter-day saints of the aristocratic tradition, the absolute-value devotees of the humanities who believe, properly enough, that the schools should help to transmit the culture of the past, but who have different ideas as to what aspects of the culture should be transmitted. Political or power values have been encountered on the basis of which, at one extreme autocratic methods to develop subservience are advocated, while at the other democratic leadership is encouraged. Economic values have long been stressed, from the early New England demand for the three R's, trade training, and theological preparation, through Benjamin Franklin's Academy and later through the development of a wide range of trade and professional schools to the present-day emphasis on vocational education and guidance. Esthetic values have been generally neglected, while social values have been governed largely by the punitive theories derived from the Hebraic-Christian tradition of Puritanism, and British legal positivism. The important task of helping young people to find any harmony of values in their life orientation has been left to fall between the mores-bound influence of their homes, the conflicting theologies of the churches, and the not very effective system of required and elective courses.

Rational. In contrast with this unsatisfactory empiricism, certain rationalistic hypotheses have been worked out and reflected in educational theory, even if they are not often clearly observable in practice. Evolutionary theory reinforced the intuitional view that nature is right and, therefore, should be followed; and the instinct hypothesis provided a temporary framework for understanding motivation, coupled with earlier motivational theory based hedonistically on pleasantness and unpleasantness which had introduced "sugar-coating" methods into the schools. A behavioral theory of choice was embodied in Thorndike's satisfiers and annoyers, which seem still to be acceptable if translated to read "objectives and conditions having positive and negative valence," or, more recently, "positive reinforcement contingencies." Psychoanalysis has deluged the journals with a motivation theory based on unconscious conflict.[10]

Experimental. Paper-and-pencil tests of interests and attitudes come close to the heart of the axiological problem, while personality inventories, ratings, social-class investigations, opinion surveys and case studies are right in the middle of it, though the researchers may not realize their location, and the results are largely unsystematic and unrelated.

As a consequence of the welter of intuition, empiricism, theory and experimentation, educators have actually become well aware of one aspect or another of the problem of values in education, but under another name. They have dealt with it as the problem of educational aims or objectives. They were forced by practical necessity to harmonize in some way the conflicting value claims of various pressure groups, theories, and research studies; and the way chosen was to name committees, from time to time, to formulate a comprehensive list of educational objectives to serve as a kind of creed. The 1918 report of the Commission on the Reorganization of Secondary Education[11] listed seven "cardinal" objectives: health, command of fundamental processes, worthy home membership, vocation, civic education, worthy use of leisure time and ethical character. This value-packed list is still a good one, though lacking in anything that could be called a basic theory, as the term is technically used. That the list was not entirely satisfactory is evident from the fact that other lists have appeared since, and various techniques have been tried out for formulating new objectives.

A direct attack on the problem of values has been made by relatively few investigators. Semantic difficulties have bedeviled the philosophers in their efforts to agree on the meaning of the traditional axiological concepts,[12] and as a consequence, a spate of new terms gushed from the pens of the social scientists.[13] [14]

VALUES IN EDUCATIONAL WORK AREAS

Theory. If educational leaders are really to deal effectively with the problem of values, they must do so in the three areas of "theory," "research," and "practice." The question of values is a significant one in learning theory and in personality theory, as psychologists, social psychologists, sociologists and cultural anthropologists are coming to realize; but scientists in these fields have not yet really begun to exploit the possibilities of the school as a social institution, or of the child in the school as a learning, adjusting organism. If educational psychologists are to assume the responsibility which is theirs, they will include findings from these fields within their province and also the cross-disciplinary concepts that are coming into favor, and no longer be satisfied with a pet list of wants or needs and vague intuitions as to the proper structure of a democratic school system. And if a satisfactory value theory for education is to be built, they will apply what is developing in semiotics, starting perhaps with Morris'[15] designative, appraisive and prescriptive signs. They will distinquish more carefully between the desired and the desirable, and learn to identify and validate their criteria for the latter. More specifically, they will learn to distinguish between the "I like" of personal taste or interest, the "I want" of desire, the "I need" of organic or social demand, the "I ought" of interiorized sanctions, and the compulsive "I must," and they will be able to put these different preferential verbalisms into the second and third person, and use them in the plural as well as the singular, on a rational, objective basis, as a result of impartial inquiry into facts and consequences, instead of deciding what others need and what ought to be done entirely from the narrow frame of reference of personal and group prejudice.

Research. When descriptive research has begun to provide (a) information about the value systems of individuals of differing ages in various economic, social, and cultural groups,[16] we can look forward to (b) studies of the effectiveness of specific educational techniques in developing behavior in the direction of objectives agreed upon as desirable,[17] and then (c) determine whether the means employed have been successful.[18] [19]

Some of the most interesting studies have employed the Allport-Vernon[20] list of values derived from the ideal types of Eduard Spranger.[21] These five value categories, with perhaps health or physical values added, are familiar enough to need only to be listed: cognitive (or intellectual), esthetic (or artistic), religious, political, economic, and social (or altruistic).

The Value Pattern. In viewing the list of values as they may affect an individual, an institution, or a society, it seems evident that there are errors of deficiency and of excess—certain values may be neglected and others pushed too far. In Western culture, the political (power and status), and economic (work and money) values tend to be overemphasized. If all can be provided for within the middle range between deficiency and excess, the pattern of living can seemingly be improved both for the individual and the community.

It may be objected that there seems to be no place for the virtues, such as honesty, self-control, loyalty, justice, and the like. But the virtues are the means for the attainment of the life values. Conduct promoting the values is virtuous; and whatever serves to negate the values is vicious. This view clarifies one of the chief problems of moral instruction. For if one concentrates on the means, for example, on honesty, a child may be baffled by the "white lies" of his parents, or if on loyalty, one may wonder about those who were loyal to Hitler. By and large, the virtues furnish acceptable guides, but the criterion lies in the relation of conduct to the life values.

In educational practice, instructional materials will no doubt be radically modified in order better to adapt to and promote individual and group values. The schools of the future will have the task of beginning instruction where the child is, not only with respect to the intellectual values which have become an educational axiom, but also beginning where he is with respect to the other values as well.

Part II
Criticism vs. Reform

6. EDUCATIONAL CHANGE AND THE DEMOCRATIC PROCESS
    Changing ends call for changing means.

7. THE DRAGONS OF FALSE BELIEFS
    Pausing to reflect—what we firmly believe may not be so; convictions may be wrong.

8. ASSUMPTIONS ARE NOT AXIOMS
    What is taken for granted as being not only acceptable in school practice, but even necessary, may be what is making all the trouble.

9. EDUCATIONAL REFORM AND THE GOOD LIFE
    Let us think through the matter of educational reform and see what can be done about it.

6.
Educational Change and the Democratic Process

Changes are rapid in a democratic, competitive society when its products make a profit, and slow when they do not. The natural sciences, through the exploitation of petroleum and electricity alone, have changed the face of our civilization in a generation, while the social and behavioral sciences, with few saleable products, demonstrate the cultural lag. Yet, it is in the field of the social and behavioral sciences that our most serious difficulties lie. Solutions for the problems of poverty, of mental health, of delinquency and crime, and even of peace and war, might well be within our grasp if there had been any real assurance that they would create wealth. The dedicated professional workers in the social science fields have labored long on little pay and meager research budgets, often misunderstood and sometimes ridiculed by the society they serve. Legislators and others have been known to confuse sociology with socialistic, economics with economical, and psychology with psychic.

Criticism. Education, which draws on the social and behavioral sciences for its reliable knowledge, is peculiarly vulnerable. Even some of the more enlightened educational critics failed to realize that their objections were only a part of the most recent of a whole series of struggles to adapt the school program to the needs of a dynamic civilization. They know little of the earlier struggles for state support, for secularization, for extending the age of compulsory schooling, for vocational education and training, for adaptation to varying abilities, and as in the case of the more recent progressive education movement, for enlarging the range of values in the objectives of the school program.

Each battle won tends to be forgotten, perhaps because it is not adequately reported to the oncoming generations. It may well be true that in no other field are the uninformed more vocal or listened to with greater interest, particularly since innovations are likely to result in the bite of higher taxes instead of the glow of larger profits. So the great debate has continued on and off, but in a somewhat unequal fashion. Critics of the schools turn out the most plausibly written articles urging indiscriminately what might prove helpful, what is common practice, and what has long since been discarded as useless.

Distorted news items and editorials appear in the newspapers. Unusual conditions presented as typical, and biased charges of various sorts make the slick magazines. But replies are not news or, with a few noteworthy exceptions, they are not in accord with editorial policy, so of necessity they appear only in professional journals. Reprints, however, have gotten through to the authors and editors, and enough information has trickled down through school officials and teachers to parents and other citizens, so that as a consequence the critics have become somewhat better informed and more cautious, and criticisms and suggestions more realistic.

Rarely now do we hear that the scholars and scientists must take over the running of the schools, that only a narrow, rigid academic curriculum should be provided, that children not academically talented should be weeded out by rigorous examinations and put to work. Educational jargon, freshman boners, and even Johnny's phonics have become old-hat. A few denominationalists still lift impassioned voices against "godless schools." The former objections of classical scholars and some others to physical education have degenerated for the most part to plaintive head shaking since they have recalled that gymnastics, not Latin, constituted an important part of classical Greek education, and have realized that in some mysterious way people's bodies and brains are connected. The recent Russian enthusiasts, too, are becoming a little more vague in their recommendations after their experiences in trying to follow the Communist party line as a consequence of the changes in the Russian educational system.

A recent visitor to Russia, trying hard to maintain his balance, wrote that "Soviet education places *primary emphasis upon basic disciplines*. Art, music, sports, shops and home economics are included in the curriculum of the schools, but the stress in the ten-year schools really has been on science, arithmetic and later mathematics, geography, Russian literature and modern languages." The poor fellow should have known, before signing his name to this blather, that exactly the same thing could be said of the American schools, with English literature substituted for Russian. He was even troubled for fear the Khrushchev reforms, with their lessened academic emphasis in favor of vocationalism, may not be a good idea—which, of course, is dangerous deviationism. Certainly those who read the papers know that the Russians have not done too badly even in "art, music, sports and shops," and who would wish to deny them a little home economics!

Collaboration.[1] Although the occasional "Disturbed Parent" or "Taxpayer" who writes letters to the editor may not know it, the great debate is really over. A good deal of twaddle will no doubt continue to be written, but the charge that educationists are conspiring to ruin the schools has fallen on stony ground. The second phase has already begun. The democratic process has been at work sifting the true from the false, and it is quite possible that some of the arguments that have produced more heat than light have actually energized needed reforms. The American people have come to realize again that good schools cost money, and they still want good schools. Bond-issue struggles will no doubt continue, but with increasing chances of success. The question of federal aid is no longer whether, but how, and how much. Colleges and universities are seeing their way to providing not only those courses which lead to the Ph.D., but also those which meet the needs of teachers, and even of future citizens who do not expect to become scholars or scientists (and there are quite a few), that they may have some of the knowledge of the world and of man that will help them find their way around in this amazing universe. Cooperative efforts between content specialists and those in education are increasing without benefit of newspaper headlines, and many of the hopes that have inspired educators for years are on their way to being realized.

The second phase, that of adequate financial support and professional collaboration, will necessarily continue. But just as it overlaps the first, so signs of a third phase, the phase of the future, are already visible. During the summers in my college years I worked on a farm with a hoe and a pitchfork and rode a horse-drawn hayrack. While there are still hoes and pitchforks, research and mechanization have already revolutionized agriculture.

Automation. During World War II, I had some responsibility for one of the Army training programs for civil affairs officers. Area and language study constituted the major part of the training. Language was supposed to be taught by the then new aural-oral procedures developed by the linguists. We employed native speakers and used a few phonograph records. Now, high schools and colleges have their language laboratories; students may dial the tape-recorded lessons needed, and transcriptions may be made of their pronunciation and compared with the original.

In some cities, the television screen brings its lessons to hundreds of rooms at a time. Each lesson is prepared and taught by a master teacher whose responsibility is not for five or six classes and 150 pupils a day, but perhaps the preparation of one daily 30-minute lesson.

Students must think and do as well as look and listen. Thousands of dollars in federal and foundation funds are already being spent in developing and conducting research on programming for teaching machines. Several companies are already manufacturing machines ranging from a simple $3.00 gadget to the most complicated electronic devices tied up with computers. For this revolution, we do not have to wait for technology to catch up. Machines can be produced at whatever level of complexity may prove most practical. We might as well face it. The most modern school today will soon be as obsolete as the one-room school with wood stove and water bucket.

The new teachers, like present-day farmers, will have to acquire different kinds of knowledge and skill. Another gentleman recently pontificated on the threshold of the technological revolution, that "the battle between emphasis on subject matter and emphasis on method has been decided in favor of the former." How blind can people be! Actually there can be no such battle. The two are organically inseparable, and a change in one necessarily produces change in the other. Wise or stupid choices may be made in content or method, but the problem is not one of emphasis but of effectiveness: what knowledge and skills are of most worth for different kinds of individuals in our complex society, and what are the most efficient means of inculcating them?

Even the best of the older methods are now being called into question. Mechanization, or automation if you will, coupled with research gives every sign of producing a major breakthrough, similar to what has occurred in agriculture. The inquiries will relate to method more than ever before. "Know-how" has long been characteristic of American engineering enterprise, and it will be sought vigorously in this area of human engineering, and will be adapted to whatever subject matter is deemed appropriate for the individual and social needs of the learners. Much of the method will be built into the machines, and the task of supervising will be a skilled technician's job, but that of providing materials to feed into the machines will not. The television programs will gradually develop masterful ways of *presenting* educational materials, and the tutoring machines will take up where they leave off by providing pupils with the necessary practice in learning facts and manipulating ideas. There will still be a place for teachers, a most important place. They will have to assess pupil ability and provide the programming best suited to their needs. They will no longer have to drill their pupils on foreign language forms, but they must be able to converse with them in the language. A knowledge of facts and relationships on which discussions can be based will be acquired with a facility never before known, and as a consequence teachers will have to be able to lead discussions with pupils who know what they are talking about! And there still remains the task of inculcating attitudes, in which the machines can no doubt participate, that will result not in evil or merely smart decisions, but in good and wise ones. Social interaction cannot be practiced individually with machines, but only socially in groups. The teacher, when freed from routine drills and mere lesson hearing, will have to spend more of his time being a teacher.

How rapidly will these changes come about? Since there is an opportunity to make a profit in the manufacture and sale of television and tutoring machine equipment, it may come about with surprising rapidity. But the machines, the programming and the promotion will not be paid for to any great extent by individual buyers who for no down payment can be promised beautiful hair and skin, a fresh smoke, freedom from indigestion, greater speed and power, or even a higher financial yield. Even with the cooperation of the foundations, they will be paid for largely by *taxes.* Like the monitorial system of Lancaster and Bell, television and teaching machines seem to promise fewer teachers, and hence reduced instructional costs. Automation may have this effect, though it is improbable. But as in agriculture and industry, it will do a better job and do it more efficiently.

7.
The Dragons of False Beliefs

Once upon a time a knight mounted his charger and set forth to slay a dragon and rescue a beautiful damsel in distress. In fact, according to the records, there were at times dozens of such knights roaming the countryside.

But there never were any real dragons, were there?

Yes, there were very real dragons, and there are now. Some are, no doubt, like the dragons of long ago—irate fathers who didn't want some ignorant hired man on a horse fooling around with their daughters. Others represent the rapacious id, soon to be done in by the transcendent super ego. Or, more broadly, the dragons may symbolize the evil and injustice in the world, to be fought and overcome by the soldiers of righteousness.

Activists are still anxious to help right the wrongs of our social order, but they now need something other than a horse, a sword and a coat of mail. One of the things they need is a weapons system to slay the dragons of false beliefs that still plague the mind of man, cause untold suffering, and deprive him of the happiness and well being that might otherwise be his.

Supposedly each person might himself get rid of his own injurious false beliefs, and some do. However, many depend on them, get used to old dragon, and come to trust him, even thinking they might be worse off without his fatherly or big-brotherly protection. What are these false beliefs?

One is the belief a person may have, that what he *thinks* must be so, that it is true, sensible, reasonable, or correct. "It stands to reason," he says of his own ideas, and "Who ever heard of such a thing!" he says of someone else's. Or he says "I don't agree," or "I am not convinced," as if these were really arguments. The false beliefs may relate to his own or another's abilities or lack of them, or to some other question of fact or judgment. If one is serious in his quest of the holy grail of certainty, he may be aided in his journey by "dialogue" and by "confrontation," and by testing the validity of his ideas in the marketplace and in the laboratory.

Another false belief is in the powers ascribed to heredity. For example, if a parent was too fat or lazy, addicted to strong drink, or never got beyond the eighth grade, such matters are used as an excuse for the child who suffers from a like infirmity. In reverse, this is the belief that a son has, or should have, the academic abilities of his father as well as his professional interests, and so should study medicine, say, or law, instead of following his own talents and interests. Thus, the parent (on the distaff side too) can take pride in the successes of the offspring.

A third false belief is the result of rejection of the old adage, *caveat emptor*–let the buyer beware. It is the belief that someone who wants you to buy what he has to sell will tell the truth about it, whether he is a con man, advertiser, trader, salesman, or owner–or promulgator. He may be a gangster, or he may be merely biased, telling the truth as he sees it. But belief in his truthfulness closes off objective inquiry.

A fourth false belief is a corollary–that a person's ideas are sound if he writes them in a book, or if he yells them at the top of his lungs ("rabble rouser"), if a lot of people applaud him, or if he speaks with deep feeling and seeming sincerity. Sober reflection may lead one to be less gullible and to weigh the evidence more carefully.

A fifth false belief is that anything that should be done should be done at once (if at all) and by direct action, even by protest marches, civil disobedience, or mob action. This seems to be the current fad. It may be recognized that mechanical and industrial processes require time, skill and training to carry through, and a careful consideration of possible consequences of one's efforts, but social processes are apparently thought of by some to be in a different category.

The sixth and last false belief to be mentioned, though the reader can no doubt supply others, results from confusing one's own desires, habits or customs with natural law. For example, revenge may seem desirable as well as sweet, and pugnacity and aggression virtuous, above good sense and cooperative effort. To win over the opponent, the prime objective of competition, is assumed as a value in itself, whether in games, business, or international politics.

It should be added that, in certain cases, one or another of these beliefs may be true. The dragon may be right, or perhaps he isn't a dragon—merely a friendly prince in disguise. But more often than not, acting on any one of them results either in complete failure or in that anomalous condition in which, as the man said, "I got what I wanted, but I didn't want what I got." And usually a great many innocent bystanders didn't want what they got, either.

It would seem that the well-meaning people, whether they are labeled capitalists or workers, deists or humanists, lawyers or social workers, statesmen or politicians, could well give a great deal of thought to slaying the dragons of false beliefs. Any success would tend to dry up the sources of many of their problems—problems of poverty and dependency, for example, and delinquency and crime, and even of war and peace.

Some of the manifestations of these problems have been dealt with locally, but by slow, primitive methods. An all-out attack on the false beliefs themselves could well be more effective. It has been said that "this is the era of the proposal and the grant." Research efforts to discover the origin, nature and means of modification of beliefs might yield surprising results. Man *can be* rational. The scientific study of natural phenomena has produced remarkable results. If a new technology can take a man to the moon, it might find a better way to slay dragons. Meanwhile, with a dedicated militia, we can keep them on the defensive.

8.
Assumptions Are Not Axioms

What is wrong with this picture?

"Joyce comes from a barren, substandard home. She is small for her age, and she greatly fears her father's aggressiveness. Her first-grade teacher says of her:

> Joyce was very immature when she came to school. We should have told her mother to keep her at home for another year. Her vocabulary was very limited; she couldn't keep her mind on anything for more than a minute; and she couldn't sit still. She surely wasn't ready to learn to read. Now she's so far behind that she knows and I know that she'll never catch up. She just came to school too soon.*

Perhaps the reader can specify two or three things that are wrong. Or if one prefers a single answer, *everything* might be it. Another single answer is quite intriguing and likely to be overlooked. It is that various assumptions about behavior are mistaken for axiomatic truths, although they are known to be false. The horror is that the situation is representative of conditions that may be found in practically every school in our land. We still try to fit pupils into the school, instead of

*Gordon P. Liddle, "The School Psychologist's Role with the Culturally Handicapped," in James Magary, *School Psychological Services in Theory and Practice.* Englewood Cliffs, New Jersey: Prentice-Hall, Inc., 1967, pp. 510-11.

adapting the school to the needs of the pupils. This is quite contrary to the most basic of educational principles, to teach pupils where they are in their development. That such conditions are possible is due in large measure to six false assumptions that are generally accepted as true, like axioms, and therefore are usually not even questioned.

Those who do question them are viewed as somehow sadly lacking, like the University of Michigan botanist some years ago, who was exploring New Guinea. He had been taken into the native tribe and so was allowed to be present at the preparation of a kind of harvest festival. There was an altar-like table on which different kinds of produce were piled; and a board with cleats tacked on crosswise formed an incline path from the ground to the table top to make it easy for one of the gods (let us call him Aba) to climb up on the altar and claim his offering. The botanist noticed that the cleats were on the under side of the board; so he turned the board over so that the cleats could serve the presumed purpose of keeping Aba from slipping. At once a little girl rushed up and turned the board back with the cleats on the bottom. "Don't you know," she exclaimed, "that Aba always walks upside down!"

The assumptions are like such completely accepted religious beliefs, taken for granted, and finding expression, on occasion, in words and action. And like this belief, the assumptions defy practices that are upside down.

Assumption 1. – Readiness. The first assumption, one which fortunately is less often considered as axiomatic than formerly, is that when a pupil enters a grade (or a class or course), he is ready to undertake the work the syllabus prescribes for it. Joyce's first-grade teacher assumed, when Joyce entered school, that she could shortly begin to read. While school pre-reading experiences are now usually provided, it is still generally assumed that when a pupil is arbitrarily placed in a certain grade, he should be able to do the work of that grade. Thus, the problem of readiness at other levels also tends to be overlooked, whether the student is deficient because of his native ability, his lack of previous instruction or experience, or his conflicting emotional attitudes.

B. F. Skinner's term, entering behavior, is a useful one here. Sometimes students need extra instruction before taking a course, and some others, by reason of high intelligence or having elected certain courses previously, could pass the course before they take it. Both conditions are obviously inefficient, and they would be considered ridiculous by any who did not take for granted the truth of the assumption.

Assumption 2. — The Classroom. It is assumed that school buildings are necessarily divided into largely identical classrooms, each built to accommodate about 30-35 children. While there are arguments and many futile researches as to the optimum class size, the general pattern is taken for granted. Administrators estimate school needs and costs, and architects design buildings on this basis, and school psychologists and mental hygiene people discuss the need for considering the influence of "the regular classroom" on disturbed children. Even though some have attacked this pattern, and ridiculed it as "egg-crate construction," and though modifications are gradually creeping in, it remains firmly fixed as axiomatic in the conceptual framework of lay and professional people alike.

Assumption 3. — The Teacher. It is assumed that in each classroom there will be a person called "the teacher." Again, estimates of school costs are based on this assumption of one teacher in each virtually self-contained classroom. Further, futile research efforts have sought to determine the personality characteristics of the good (and the poor) teacher. This assumption is also treated as an axiom. It is taken for granted, and it just does not occur to lay or professional people to think otherwise.

Consequently, the possibility is overlooked that lecture-demonstration (explaining), monitoring (improving pupil performance) and leading discussion (planning, etc.) may require quite different talents. And little has been done to train people in the specific skills[1] they need to use as teachers or to provide a desirable variety in instruction—by the use of teaching teams and aides, and persons of varied background, even by individual study, to say nothing of teaching machines and television.[2]

Assumption 4. — The Knowledge Objective. It is assumed that verbal knowledge is the sole objective of the school, that motor skills are few and supplementary only, and that social skills should be taken care of by "discipline," or else by some kind of semi-medical diagnosis and treatment.

Programmed learning has revealed the importance of defining behavioral objectives,[3] and studies of learning suggest that social behavior can be taught. But these ideas, for the most part, leave school practice untouched, and students continue to be drilled on factual knowledge and "inert ideas," most of which are quickly forgotten, while punishment or permissiveness rule the roost in dealing with emotional and behavior problems.

Assumption 5. − The Grade.[4] Grades, like classrooms, are assumed to be as integral a part of schools as branches are of trees. A school without grades is unthinkable to most people. Even the experts, for example, talk about fifth-grade ability, knowing full well it is only a fictional average, and that the abilities of the children in the fifth grade range from that of some in the third grade to some in the eighth grade. Originally, it was an administrative convenience instituted a little more than a century ago to economize on instruction by providing for groups of children to be taught the same thing at the same time. It has become a diabolical device into which we try to fit the pupils, and by means of which they will proceed with seeming smoothness each year from one grade to the next. And, like Joyce, they never catch up.

Ability grouping will no doubt continue until it is realized that children learn at different rates; hence, the time units of instruction are inappropriate. Credits in high school and credit hours in college are the analog of grades in the lower schools—credit for time that must be spent in class, somewhat like the time that must be spent in prison before the unhappy inmate can be released. But in schools there is no chance of a reduced sentence, parole, or pardon, only for escape by dropping out.

Eventually, it must be realized that instead of holding time constant and allowing competencies to vary, competencies are to be held constant and *learning time varied.* It is hardly possible to appreciate the satisfaction schooling will bring to children and young people when they are allowed to work at their ability level and when they can see the progress they are making, instead of being constantly reminded of failure for which not they, but the schools, are responsible.

Assumption 6. − The Mark. It is assumed that differences in human ability necessarily result in some students doing well, some about average, and some poorly.[5] The probability curve or curve of chance is the symbol of this assumption, which is considered axiomatic.

Indeed, it is so thoroughly believed in that when a large proportion of students do equally well (or poorly), either insignificant differences are magnified to get a distribution, or the test or examination is considered at fault, and the next time a larger proportion of hard or easy questions is used. It results in the anomaly of the norm-referenced score,[6] as illustrated by the fact that many bright students prefer not to be placed in the top "honors" group, for if they are, they might get a B or a C; whereas if they were in the regular class, they could be sure of an A. Instead, we could well expect a criterion-referenced mark or score, which depends only on the learner's proficiency, whatever his age or grade.

The use of marks fits nicely into the system of grading and annual promotions, for since the slower student can't keep up, and like Joyce, when he gets behind can never catch up, it simplifies things and salves pedagogical consciences to "evaluate" his achievement and give a low mark. Somehow, it never seems to occur to anyone that teachers are thus being paid for not teaching students.

Stimulus from Outside. The time will come when some critics of education will forget their pet peeves about what children are being taught in the schools, and really look into the situation. When they do, and when they find that as things now stand the curriculum makes no great difference because little is learned anyway—when this happens, there will be a real revolution.

Managers of large industrial and governmental concerns will not think highly of school administrators who complain that a program that adapts to individual differences is difficult to arrange. Trainers in the armed forces and in industry, who are already beginning to talk about education, will not be dissolved to tears by the teachers' complaints that certain students get behind. "Get behind what?" they are likely to ask, and further, "If you consider this content important, why not *teach* it to them?" Psychologists versed in the nature of learning are not likely to be enthusiastic about the use of educational procedures out of the distant past, procedures which never have worked well, and still don't. When one asks about reinforcement contingencies, teachers are likely to be baffled, though they may recall reading about them in the teacher-education institutions they attended. But they did not see any relation between them (and much else they learned then) and the actual job of teaching.

What Is the Answer? What can be done to get school practices going right side up instead of upside down? The obvious thing is to get rid of the myths and false assumptions that serve to maintain the present topsy-turvy structure. No one group can do this alone. But it should be possible if the more enlightened administrators, teachers, school psychologists—and students (who are now beginning to become aware of some of the phony practices) get together locally and on state and national levels, and through active committee work, start housecleaning, move the antiques up into the attic, and begin the modernization program that is now long overdue.

A number of schools are trying out one scheme or another—programming, television, team teaching, teaching aides, ungraded schools, and so on, which is a very good way to start. *But not much improvement can be expected by inserting one or two of these in the old setting; the false assumptions must be abandoned and the system restructured.* Consequent developments would be a boon not only to the culturally deprived, but to all young people in our schools and colleges.

9.
Educational Reform and the Good Life

The so-called great debate on education is now fortunately about over. Gradually, the tumult and the shouting died, though occasional sniping will no doubt continue for some time from the Johnny-come-latelies. Those concerned, however, are gradually becoming aware of the changes that are really needed, as suggested in the preceding four chapters.

THREE STAGES

The year 1963, in a way, marked the end of the old and the beginning of the new with the appearance of two volumes on teacher education. In that year James D. Koerner[1] may be said to have rounded off the period of lay criticism with an elaborate critique but with the familiar "back to the disciplines" theme. And James B. Conant[2] opened up the new with one of the most controversial of his reports—*The Education of American Teachers.* There is some doubt as to whether Conant can properly be called a lay critic. As Harvard professor and president and ambassador to Germany, he qualifies, but his four or five years of study of educational problems supported by foundation grants, as Marani[3] points out, may qualify him as a member of "the establishment." His insights and challenging recommendations, however, seem to place him in a category by himself as marking the transition to the second stage of education reform, that of cooperative effort.

The transitional stage, like the first phase, is somewhat chaotic. Conant himself wrote that he hoped the book would provoke controversy, but he is a friendly critic albeit at times a devastating one, and the controversy, which began at once, has been on a distinctly higher level than what preceded. Battle lines have tended to fade out. Former opponents have found themselves in agreement, and propositions have come to be debated largely on their merits. Some proposals relate to matters about which there is common agreement theoretically but point to deficiencies in practice. Others indicate well-known weak spots but suggest questionable solutions.

Implicit in Conant's discussion are three presuppositions, the first of which is that systematic courses as now organized both in school and college are standard operating procedure and will continue indefinitely. Hence, it would follow that improvement in instruction, if any, must come by reshuffling these courses, making such invidious distinctions between them as "necessary," "desirable but not needed," and "worthless," ascribing less or more credit to them, or trying to get better teachers to teach them. Yet Conant is outspoken in his denunciation of the course or credit-hour as a unit of measurement, and elsewhere suggests the interesting possibility of holding proficiency standards constant and varying the length of time of instruction. It is to be hoped that future controversy and collaboration will recognize that what a student knows and what he can do are what matters—rather than the number of hours or courses he has "had."

The second of his presuppositions follows from the first. It is that instruction is carried on only by *the* teacher in *the* classroom. This familiar speech form tends to direct the thought of those who use it away from such ecological variations as the shop, gymnasium, studio, library, laboratory, conference room and auditorium as well as from the playground and the outside world as explored on field trips. To reveal something of the insidious influence of this speech form, Conant himself, in discussing the criteria for certification, gives no consideration to these varying locales when he categorically affirms his belief that "the ultimate test of teaching should be *how the teacher actually performs in a classroom* as judged by experienced teachers." (Italics his.) Such stereotypy tends to block off consideration of team-teaching and of departmentalization, both of which he discusses, and assumes the perpetuity of the self-contained classroom, which actually, he opines, will not continue long above the third grade. Yet, in his delineation of needed practice-teaching experience, he recurs to the stereotype with recommendations which make no mention of the quite separate skills required for such different teaching procedures as the lecture, demonstration, recitation (i.e., traditional "teaching"), discussion and monitored performance. The value of audio-visual materials is minimized, and TV and programmed learning practically overlooked, as is the possibility of the fading out of the present grade-promotion system as a consequence of the development of continuity of instruction through the years that will gradually grow out of programs of advanced placement.

The third of Conant's presuppositions is that the objective of teacher preparation is good teaching as, of course, it is. But the criterion is not necessarily what looks good in "the classroom," even "as judged by experienced teachers," unless the "ultimate test" is viewed as that which results in *pupils'* learning what they can and will use and transfer to later in-and-out-of-school-situations. Again, Conant recognizes this, as when he points out that the schools are "involved in more than imparting knowledge and developing skills. . . . (They) are charged with the responsibility of developing certain attitudes." And, again, he puts his finger on the criterion for a selection of the professional knowledge a teacher should have, though he limits himself to psychological principles, when he says the teacher might well be able to "deduce such specific predictions as 'If I (as a teacher) do so and so, such and such will probably happen,' or 'If he (the pupil) behaves in this or that way in situation X, he will behave in a certain way in situation Y' " (pp. 135-36). To be able to make just such predictions, then be able to do or say what is needed to produce the behavior desired, whether in "the classroom," in conference, or elsewhere, or in rendering professional judgments in faculty committees on the curriculum or "discipline" or other problems, is precisely what programs of teacher-training are for. And yet somehow this usually gets lost when teacher preparation is discussed. It may be that future collaborators will consider the value of systematic courses, say, in the social foundations, with this criterion in front of them.

Examples of the second phase, that of cooperative effort, are many; and, of course, to some extent they preceded the first phase. They include the work of various committees and conferences at the local, state and national levels, in which subject matter specialists and educationists participate. The consequences of collaboration often lead in quite different directions from those advocated by the earlier lay critics.

TECHNOLOGY

As the first phase is moving off the scene, and the second begins to occupy the center of the stage, the third has already made its entrance. It bears the name of educational technology, which refers not alone to teaching machines, educational television and electronics. Like the pronouncements of the lay critics in the first phase, the hardware may have had the effect of stimulating change. But much more is involved, namely, a *functional analysis of the whole teaching-learning process.*

The question of the use to be made of the new media raises the further question of the respective roles of the new and the old. As a consequence, the search is on for specific instructional objectives much more clearly stated than heretofore. How much more reasonable it would be to set forth clearly what we intend to teach our students, i.e., what we expect them to know or do, and then teach it to them, than to follow the customary procedure of stopping when the bell rings or the term is over, and giving them a mark to show that many of them haven't learned it! Various attempts have been made over the past fifty years to adapt instruction to children and young people of differing intellectual ability, ranging from non-promotion and sub-grouping of those in any one grade to schemes for individual instruction, as illustrated by the Dalton and Winnetka plans. But now, as a consequence of the invention of the teaching machine and of programmed learning, individualized instruction on a large scale for the first time becomes really practicable.

Other questions arise. How effective are many of the time-honored school practices and procedures—the self-contained classroom and the grading and marking systems, the so-called Carnegie unit for high schools and the credit hour for colleges, the present division of labor of the teaching staff and the division of the school building into a number of equal-sized classrooms? And how effective are the traditional methods and media, the teacher's talk, the recitation, the library, audio-visual materials, and even the textbooks?

These time-honored devices are suspected of not producing up to capacity, or perhaps some of them have out-lived their usefulness.

Investigators are seeking ways to teach that will enable students to apply what is taught in their daily lives instead of having it remain, as it so often does, a mass of unassimilated facts that are soon forgotten. The goal of excellence is more than a cliché, and the ideals of a liberal education, seemingly as fantastic as a trip to the moon, begin to have the ring of possibility.

DISCIPLINES OR FACULTIES?

Will there be a fourth phase? If so, what it will be is any man's guess. But George Gallup[4] has given me the courage to suggest a possibility that I have been considering for some time. It might be called the Direct Method. In common parlance one of the important objectives of education is to teach young people to "think," to use their minds; or, more specifically, to learn to perceive, to form concepts, to make judgments, to foresee consequences, and to take effective action. This end, we have been taught to believe, is to be attained by instruction in the school subjects, or as some prefer to call them, the disciplines. This is axiomatic. But suppose in proper scientific fashion we question this axiom. Suppose we ask if there are other ways and suggest as one hypothesis that the way to attain this objective is to do it directly, and not indirectly by way of the school subjects.

Since I have seen virtual monotones taught to carry a tune by the use of mouth and throat exercises, and students with no sense of the third dimension taught by practice to perceive in depth, I have speculated on the possibilities of extending the idea to other functions. Gallup assumes that the third or technical phase is assured, but as the next step he foresees classes in such subjects as problem-solving, decision-making and creativity, the goal being to develop the full potentialities of each individual. The subjects would still have their content value, but they are deemed inadequate when it comes to developing the general capacity for rational thought.

In view of the rumpus already raised by the advent of educational technology, one can well imagine the storm that will be occasioned by his suggestion to upstage the disciplines and train the faculties, once its implications are realized, and before his stimulating hypotheses are tested.

Be that as it may, what is now needed is not so much a try-out of

TV or programmed units, nor yet the introduction of economics in the third grade or French in the seventh or calculus in the twelfth, although experimentation with curricular segments is desirable. Rather, what is needed is careful planning and experimentation in the coordinated use of different methods and media for different instructional tasks. New kinds of school systems will be developed, with new designs for instruction. These are definitely in the offing.

With a reduction in the number and intensity of the blasts from the lay critics and increased cooperation of psychologists and subject matter specialists and educationists, educational technology will not only be able to cope with the population explosion but also will give the people of the world a better education than their fathers or grandfathers ever had.

Most of what has been said refers to the cultivation of the intellect. If we stop here we are guaranteeing a future population of abler engineers, scientists and administrators and a labor force less dependent on unskilled jobs. But unfortunately we are also guaranteeing a future population of abler crooks, criminals, manipulators and even dictators. On the other hand, those reactionaries who press for a return to more thorough and widespread instruction in science and in the humanities are admitting that the kind of education that has produced this turmoil known as the twentieth century is the kind they want in the future. We are in a quandary: there seems to be little hope in going either forward or back.

VALUES AGAIN

Aside from the cold and hot wars and other social ills for which there is as yet no known cure, and with which we are therefore trying to learn to live, there are minor symptoms of malaise which may point the way out. Joseph Wood Krutch[5] quotes a magazine article in which a well known commentator wrote: "[In Moscow] the day-to-day routine of most citizens is inexpressibly dreary. No local citizen has ever read a gossip column or played canasta. No one has ever seen a supermarket, a drive-in movie, a motel, or a golf course. No one has ever shopped by mail or paid a bill by check. No one has ever seen an electric toaster, a sidewalk cafe, a shoeshine parlor, or a funeral home. I never saw a girl with dark glasses or encountered a man with a cigarette lighter." And without these evidences of the high level of our culture, how dreary the life of man on this planet must have been for the first few thousand years! How fortunate are we to have delayed our entrance until we could find happiness in the products of this modern age!

What is lacking is a proper consideration of values which have been seriously disturbed by world conflict and rapid industrialization, involving the contact of widely differing value systems. If we look to pure science for our answers, we find it is objective and impersonal. The humanities record the best that has been thought and said, but also much of the worst. In a democracy we believe man should be free to choose, so long as he does not—and here we are faced with all the provisions of the penal code, which may be summarized: so long as he does not do injury to himself and others. With a considerable area of agreement, Western society still wavers on the meaning of injury. And with all its intellectual advances it does not yet know how to nurture many of its citizens so that they do not want to injure themselves and others.

Yet it is becoming more and more skillful in influencing their other wants. Commercial advertisers have taught people to cherish the gadgets listed by Krutch's commentator, and they have done so as a consequence of many careful studies of attitude formation. Politicians employ various schemes, empirically derived, to make people want to vote for them. And talented leaders have even worked out ways to make men want to kill and to die.

But these are but islands in an uncharted universe of ignorance. Man must decide, and he does. But in unknown, capricious and chaotic ways his decisions have already been made for him, perhaps not by the advertisers, politicians and leaders at all. He has been "conditioned," to use the psychological term, to choose as he does. And the results of his choices are uncertain—they may be happy and they may be disastrous, both to himself and to others. Or they may be harmless, but far less satisfying than they might be. Yet, amazingly enough, relatively little scientific attention has been given to this most fundamental of human problems, partly perhaps because many believe it insoluble, and partly because many still hold to the fiction that man makes his own choices despite the cultural influences that are brought to bear upon him.

The freedom of the will is an old problem that needs new analyses. The atom was for a long time thought to be the smallest indivisible particle of matter. But research has revealed within it many interacting particles. Biological research has rendered obsolete the old disputes about the nature of heredity. Suppose the same amount of money and effort were expended on research on the problem of wants and values as a basis for choice and action, and on the processes of attitude formation, as have been given to atomic and genetic research. Such research would need to be both pure and applied, pure to discover the facts of nature, and applied to discover ways in which the facts of nature can be manipulated in order to obtain the results sought.

A little over a hundred years ago Herbert Spencer[6] wrote the essay with the challenging title, "What Knowledge Is of Most Worth?" A little over thirty years ago, George S. Counts[7] published a book with the still more challenging and more disturbing title *Dare the School Build a New Social Order?* So disturbing was it that the social order immediately repressed it into the depths of its unconscious—and forgot all about it. It is now time for a little deep analysis to recover this question and perhaps to reword it to read, "How Can the School Help the Social Order to Build Anew?"

Research, like other human activity, tends to move to where the money is. With a few million dollars given to investigations in the area of wants and values, it is possible that we could gradually pull ourselves out of the quandary. We need neither go back to the old educational ways, many of which are unfortunately still with us, nor need we fear the new and more effective ways of cultivating the intellect, whether by the new technology or the "direct method," or both. Permeating our education, whether old or new, would be a continuing emphasis on the making of good choices. We could not only learn ways of inculcating attitudes that, for example, will prevent juvenile delinquency, but also, and on the positive side, ways of building a good life.

The age-old goal of human happiness may not be just around the corner. But if wrong choices are minimized, and they can be, we can get a little closer to it. Not to make the effort is to concede defeat, and the result will be nothing less than to hasten the collapse of Western civilization. If the effort is made, we may be able to do little more than hold our own. Or we may at least, like medical science, succeed in banishing some of the afflictions that have for centuries made man a little less than he might be.

Part III
Teacher Preparation

10. CHANGE, PROGRESS, INNOVATION AND REFORM
    Educational practices must continue to be reformed if they are to be effective in helping young people to satisfy their varied needs.

11. THE EDUCATION OF TEACHERS
    If reforms are to be effective, they must be implanted in the competencies of individual teachers.

12. A CRITICAL LOOK AT GRADUATE STUDY IN EDUCATION
    Not how many hours of credit, but improved performance as a consequence of the training should be the criterion for evaluation.

13. CERTIFICATION AND THE AGE OF TECHNOLOGY
    Teachers are less and less generalists, certified to do everything; many need to become specialists trained to do well the tasks that need to be done.

14. THE CREDENTIALS MILL IN A TECHNOLOGICAL AGE
    Students should receive credit not for sitting-time in school, but for the competencies they have acquired.

10.
Change, Progress, Innovation and Reform

Before getting down to specifics in the matter of educational reforms, it may be well to make a few distinctions which, though familiar, are likely to be overlooked. Change is, of course, implicit in reform, but change may occur as a result of chance conditions not subject to human control, and may be seemingly erratic, without direction. Is all change *progress?* While this question is customarily answered in the negative, for it may be for better or for worse, those who promote a new process or product are naturally partial to the change they seek. "Something new" has an almost irresistible appeal, and it may also serve as an escape from past practices, that is, from the force of tradition, which is often thought of as something good in itself. Of course it may be. But there would seem to be about a 50-50 chance that a change will be inconsequential, or harmful, or even dangerous. And most annoying of all, some consequences of a change may be bad and others good, and as in educational matters, it may take research to find out which is which.

Progress, on the other hand, implies a continuing process having some direction, usually purposely brought about by human agency, and certainly considered advantageous to the persons concerned. Innovation applies to the addition of something new which is expected to improve the situation; and, if well-planned and skillfully operated, it probably will. Reform implies that some on-going process is ineffective or has harmful by-products, and does not satisfy the purposes for which it was intended, and so needs repair or renovation to operate satisfactorily. It further implies directed change with a view to improvement of some sort or other, improvement being defined as change to something more satisfying than present conditions to the persons concerned.

In the matter of reform, the present assumption of many young people that they should be consulted in all matters that affect them in any way, whether they know anything about them or not, illustrates what may be the chief difference between the mature and the immature. It has been pointed out that the reform-minded youth lives in a two-dimensional world made up of things as they are and things as they ought to be. The adult commonly adds two more dimensions, the past and its learned or remembered failures and successes, and the future with its possible consequences and side effects. The adult therefore tends to be more cautious, preferring at times to stay with the evils that he knows, instead of moving on to those that he knows not of.

An important question at the outset is who is to be benefited by the reform, and by how much. Is the "greatest good for the greatest number" the criterion, or the satisfaction of the desires of a small dissident group, perhaps at the expense of the others, so that in actuality a minority rules?

A reform may involve some innovation that is limited in scope, having little effect beyond the borders of the immediate group. Some reforms have the character of intrusions, having a favorable effect on some and an unfavorable effect on others, like a labor-saving device. An innovation may work well or it may not—it may "have bugs in it" or be improperly operated, or it may not fit in with the old equipment or the old, familiar routines. The provision in a number of schools a few years ago for language-laboratory equipment illustrates all of these possible conditions.

A reform may be thought of as intervention, as a new, perhaps more effective part fitting into an old process and making the whole more efficient or otherwise attractive. This process would contrast sharply with revolution, which implies quite different parts and patterns of operation. Thus we speak of agrarian *reform* and of the industrial *revolution*.

Although we Americans live in a revolutionary age, we seem still to be somewhat naive about the early planned stages of revolutionary change. We sometimes fail to recognize them for what they are, even though the revolutionists themselves are usually quite frank about their goals, some of which seem so impossible and so ridiculous that we do not take them seriously, and hence do not act until it is too late. China and Cuba are two rather obvious recent examples. The Young Pioneer camps and agrarian reformers of an earlier day seem much more reasonable than the recent rioting in the universities. Some consider it a matter of interest that the revolutionists hide behind the protections of the Constitutionally derived freedoms of the Establishment they seek to destroy. But this is not new, nor would be the speed with which the guarantees of freedom are removed when the one-time revolutionists become the new Establishment.

While it is high-time that we learned the ways to offset the imposition of dictatorship and minority rule, the *paths* described in this book are based on the assumption that we the living are worthy and competent recipients of the accumulated wisdom of the past ages, and that we will be wise enough and strong enough to maintain our heritage.

The reforms here contemplated may be classified as *instrumental, philosophical* and *instructional.* The *instrumental* reforms include such matters as financing (e.g., the property tax vs. the income tax), local, state and national support and control, and administrative matters, e.g., state organization, metropolitan decentralization, and the size and distribution of school districts. Since these deal with costs and with power distribution, they receive a good deal of public attention, and they are important. But they are arrangements that are made so that the function of the school may be served, while that of education itself should receive more attention than it often does from the more intelligent people of the community.

The *philosophical* reforms are those which relate to a consideration of values to be emphasized and provided for. Here, as also in the utilitarian areas, there are bound to be continuing conflicts and readjustments consequent upon political and social change in different parts of the country.

The *instructional* reforms, with which we are here primarily concerned, and which tend to receive too little general attention, are those in school plant and equipment, in curriculum and method (though these are in part philosophical), and in evaluation, and consequently in teacher education and training. Here there are many paths, some overgrown with grass and weeds, that should remain that way, while others are faint and difficult to follow, some of which should be opened up and their turnings well-marked. And some new ways should be surveyed, not following the old macadam river road, but cutting across country like the new superhighways, and leading more directly to the goals that lie ahead.

And in all areas of induced change, we will do well to avoid the false beliefs and the assumptions that are not axioms, and be careful to escape from the cliché that the end justifies the means. We know that means and ends are inseparable. The consequences cannot be added up separately. If the stated desirable ends are actually attained, the evil influence of the means employed must be subtracted from the results. And how much worse when the ends are worthy but not attained in spite of the evil means employed. But alas! This is just what we find today in many of our school practices, and what dedicated men and women must labor to root out if we are to survive.

If reforms are needed, and they are, who is responsible for instituting them? Who shall serve as change agent? Here there is a great deal of evasion and buck-passing. Teachers, as a rule, don't like change, sometimes merely preferring accustomed ways, and sometimes becoming anxious about the stability of their employment. Principals and superintendents often maintain a precarious balance, and quite understandably don't want anyone to "rock the boat." And yet many reforms are dependent upon the cooperation of these professional people. Boards of education and taxpayers are properly sensitive to costs, and some parents tend to favor the school practices with which they are familiar, while others are fearful of having their children serve as experimental animals.

So stated, the situation looks bleak indeed. But, fortunately, there are enlightened people in all these groups to give support to what needs to be done. And in addition, there are the psychologists whose training—though often inadequate—provides a basis for developing educational technology. Reform from within would seem to be preferable, but if it is not forthcoming, there are other possibilities.

There are somewhat ominous combinations of publishers and manufacturers of instructional materials who are looking for expanded markets. And even more ominous reform from outside is possible—what is called "performance contracting,"[1] by which a private corporation will operate a part or all of a training or educational system under contract to local government. Under these conditions, any failure is not to be blamed on the learner, as is now customary, but on the corporation, which will lose money if it does not produce the guaranteed amount of student learning. With the probable reduction of defense contracts and of aerospace research, a number of corporations are looking around for future outlets for their energies and see the schools as a possibility.

And, lastly, there are the students themselves, who are beginning to take a hand in determining their own fate. Like adults, they may sometimes be wrong, and they may be unschooled in the way to get things done and in the democratic processes—but whose fault is that! They are our allies, and their support is welcome. Unfortunately, they have learned some words from the revolutionaries—"confrontation," "demands" and "non-negotiable," for example, and some highly undemocratic techniques that serve to break the monotony of life and provide some excitement. More ethical equivalents for these practices can perhaps be found while the young people learn about the other two dimensions, the past and the future; that is, about probabilities and consequences, and financing, and most of all about responsibility.

In some cases, time may seem to be of the essence, and a crash program may be needed to get things started. But this is costly and inefficient, and the errors made may produce more opposition. We know nothing better than the slower, step-by-step planning including open communication and progressive clarification, training of the participants in the skills needed, try-out, and continuous correction through feedback. Considerable progress can be made, as will be shown later, merely by renovating an obsolescent enterprise in such ways as Conant and others have pointed out. But it is to be hoped that innovating practices can eventually be introduced—not just one, but several—in a multi-variable approach which, like earlier reforms, will gradually become common practice. Then the schools will be doing the kind of job they are capable of doing.

11.
The Education of Teachers

No phase of education, from the nursery school to the graduate school, has been immune from attack recently; but, unfortunately, the critics, each imbued with his own value system, cannot agree on what is wrong, so they naturally cannot agree on what should be done to improve the situation. They have given teacher education the full treatment, and if they do not advocate its abolition, some give it a rather low rating. Certainly, if reforms call for new content and methods, teachers should be prepared to handle them. Otherwise no change may be expected. Practice teaching is usually considered of greatest importance, even though the underlying assumption is that traditional class procedures will continue indefinitely, untouched by the new media and the new designs for learning. Other recommendations usually do little more than propose a reshuffling of required courses, or a minor change in the number of required credit hours.

Present Requirements. School or college of education offerings are divided somewhat loosely into three parts: the undergraduate, pre-certification program leading to a B.A. or B.S.; an intermediate, miscellaneous period leading to the M.A. or M.S.; and top-level graduate study capped by the Ph.D. or Ed.D. The levels are not always sharply defined; students from all three are occasionally enrolled in the same course, and the textbooks for the first level often contain erudite discussions that might be more appropriate at the upper level.

As to the first level, there is no discoverable consensus among education professors as to what psychology, sociology, or history and philosophy of education a newly certified teacher should really know; yet these are often referred to as foundation courses, and make up the generally required core of certificate training. Furthermore, an instructor rarely shows the student why these subjects are required or how they apply to educational practice. And there is no indication as to what content can well be left for graduate work later.

The intermediate level is largely for specialized training or upgrading purposes. That it enhances the teacher's value is presumed, since an increment in salary is often provided. But little or no effort is made to discover whether the 24 hours of added credit actually increase the teacher's competence. In some schools it is little more than a fifth undergraduate year; in others, where the degree of master of arts in teaching (M.A.T.) degree is in vogue, together with practice teaching, it is merely the equivalent of undergraduate professional training for those who already hold a baccalaureate degree. Such variation, aimed to adapt to the various needs of the students, is highly commendable, but it implies considerable uncertainty as to what the needs really are.

The demands of the doctorate range along a continuum from research on a highly restricted problem to the consideration of a number of practical and theoretical educational problems. Presumably, the professional doctor of education degree should be the one awarded by schools of education, just as the doctor of medicine is awarded by medical schools. This would leave the doctor of philosophy, with its research emphasis, for work in one of the related disciplines, psychology for example. For various practical reasons, however, the Ph.D. is also given in education; but the distinction between the two is far from clear, though the Ph.D. seems to be preferred by the students. The question therefore arises as to where along the continuum the doctorate in education, whatever its name, should lie.

A Job Analysis Needed? The answer should be discernible in the definition of its purposes. Kerlinger[1] analyzed the situation, and asserted that the basic nature of the doctorate, and specifically of the dissertation, is "critical inquiry." Originally, however, it was introduced to provide practice for the student in what he would be expected to do professionally, whether it was to engage in theological disputation or to practice law or medicine.

Perhaps what is now called for at all three levels is a careful job analysis of the role expectations in the various educational positions, to discover the knowledge and the motor and intellectual skills they require. Following this would be an effort to discover the best ways to teach the candidate the requirements of the employment for which he is preparing.

Fears that this would result only in technician training would be groundless, for if the analysis found that additional competencies involving various kinds of judgment or critical thinking would be needed, these competencies would be included in the instruction. Then, instead of an argument about what should be the character of the dissertation for either degree or the nature of the instructional program at any level, there would be a search for ways to teach the needed abilities.

It is presumed that the same research procedures, if followed at the other levels, would be equally fruitful; the results would define the character of the preparation required. It is not likely that the basic content of the resultant programs of training would vary widely, but selections could be more wisely made, and applications could be more pointed and effective.

CONANT RECOMMENDS

People have few recollections of their own school days that would enable them as citizens, or even as parents, to make any very valuable suggestions for the improvement of teacher education. And yet they may be asked to do just that. Some no doubt recall the controversy stimulated by James B. Conant's report on *The Education of American Teachers*[2] and of his inclination to look to the lay public for support.

In contrast with the lay public, educationists are professionally familiar with the vast and intricate organization that is public and private education today. Far from being opposed to change, most of them are constantly encouraging it, as evidenced by their publications and by the changes they have helped to bring about. But they are naturally discriminating. Before advocating change, they ask what evidence there is that it will produce the advantages claimed for it. Is it worth the cost? They question a package deal because it contains all manner of recommendations, some badly needed and others of doubtful value.

Collectively, their knowledge and experience are far greater than those of Dr. Conant and his staff, or of many others who have written articles criticizing educational practice and have presented interesting, innovating ideas for improvement.

It is important that the lay public know what is going on and be informed, concerning the recommendations put forward. Most of them, perhaps with a little working over, point to objectives mutually sought: a few, however, may seem less likely to have the desired effect.

Certification. Take, for example, the recommendation giving the power of teacher certification to the training institutions. At the present time, there are some 1,200 colleges and universities of all kinds preparing teachers. All or part of the responsibility could be given to these 1,200 institutions, to the 50 state departments of education, to extra-legal agencies like the Northwestern Association of Secondary Schools and Colleges, or to some special agency like the National Education Association (NEA) or the National Council for the Accreditation of Teacher Education (NCATE), or a combination of them. There is no doubt that fault will be found with whatever plan is followed. But the American way seems to be for the professions to look after themselves in these matters. Although certification and accreditation procedures are continually in the process of improvement and adaptation to changing conditions, many educators believe that it is somewhat short of realistic to give practically sole responsibility for certification to each of these 1,200 colleges, with no particular attention to their own accreditation, and then to insist on reciprocity among states.

Training Programs. Programs for the professional preparation of future teachers are continually being modified in the light of changing conditions. There are three parts of any such program: general or liberal education (majors and minors, distribution courses, etc.), the subject(s) to be taught, and the professional training. Any one of these three may be called "education" according to the context. There are honest differences of opinion, not about the necessity of including all three, but about the relative emphasis that should be given to each.

To ask faculties to justify their present course requirements might lead in some cases to desirable revisions, but almost any requirement that is in effect can be justified. The weakness is that changes would, at best, result merely in shuffling courses about and would not solve the main problem; the needed level of competence of each student cannot be assured by adding and subtracting credit hours. But it could be assured by agreement on the content and level of proficiency required, followed by the instruction needed to bring each student to that level, whether the time it takes is shorter or longer than a prescribed number of hours.

Dr. Conant often got as close to this as the Mayan Indians did to the invention of the wheel, but he never quite put it in the form of a numbered recommendation. For example (p. 80): "My suggestion is simply that a standard of performance in English composition be set . . . ," but he would expel the student who failed, or would make him hire a tutor at his own expense to reach the standard. And again (p. 181): "In each case a level of proficiency would seem to be relatively easy to define, and once it is defined, a student's success or failure in meeting the level could be demonstrated through proficiency examinations." And yet again (p. 141): "Professors of education have not yet discovered or agreed upon a common body of knowledge that they all feel should be held by school teachers before the student takes his first fulltime job."

Not only professors of education, but faculties generally, have evaded any clear delineation of objectives, and also any persistent instructional efforts to see that the objectives they have are met. Yet this is what is needed in all three parts of a program for the education of teachers. Lest excessive demands prolong the training periods unduly, further distinctions must be made between what is deemed necessary for certification and what can be left for graduate work.

If more attention were given to educational objectives, less would be needed for various minutiae.

Many institutions provided teacher training combined with the master's degree before the Fund for the Advancement of Education dreamed up its subsidized master of arts in teaching. If, as some argue, the four years of college are needed for courses in general education and the subject(s) to be taught, then obviously a fifth year is necessary. It would seem that, although there should be nothing sacred about the traditional four years, they are sufficient for most students to devote a fifth or sixth of their time to professional training. To help decide whether this period of time is sufficient, it might be well to relate it to the present well-known standard operating procedure and see what modifications are called for.

In brief, the program usually includes four parts:

1. Social foundations of education, with elections from educational philosophy, history, sociology and comparative education. Such a background is helpful, particularly in making professional judgments, in conferences and in faculty committees, and in considering matters of school policy.

2. Psychological foundations of education. These include educational psychology, measurement, statistics, mental health, child development and learning. From this section the student obtains some idea of the nature of the child to be educated, the intellectual and other differences between children, and the characteristics of the learning processes.

3. Methods, sometimes general, but more often related to specific subjects. With the coming of the new media of instruction, this part calls for drastic revision. Programming has emphasized the fact that different teaching tasks require different skills which have to be developed: e.g., lecture-demonstration as on TV, leading discussion, monitoring (interrupting to correct pupil performance as in motor skills, the arts, and in the language laboratory) testing, and directing groups as in team games, music ensembles and dramatics.

4. Practice teaching. The academic upgrading of the persons in charge of practice teaching, as Dr. Conant suggests, is desirable whether or not they are called clinical professors. Ideally, they should be able to teach the methods courses, step into an elementary or high school classroom and take over, or pick up the pieces, if necessary.

OBJECTIVES OF THE PROGRAM

As it stands, such a pattern seems enough, but improvements should be possible. Any recommendations aimed to improve instruction in these three areas and to make practice teaching more valuable should be considered.[3] However, as now organized, the sheer number of courses makes it impossible for a student to elect all, or even a major fraction, of them. To meet this difficulty, proposals have been made to combine what is deemed essential in systematically organized block courses. But, as has been pointed out, few have addressed themselves seriously to the task of determining what knowledge and skills are most needed. A further weakness is that students are certified even though they get quite low marks, indicating there is much they have not learned in the courses they have taken, although it may, of course, be that what they have learned is essential and what they have not learned is unimportant.

In any case, it is desirable that careful studies be made of the teaching-learning processes and their consequences in teacher performance and pupil behavior. Basic to such studies would be what is referred to as a functional analysis of objectives in order to determine explicitly what the teachers who are the products of a training program are expected to know and be able to do. Professional jobs are necessarily more differentiated than they once were.

A Whitmanesque *Salut aux Ecoles,* suggests that the diversification already in effect is even now quite extensive:

I see toddlers in the nursery school and octogenarians in adult classes, and all those between;

I see the feeble-minded and the genius, the culturally deprived and the privileged, and all those between;

I see the physically handicapped, the deaf, mute, blind, crippled, neurotic, feeble-minded and emotionally unstable, and those with speech and organic defects, being taught as they must be taught;

I see teachers both present and future, different in social class, ability, temperament and talent, and supervisors to help them with their difficulties;

I see administrators, professional leaders, principals in elementary schools and in secondary schools, conferring, always conferring, with parents, teachers, children, custodians, with delegations of citizens, with you and me; and school superintendents talking at Rotary luncheons, preparing budgets, planning school buildings also conferring, always conferring;

I see new specialists, psychologists, counselors, curriculum supervisors, visiting teachers, librarians, audiovisual specialists, research workers, educational technologists, skilled, busy, working each in his own way;

I see research workers, translating words into numbers and back again into words, always seeking to answer questions, your questions and mine, about our children, about ourselves and our world;

I see teachers of different subjects, of mathematics, of science, of language, teachers in classrooms, in studios, in shops, and on playgrounds, skilled, busy, working each in his own way for you and for me and for America.

Such an enumeration, perhaps more than any other one thing, tends to induce a certain feeling of humility in professional and lay persons alike, and make them cautious in generalizing about the needs of "*the* child in *the* classroom," and about educating his teachers. True, many of the jobs are not done so well as they might be. But at the same time, it makes one proud of the American heritage of the schools and of the hundreds of thousands of men and women who have worked and are working to transmit and develop that heritage. It makes one wish to participate in the task actively, wisely and effectively. To do this, certain conditions are required.

Conditions to be Sought. A first condition is one of less guesswork and more research. And along with the customary research, reporting conditions as they are, there must be more of the dynamic kind which seeks to find out what happens when certain things are done, when certain factors are changed.

A second condition is one of less debate and controversy and more discussion and exploration. Lay and professional opinion will be most effective if various recommendations for change are discussed individually in conference and in committee, and in collaboration, particularly those recommendations which, if carefully implemented, seem most likely to improve the status and educational opportunities and the effectiveness of teachers and other educational workers.

A third condition is one of less empirical generalizing and more careful thought. Juggling regulations in the teacher education program, except for those that are way out of line, will keep faculty committees busy, but will have little or no other appreciable effect. The same holds for any new regulations for certification and accreditation. Except as specific corrections are made by the profession to meet specific needs, they will likely be equally futile, serving only to confuse and to introduce a different set of disadvantages. No doubt many improvements can be made on an empirical basis, but I venture the opinion that there will be no real breakthrough until adequate learning replaces the letter grade as the culmination of instruction, and until proficiency replaces the credit hour as a criterion of competence.

12.
A Critical Look at Graduate Study
in Education

A teacher I once knew occasionally used a transitional sentence which characterizes a great deal of social criticism: "Having looked the difficulty square in the face, we will now move on." Like most social enterprises, graduate study in education deserves a bold, hard, critical look; but it deserves more. Graduate education is very important because the graduate professors and those they train are highly influential in determining the course of education, for better or for worse, both in this country and abroad.

A number of phases of graduate education that deserve a critical look I shall not touch upon—subject matter content, for example, and staffing, and finance. It may well be that our masters and doctoral students are not sufficiently well-informed in the natural and social sciences, and the humanities, or even in the psychological and social foundations of education—particularly educational history and philosophy. The responsibilities of teaching by research fellows, as well as the apportionment of funds for teaching and for research, also deserve study. I wish to call attention, however, to some of the present instructional practices and procedures of the graduate program in education.

I might say at the outset that these practices and procedures seem satisfactory enough. But perhaps this is because they are so familiar, and because they tend to copy the highly respected liberal arts pattern. But customary social practices are not necessarily desirable, and the liberal arts pattern has recently been subjected to severe criticism.[1] It has been found unsatisfactory even for the liberal arts college itself; and many of its weaknesses are compounded when employed in graduate and professional schools.

THE PROFESSIONAL OBJECTIVE

For professional education, the key to the fault is to be found in the term "graduate study," which tells only half the story. Professional education involves study, of course, but it should be more closely affiliated with professional training than with the work of the typical graduate school, which is primarily aimed to develop scholars and scientists in the several disciplines.

Professional schools have this aim, too, but their primary function is to develop *professional* competencies and to improve performance in the various professional tasks—in the case of education, in teaching, supervising, guiding, evaluating, researching and administering. For these purposes, *to know* is essential but insufficient; it is also necessary *to do.* And since most educational preparation is carried on following a bachelor's degree, the range of skills required is necessarily from that of technician to that of a top-level operator and decision maker.

Instead of bending all their energies to this twofold professional objective—needed scholarship and technical skill—the graduate programs, with some notable exceptions, follow the track of custom with lecture courses and examinations, and with the usual marks of multiple meaning which, however, indicate that a large proportion of the students are definitely less than proficient. And no effort is made to discover whether those who are subjected to the graduate program are any more competent than they were before undertaking it. Of course, it "stands to reason" that they are. And the "credit hours" on the student's transcript provide an objective criterion for superintendents and school boards to use in granting salary increases.

Criticisms of current practices are implied in the changes here recommended:

RECOMMENDATIONS

First, designate the specific objectives of instruction for each course—the terminal behavior expected.[2] Professors usually shy away from this idea, satisfying themselves with generalities that have long since lost their glitter. This recommendation takes its cue from the programming procedure, though it is equally appropriate whether programming is used or not. But, as a rule, it is much easier and far more enjoyable for a professor to enunciate and expound than it is for him to face the double question: As a result of my instruction, just what should the students know, and specifically what should they be able to do?

Second, search for ways to provide the needed instruction and make it as efficient and effective as possible. Lectures are not out, nor are discussions and seminars. But additional techniques are needed. Illustrations of the possibilities are to be found not only in the new media,[3] but also in providing objective samples of individual performance, like the recording of guidance sessions or, for administration, the handling of a pre-arranged in-basket. The case method, as used in law schools, has undeveloped possibilities, as do other simulation techniques.

Third, assess the "entering behavior" of all students. This can be done when the objectives are known and the content thus objectively defined. A record of previous courses students may have "had" is not sufficient. Assessment should be in terms of what students can and cannot *do.* Those who have vocal, verbal, or social habits that would reduce their effectiveness (the correction of which is not an appropriate objective of the course) should be so informed, and advised as to what steps they should take to correct them. Included would be defects in speech and writing. If the course requires that students write essays either for examinations or for term papers, and some do not know how, these should be taught to write essays. A deficiency would be removed when a later assessment, or a statement by the special teacher assigned to the case, indicates that the student has attained the requisite competence.

Fourth, revise the marking system. A more adequate marking system is needed than the one we have limped along on for so many years. It should be in the nature of a check list to indicate that the student has attained the specific proficiencies needed. Each item could be represented by a scale ranging from complete ignorance or inability, to the highest level of professional competence. But a student's place on the scale should be quite independent of the performance of other class members. Somehow, the profession must be sold on the idea of the *criterion-referenced* in contrast with the customary *norm-referenced* mark. A course is not passed until the criterion-referenced mark is up to the agreed-on point on the scale—like so many words per minute in typing or stenography. It is granted that professional educational skills cannot be measured with the precision of sensory-motor skills; but, on the other hand, the practice of turning out incompetent teachers and salving the professorial conscience by giving a low mark should cease.

Fifth, reduce the emphasis on disconnected facts and on what Whitehead has called "inert ideas." The multiple-choice test is, in part, responsible for this emphasis. As an example of what present practices can lead to, the word got around in one department to study the footnotes. It had been discovered that on a previous examination there was a question on a footnote in one of the readings. Even at the graduate level, in their efforts to outguess the instructor on what will be called for on the examination, students resort to all manner of questionable schemes, not the least of which is a final effort to try to memorize quantities of facts that will soon be forgotten.

This situation would be improved by the careful delineation of the course objectives, as suggested above, and by the use of a relatively simple device. We can assume that, in addition to the essentials in the course objectives, there are a number of interesting and more or less important supplementary facts—say 100 of them. If a person does not know *any* of these, he is an ignoramus. Let's say he should know 25 of them, or 50, or 75, but it makes little or no difference which 25, 50, or 75 he knows. This situation would be especially likely in content subjects like history or geography, but in most others as well. On an examination, the 100 (or a sampling of them) might be called for. But a student would score no higher for getting more than the previously stated 25, 50, or 75 per cent. (However, he could properly lose credit for any he got wrong; that is, for not knowing what he did not know.) The reduction of pressure would have a salutary effect, and the time the student did not spend on boning up on unnecessary additional facts could be given to some more creative activity.

The final examination (and quizzes as well) would be divided into two parts: Part I would be a *mastery test* on the previously stated specific objectives. Part II would be on the supplementary information.

Part I would not be "passed" until all items (or, say, 90 or 95 percent of them) are answered correctly. Opportunities for make-up would be provided, using the same or equivalent form of the test. Part II would be "passed" if the previously stated per cent of the items are answered correctly, but no higher score would be obtained by answering a lot more, which would be considered as evidence only of a fly-paper memory, or of a misspent youth!

Thus, marks could be assigned as follows, assuming three passing grades, A, B and C:

C—Part I (mastery) passed, but not Part II;

B—Parts I and II (supplementary) passed, or Part I and a Project (see below);

A—Parts I and II passed and a Project satisfactorily completed.

The project, previously alluded to as some more creative activity, might be a historical, biographical, critical, or experimental study; or an analytical report of some educational institution or of some innovating practice, or the like.

If the famous man from Mars were to look in on our present system of graduate study in education, I am sure that he would be surprised that the results aren't worse than they are. It would seem that the graduate school should be able to guarantee its product. Instead of merely hoping that its graduates will get by on the job, it seems reasonable that it should see to it that they know and are able to do what is needed in the performance of professional tasks that are likely to confront them, and are capable of handling the kinds of decisions they will be called upon to make.

It is unlikely that the stimulus for such a change will come from within the graduate schools. The logical source is the employer of their product. Elementary and high school teachers and administrators could exert this pressure, for they would be the ones to profit from the change. The scheme could even be tried out in elementary and secondary school classes. In this effort, school psychologists might well cooperate, since many of the maladjustments with which they are called upon to deal are school-made—a mishandling of pupil differences. It is surprising that the matter of behavioral objectives tuned to the capacities and previous learnings of the students has had such relatively little attention in the past. The time has come for a change.

13.
Certification and the Age of Technology

If we could once lay aside the traditional spectacles with which we customarily view educational problems and take a cold, unbiased look at the procedures employed in teacher training[1] and certification we would see why the instructional tasks have never been adequately handled, and never can be under present circumstances.

True, there have been and still are teachers who make the best of a bad situation and do remarkably well, all things considered. They are sometimes referred to as "gifted teachers." Just how many there are in a hundred no one knows. Some people can recall one or two they have had, although their classmates might not agree. Pupil characterizations of their teachers have run the gamut from "sourpuss," " old meanie," "crab," and "s.o.b.," to "sweety pie," "mamma's boy," and "old hickory,"—from "he (or she) won't let you get away with a thing," or "is always complaining about something," to "explains things so you can understand," "encourages you and makes you want to work harder." Latter-day eulogies are likely to run something like this: "I don't remember a thing he tried to teach me, but what I did learn was how to study," or "that it pays to be honest," and so on.

Let's face it! The "gifted teacher" is a fiction, an imaginative construct, a never-was, or perhaps a seldom-was. Of course, there are many good teachers, but they are rarely good at *everything*. They may be good at explaining things, but slow at returning corrected papers. They may have an excellent French pronunciation and a charming smile, but are unable to keep order. They may be friendly and well-liked, but not too well grounded in the fundamentals of their subject.

The truth is that the teacher's job is an impossible one. Some do it surprisingly well, all things considered, but they do not do it well enough. They can't. No one person can be a competent subject matter specialist, an able expositor and demonstrator, an inspiring discussion leader, a planning-group leader and individual tutor, adapting instruction to individual differences and stimulating originality, creativity and love of learning; and also confer with parents, keep records, discipline the unruly, mete out punishment, give tests, pass and fail pupils, and be admired and loved by all!

And how can they be expected to do all these things for all the children they have to deal with in "the class"? A class is not a group. It is a chance assortment of young people who happen to be about the same age, who live in the same part of town or on the same bus route. They have a range of ability of five or six or more years. Their home backgrounds are as varied as their future vocations and their "ideals." A few teachers can do some of the necessary things well for a time. But the life has its effect over the years. Often the best ones, it has been observed, are being "lured into other fields," not always, I suspect, because of "higher pay or brighter futures," but rather because the work is more congenial. For one reason or another, many of the more competent do not "stay in teaching"; many of the less competent remain and become sour old maids, whether married or not, or petulant bureaucrats.

With the differentiation of the teaching function, which the new media make possible, the heterogeneous array of responsibilities can be broken down into manageable parts with no loss to anyone and considerable gain in the direction of the main task, that of pupil learning; that is, making the desired changes in the children and young people who come to the schools, which is what education is for.

When something is done along these lines, it will be possible to make a few intelligent judgments about the preparation of those who will be responsible for the different tasks.

There is one aspect, however, to which attention should be called; and that is the traditional method of measuring teacher or pupil competence in terms of time spent in classes instead of in terms of degree of proficiency.

With the development of individualized instruction that now, at last, programmed learning brings within the realm of actuality, it is possible to devise instruments which measure abilities directly, provide instruction at the point where each learner is, and allow him to go on from there, whatever grade, school or college he may be in. Field sports and stenographic skills are fortunate in having standard units of measurement—feet and inches, minutes and seconds. But where units do not exist, as in mathematics and language abilities, for example, a scale of proficiency could well be devised ranging from zero to, say, 1000—which would be something a little above the highest presently attainable competence. Gradually, norms for different purposes could be developed from the absolute achievement scores, and interesting studies could be made of the relative competence attained by different age or other groups.

Such a rational scheme would have a salutary effect on the current proliferation of courses. It would also make it possible to discard almost entirely the highly unreliable marking system. And more important still, such a scheme would make it unnecessary for intelligent men, scholars in their own right, to argue about how many years a student should spend on a subject, or how many credit hours a young person should have in this or that to be qualified to teach.

14.
The Credentials Mill
in a Technological Age

Today both young people and adults in diverse walks of life seem to be at the mercy of individuals, institutions and organizations which have the power to issue or withhold the credentials necessary for one kind of advancement or another.

The familiar letter of recommendation from a teacher or previous employer is recognized as a doubtful blessing, and hardly as an objective prognosis of future success. So this letter is supplemented by test results and reports on school progress, regardless of whether these have any particular bearing on the activities in which the individual is expected to engage. Letters and transcripts sometimes advance a student toward his goal with the speed of a police escort, and they sometimes inhibit progress as effectively as a ball and chain.

CREDENTIALS LACK CREDIBILITY

Dropouts are urged to go back to school and finish the eighth grade, high school, college, or the work on a graduate degree in order to obtain the all-important credentials that will open the doors of opportunity. Yet few inquire what added competencies an individual gains from the credits or credit hours he receives for the extra time spent sitting in classes.

Is it only that he is a little more mature and so can work more consistently; or, as in the case of teachers, is it that those who do graduate work thus reveal a superior professional interest and dedication? Is the evidence really reliable, or are the required courses actually considered quite useless except as they are necessary to obtain the credential, the "union card"?

The word *credential,* like credit and creed, derives from the Latin *credere,* to believe or trust. To accredit a person (or an institution), as in the case of financial credit, implies that some responsible agent believes in and trusts him. To a certain extent this is true, but in the case of educational accreditation, the basis for such belief and trust is often unsound, and the trust is misplaced; otherwise there would not be so many incompetent teachers. Furthermore, there is rarely any evidence that the work required to obtain such credentials will increase an individual's competence. In short, it is a patchwork, mechanical system that has expanded over the years for administrative convenience, and has been applied wholesale with little or no regard for the individuals most concerned—the students and the prospective employers.

Critics who have objected to the use of mechanical teaching devices, chiefly teaching machines and television, and also programmed instruction, would do well to observe the *mechanical operation of the credentials mill,* an anomaly in this technological age. Is there not a less shaky way to testify one's belief and faith in a student's general competence? Could not schools and colleges and the accrediting agencies as well even go a step further and actually *guarantee* their product?

CREDITS NO GUARANTEE

The place to start would seem to be with the familiar proposition that school subjects are *means* to a diversity of educational ends. But we should not assume that any student, merely by taking the subjects, will secure the ends and attain the objectives sought by the instruction.

However, if in each subject or curricular activity from K through 12 and beyond the student has specific practice in ways he can best use his mind in the various required tasks, he will presumably form satisfactory working habits. Such habits should stand him in good stead not only in academic pursuits, but also in the many diversified occupations in which people engage; although, of course, special training in any one occupation is also desirable and usually necessary.

Such practice cannot depend on the requirements of the subject alone, but must also derive from the ends for which the subjects are means. It calls for a clear and specific determination of objectives, which is basic to modern educational technology in general, and to programmed instruction in particular.

High school and college teachers have consistently declined to formulate specific objectives. Perhaps this is because there has been too much emphasis on knowledge of content to the exclusion of psychological processes. If some kind of psychological pattern were incorporated into the instruction in the several school subjects, and if appropriate measuring instruments yet to be devised were employed, one could be assured of knowing the nature of the progress that students are making, not only in their control of content, but also in their ability to use their minds—to think. Credentials would then be based not on credit hours for the time spent, but on progress along a continuum, both in content they have studied and in other situations as well.

CREDENTIALS BASED ON COMPETENCIES

As a tentative approach, nine imperatives are listed below, each of which is an injunction to engage in an activity that can be practiced in different contexts. The activities are listed in the order of their approximate complexity. There is no sharp line separating them, but each is basically different from the next. Each will be commented on briefly in order to clarify what is meant or implied by the term used. Each may be seen to apply to some item, event, pattern, structure, formula, proposition, or other situation perhaps as simple as a stone, or as complex as a system of philosophy.

In this presentation I am obviously indebted to Mager,[1] whose work is invaluable but a little too restricted, and to Bloom *et al.*,[2] whose *Taxonomy* becomes overly complicated for our present purposes. It seems highly probable that students can be taught in ways which will enable them to generalize these activities, and that the improvement in their ability to do this, in different contexts, could be measured. Such improvement would be the objective of the training provided for obtaining the credential sought.

1. *Observe.* Observation is the basic activity of sensing. Students of all ages can be encouraged to see and hear what is around them—flowers, trees, buildings, furniture, animals, birds, people, signs and symbols including word endings, musical tones or notation, and facial expressions, errors, attitudes and social groupings. Louis Agassiz, the noted Swiss-American naturalist, had his biology students at Harvard spend three or four successive class periods describing a fish, so important did he consider observation to be. Some of the greatest discoveries have come about because the scientist noted something unusual, some incongruity in what was going on in his laboratory.

2. *Identify.* In communicating an observation, one needs only to point, draw, or describe in his own words. To identify, one must *perceive* some recurring phenomenon for what it is, attach a name tag to it, recognize it when he sees it in other patterns of relationships, and so give some kind of meaning to the sensory object.

3. *Discriminate.* Building *concepts* involves classifying things into categories and recognizing larger and smaller differences that make a difference in their categorization. The student learns to discriminate between different kinds of birds, wood, machines, music, paintings, triangles, language usage, processes, performance and behavior. He comes to recognize the criteria and principles on which the distinctions are made, and learns what is involved in the rules of exclusion and inclusion of generalizations and abstractions that form concepts.

4. *Report.* A person is expected to be able to *state* or represent symbolically what he has learned, his knowledge of things and their relationships as facts, events, propositions and the influences they have on each other, which is understanding. It is one of the tasks of the school to impart such knowledge, often referred to as "transmitting the cultural heritage," for which lectures, textbooks and examinations are the common instruments admirably suited to this purpose. Whether in the form of inert ideas or vital information, facts are "in," in all school subjects (and in life generally), with perhaps less attention than would be desirable given to selecting the facts and considering how they may best be taught.

5. *Apply.* While some knowledge is desirable for its own sake, much of it has an instrumental value: it is to be used for some purpose—to solve problems of a theoretical or practical sort, for

example. But theory tends to get itself separated from practice; when students do not know how to use what they have learned, application is the appropriate instructional objective. An effective approach is by way of the principles of (a) stimulus generalization—learning to do something in one situation and also in situations that are somewhat different, and (b) response generalization—learning to modify one's response in view of the changed nature of the situation.

Application usually involves a common condition or principle in situations which otherwise may be totally different. Hence in vocational training, a certain skill may be taught as if it were a separate item, not an example of an underlying principle. The *what* drowns out the *why*. The situation presents the teacher with a quandary—whether to teach the principle or rule first and then the examples deductively ("RULEG") or, inductively, to teach the examples and so establish the rule ("EGRULE").

6. *Solve.* One may apply what he has learned almost automatically without giving particular thought to the matter. But when transfer and application do not thus occur, when there is the familiar "felt difficulty," the situation becomes a problem to be solved. Students are frequently required to solve problems within the boundaries of a particular subject, e.g., in arithmetic, geometry, or chemistry, but the procedures are not always explained. And how the experience can be applied more generally in other situations is rarely mentioned.

7. *Reflect.* Reflective thinking might well be coupled with problem solving, except that a great deal of thinking goes on which is not dealing with a specific difficulty, and is neither fantasy nor reverie, but a kind of inquiry or wondering about things. Seemingly, there should be practice in formulating criteria to evaluate the quality of thinking—ethical, esthetic, or, more narrowly, cognitive. Or, following Guilford,[3] it might be worthwhile to provide opportunities for divergent as well as convergent thinking, to give time for students to ponder, to consider "all the angles," to think up possibilities, to be critical or creative, to restructure their experiences leading to the educational goal of individual fulfillment; in short, to meditate.

8. *Improve.* A pattern of activities or motor skills is repeated with variations intended to improve it. Among these are the narrower trade or vocational skills, for which applicants may need credentials, though the training is usually provided within the industry or on the

job. Progressive approximation to the required degree of excellence through repetition and reinforcement is seemingly the most useful formula. And, to save time, directions are given instead of waiting for the correct response to be made and then reinforcing it.

Perhaps the most important teaching task is to give competent guidance and direction to the ensuing practice, and so ensure the needed improvement. However, it is usually left to the teachers to exercise their ingenuity in devising effective verbal and other stimuli for improved responses, whereas a larger number might well be prepared and made available, especially to beginning teachers. Similar attention could well be given in instructing teachers in the performance of a number of teaching skills.

9. *Remember.* The importance of remembering, which is stressed in all the previous eight stages, suggests that repetition and drill have tended to be overemphasized at the expense of other values—what is significant and why. Repetition can take the form of considering things from different points of view, and some of the lists of facts to be remembered might be replaced by experiences, with variations on a few important themes.

CERTIFICATION FOR PROFICIENCY

The abilities here enumerated are those involved in thinking, the activity primarily required of those seeking credentials of one kind or another. In particular, the act of thinking is required of teachers as professional people who presumably will relate these abilities both to the content and to the learners they are expected to teach. Yet there is little evidence that these abilities are in any way developed or improved by the usual courses required for teacher certification. And, further, there is no evidence that the certified teachers have acquired the skill to develop these abilities in their students. Certainly, we have no reason for complacency with respect to the traditional adding-machine method now employed to determine and certify professional competence.

It is beyond the scope of this chapter to indicate ways in which these abilities can be developed and measured; suffice it to say that promising results have been obtained in preliminary experiments in developing three-dimensional visual perception, and there is every reason to suppose that other processes are amenable to a similar direct approach when the techniques are developed and employed in relation to the several subjects. With anything like the attention to detail given to operator skills that is characteristic of other professions, and with an appreciation of modern technological methods, it should be possible to develop proficiencies and to identify them in a far more effective manner than that employed by the credential mills as they now operate. And, even for teachers, in a few years, we should be able to guarantee the product.

Part IV
Toward an Educational Technology

15. WHAT IS EDUCATIONAL TECHNOLOGY?

    A technological systems approach to educational perform-
ance involves analysis and synthesis of a series of instructional and
learning tasks designed for greater effectiveness.

16. BEHAVIORAL OBJECTIVES IN EDUCATION

    Students can well be informed specifically as to what they
will be expected to do as a consequence of instruction, and then
taught to do it.

17. ON MARKS, GRADES AND SCORES

    Expectations as objectives can be indicated at points along a
continuum on which the student's measured (or estimated)
proficiency can be marked.

18. ON MARKS, NORMS AND PROFICIENCY

    Purposes of marks and the advantages of criterion-referenced
marks as an indication of student proficiency over norm-referenced marks dependent on a comparison with others.

19. GRADES AND OBJECTIVES IN HIGHER EDUCATION

    The functions of a marking system at the college level can be
better served than they now are by the credit hour device.

20. LEADERSHIP, THE NEW MEDIA AND THE OBSOLESCENT
    CLASSROOM

    Prospective leaders considering first steps for reform will
consider curricular objectives and the implications of a multi-
media approach.

21. TEACHER AND TELEVISION

    Instructional television for individuals and groups, in class or
at a distance, can improve instruction in knowledge and skills and
in attitudes and values.

15.
What Is Educational Technology?

Educational technology really got under way with B. F. Skinner's teaching machines, and perhaps partly for this reason, and also because the term technology had been used in connection with automation in industry and with the mechanics theory called cybernetics, it has unfortunately meant to many people a kind of production-line education. But the actual situation is quite otherwise, for it has much greater concern than traditional education for the wants and needs of the individual student.

TECHNOLOGY AND SYSTEM

The word "technology" really means nothing more dangerous than applied science, the expert use of accumulated specialized knowledge directed to the problems of living. The word comes from the Greek *technikos*, from *techne*, a practical art. In Latin it becomes *texere*, to weave or construct, hence textile, architect and text. The -ology is, of course, the same ending from the Greek *logos*, meaning knowledge or science, that we have in biology, psychology and in other sciences. The term properly applies to some kind of construct or system operating in a way that will attain some specified ends. In the natural world we are familiar with the solar system, the nervous system and others; and, in the man-directed sphere, the feudal system, the school system and so on. The larger systems include smaller subsystems, and the aim of technology is to develop and harmonize their parts in the interest of attaining the objectives more efficiently and effectively.

Tools and machines are employed where they are more effective than human labor—earth movers and typewriters, adding machines and computers. But human participation is implied as in the phrase "man-machine system," although even man's direction and control are relinquished when possible.

The term "cybernetics" in 1947 was given by Norburt Wiener[1] to the "entire field of control and communication theory whether in the machine or the animal." It comes from the Greek word meaning "steersman," and implies control through a feedback mechanism like the governor on an engine, and like the familiar thermostat which communicates or feeds back the temperature of a room to the furnace, which comes on or goes off accordingly. W. B. Cannon,[2] working in the field of physiology, pointed out that the autonomic nervous system has a similar function, which he called homeostasis.

Obviously, renovative and innovative educational reforms can be carried on without much of any technology, and without employing a systems approach. But they are likely to be patch-and-tinker efforts in contrast with a more thorough study of the total pattern of instruction, with a view to a more efficient and effective arrangement of the components of the whole system and of its subsystems. An open system of exchange of information between systems and their parts, including the individual organism, permits change and learning, i.e., modification through feedback, which may be said to be the basic cybernetic principle.

Besides feedback, as a basis for regulation and as a source of criteria for improving a function, the most important concept is the *objective,* the specified end or goal of the process. But, strange to say, in education it is one of the most neglected. Teachers are often quite vague about what they expect their students will be able to do as a consequence of the instruction provided. And if they don't know what they are trying to do, aside from "covering" a certain number of pages, they will hardly be able to decide whether they are doing it efficiently and effectively. Skinner[3] is even more drastic:

> ... When we know what we are doing, we are
> training; when we do not know what we are doing,
> we are teaching. Once we have taken the important

first step and specified what we want the student to do as a result of being taught, we can begin to teach in ways with respect to which this outworn distinction is meaningless. In doing so, we need not abandon any of our goals. We must simply define them.

Some people choke over the idea of predetermined goals and aver that the purpose of teaching is to allow students to develop their own goals and their own personalities. This aim is, of course, a laudable one, though it hinges largely on the curriculum—educational guidance, and the choice of courses provided. Once a course is chosen, the implication is that the student will learn something of what it is set up for—whether French, mathematics, sociology, or something else. If there are choices possible for the student within the general area, one of the stated objectives could well be: to help the student explore the field to discover his own special interests and needs. As Skinner said in the passage quoted, "We need not abandon any of our goals. We must simply define them."

System. A system may be defined as "a bounded organization of interdependent and interrelated components maintained in a state of relatedness to each other, the total system, and the environment for the purpose of accomplishing stated goals." A management system includes "planning, organizing, motivating, and controlling human and material resources, and relationships among resources, to attain the predetermined goals."[4] An instructional system consists of "an integrated set of media, equipment, methods and personnel performing efficiently the functions required to accomplish one or more training (learning) objectives."[5]

The "implementing, decision-making roles . . . are concerned with optimizing outcomes . . . identifying and organizing goals and objectives . . . organizing and employing resources, and evaluating results."[6] A typical school system, however, is not set up for planning and reform, but rather for keeping the routine going. Those operating it usually prefer to meet situations as they arise, and cross bridges when they come to them.

Research and development people may emphasize development without assurance that the changes they install result in any improvement, or they may spend so much time on research that they don't get anything done. The educational technologist, with his psychological and technical knowledge, will presumably maintain a balance, employ a systems approach, engage in preplanning, specify instructional objectives, and evaluate as he proceeds.

Whether or not it has been for use in machines, programming has emphasized the need for continuing evaluation followed not by judging and marking students, but by revising the program, i.e., the instruction, so that the students will be able to meet the instructional objectives. Programs, therefore, are empirically tested, that is, tried out on the kinds of learners they are intended for. The somewhat flexible criterion formula is 90/90, meaning that 90 per cent of the students master 90 per cent of the material. This does not apply to aptitude tests, which are constructed so as to indicate probable future performance, nor to achievement tests, which indicate the level of present performance. It applies to the instructional program itself, to the knowledge and understanding the learners have as they proceed. It is the quality control of the saleable product, the program, which provides a kind of guarantee that does not seem to be considered necessary for textbooks and teachers.

Even more attention will be given to this matter if the movement for performance contracting continues to develop. As already indicated, performance contracting is an arrangement whereby an industry or a community draws up specifications for teaching certain knowledge or skills, and receives closed bids from different educational and training agencies who contract to inculcate the specified competencies. They are paid only if they are successful, not on the basis of elapsed time spent in the effort. One wonders what would happen if schools were required to guarantee their product in this fashion.

Reforms will be based primarily on empirical evidence and will emphasize not only knowledge, but also psychomotor, cognitive and social skills. As a consequence, the subsystems will function less haphazardly and independently, and system and environment will be more compatible, as will be the system and its purpose.

System Analysis. [7] A scrutiny of the total pattern of the system is of first importance. It is necessary to identify the components and determine the relations between them, and then to synthesize or recombine the components in more effective relationships. For a system, synthesis is usually working out the problem of who does what and when. For example, there should perhaps be closer relations among admissions, counseling and vocational guidance; or in teacher-training programs. among foundations courses, methods, practice teaching and placement. Models and flowcharts are helpful; for, like all diagrams, they are analogues of the reality with which one is dealing. In practice, they may not be followed very closely, however; the interests, qualifications, and talents of people in positions with the same title may vary, so it is wise to design any operations to take advantage of this fact.

INSTRUCTIONAL MEDIA

In the early schools in this country, slates, as a medium of instruction, came to be replaced by blackboards and writing paper; and these were supplemented by readers, textbooks and a few other volumes, constituting the total instructional resources on which teachers could draw. Following the printing press, the camera and projector began to provide some variety, until now we have an embarrassment of riches—both hardware and software.[8]

Hardware. The machines that share the instructional tasks have stimulated a number of innovations and a great deal of needed research. Audio-visual aids were first in the field—slides, filmstrips and motion pictures, along with phonographs, tape recorders and sound track films. All these have been used to help sharpen perceptions and to enlarge and clarify concepts, the chief weakness being in logistics—transporting machines and films and keeping them in repair.

Transmission at a distance was made possible by the invention of the radio. But before its possibilities could be fully realized it was upstaged by television (Chapter 21) with its two contradictory advantages—immediate transmission and videotape recording for delayed presentation. Efforts have been made to rescue a few of the airwaves from the banalities of commercial programs for the use of educational television (ETV), but with only moderate success. This is partly due to the costs, and partly to the difficulties inherent in producing good instruction: it is easier to reproduce instructional mediocrity than to take full advantage of the medium. Videotapes can be used advantageously instead of sound track film. It is ideal for enabling students to observe, identify and discriminate structural patterns and feedback on individual skill and group behavior, thus aiding in shaping performance.

Just as television has upstaged the radio, so the rapid development of computers has reduced interest in simple teaching machines. The early inventions of Pressey were viewed more as scoring devices, though they were also used to teach. It was the invention of B. F. Skinner[9] that attracted attention to their possibilities. Viewed on the one hand as a devilish device that took the soul out of teaching, or as a mere page turner, and on the other as the wave of the future, the teaching machine opened up possibilities for modifying practice that teachers and investigators could deal with. Even when they were used merely as adjuncts to the traditional school routines, students did as well or better than those subjected to the uncertain ways of the "living teacher." And, even now, with the provision for feedback and reinforcement, they seem to be more effective for some purposes, particulary at elementary school levels and in the area of special education, to say nothing of oral language learning.

Computer assisted instruction (CAI) or computer managed instruction (CMI) are still in the experimental stages, but look promising. For instruction, chief consideration must still be given to the construction of programs. The computer programmer should at least be a competent educational psychologist, if he is to set up programs that will adapt with increasing precision to the specific and momentary needs of each student. And the goal is nothing less than this. Computers will automatically determine a student's aptitude, maturity, background—even his dexterity and his personality traits. Teachers can specialize in conceptual instruction at the known readiness level.

Software. The most important thing about teaching machines—and computers as well—is not the machine itself, but the program, that is, the data and explanations that are fed into the machines, and the questions the students are expected to answer.

The teaching programs are provided in book form and are made up of successive steps or frames, with various devices for students to check or write in their answers.[10] Skinner did not favor the familiar multiple-choice form, in which the students are expected to distinguish the right answer from two or three wrong ones on the basis of having read certain selections (or panels) providing the information. He claimed that this procedure actually teaches the wrong answers. He prefers the completion form, in which students supply the key words to fill in the blank spaces, based on their reading of the program. He also favors the "linear" pattern that is followed by all students, each one taking the same small steps, but each at his own rate. Others prefer Crowder's "branching" patterns in which, on the basis of their errors and successes, students are shifted to easier or harder questions as they go along. Efforts to find out which method is better proved unavailing for the annoying reason that the difference is indeterminate: there is no way to tell whether better scores are due to the format or to the quality of the program.

So these two, and various other forms, are now used according to whichever seems best adapted to the content and to the needs of the learner. Many students like programmed instruction because of the opportunities for self-correction, and for the independent study it provides. It seems particularly well suited for teaching concepts and providing practice and drill, especially for review or as a refresher for the basic concepts of a course previously taken, thus teaching what students will need to use in a more advanced course. A number of full-term and full-year courses, however, have been successfully programmed.

But it is not easy to make a good program, and many poor ones are on the market.[11] The aim is to anticipate and overcome the learner's difficulties as he follows a reasonable continuity in the direction of the educational objectives. The frames call for paper-and-pencil responses, under given conditions, and these responses are taken as evidence of success or failure on the several items. As criteria, however, they might not be the equivalent of job success, where the conditions are likely to be different. But this and many other criticisms of programs hold equally for traditional instruction. Three chief differences between programmed and traditional instruction are (1) the provision for individual study and individualized instruction; (2) the ideal of 90/90 mastery, with the rejection of the usual letter marking system; and (3) the measurement of proficiency whatever the learner's age or grade, the absolute, criterion-referenced score with the rejection of the relative, norm-referenced score that depends on what other students do—on the capabilities of other students as registered on the probability curve.

Needless to say, books, manuals, journals, displays, tests, checklists and other kinds of software are still in use, and will be indefinitely.

Effort is now directed toward what is referred to as multi-media instruction—for different kinds of subject matter and for different kinds of students.

TASK ANALYSIS

System analysis, as we have seen, refers to a study of the total pattern, and the ways the component parts fit together. Task analysis requires that the tasks or responsibilities of the individuals concerned also be analyzed, which implies pre-planning of the instructional process to make it somewhat less extemporaneous than at present—a more detailed study of what each person or machine contributes to the output. For a gifted and inspiring teacher who may take off from some event of current interest to bring home some important truth, the necessity for careful planning may seem an unjustifiable constraint. But planning need not eliminate spontaneity; indeed it may even provide additional possibilities for it.

Various strategies are employed to control the quality of the instruction by selecting the relevant and the efficient. This refers chiefly to effectiveness in content and method, which will be touched on later. The instructional emphasis chosen may reveal "stimulus orientation," i.e., perceptually identifying and distinguishing similarities and differences in the objective phenomena to which the student will respond. Or it may reveal a "response orientation," with special attention devoted to acquiring certain knowledge and developing skills and attitudes.

Probably the most valuable contribution of programming in particular, and technology in general, is the insistence on the need for explicitly stated learning objectives. Only gradually are people coming to realize that the traditional, easy-going talk-assign-test, with little or no attention given to specific educational goals, is one of the main causes of many of our educational ills—from bad grammar to dropouts, and from irrelevance to vandalism.

Behavioral Objectives.[12] In the case of sensory-motor skills, the behavioral objectives are the visible, overt accomplishment of the learner—he saws or hammers, swims or skates, as he could not earlier. But for the thought processes, as discussed in the next chapter, the overt behavior serves as more or less satisfactory evidence that the inner, covert goals of learning have or have not been attained; though as we have seen, paper-and-pencil accomplishments may or may not guarantee success in related practical situations.

Terminal Behavior. Presumably, the behavioral objectives describe certain things the learner will be expected to do at the completion of some unit of instruction. In the jargon of the technologists, they are the "output" of the process. Whether or not they are attained depends on the "input"—the nature of the learner and the experiences which a teacher, as learning manager, provided for him.

Intermediate Behavior. Except for the simplest of single-unit tasks, there will be a learning period with a series of intermediate or interim objectives presented in some reasonable sequence, revealing a line of progress from where the learner is at the start (his entering behavior) to the final goal—his terminal behavior. The sequencing of the units of instruction may be based, as it has been in the past, on one or more of a number of organizing principles: chronology, easy to difficult, simple to complex, familiar to unfamiliar, or the reverse; specific to general (EGRULE), or the reverse (RULEG), with careful provision for permanence (retrieval) through repetition and the establishment of meaningful relationships.

Entering Behavior. The traditional grading system was supposed to regulate this variable. Those who had passed grade VII were supposedly ready for grade VIII, or those who had had math 31 were ready for math 32. But, as everyone knows, the abilities of students who enter a grade or a course vary over a wide range. Little or no effort is made to discover the student's entry level performance (ELP), or prerequisite knowledge repertoire (PKR) as it is sometimes called—the knowledge and skill each possesses at the start. Those who have what will be needed can go ahead (sometimes quite a bit ahead). Those who do not have it, most of them at least, go on anyway and gradually get farther and farther behind unless the teacher takes the time to teach them, which slows down the progress of the others. Results from tests of ELP suggest that individualized programs may well be used to insure more accurate group placement.

Besides the prerequisite knowledge and skills, certain other preinstructional variables that tend to be neglected are again beginning to receive the attention that is their due, and are even being programmed in CAI. These are personality-type basic aptitudes, general readiness as determined by age and developmental level, and specific learning sets that may facilitate or interfere with the student's progress.

INSTRUCTIONAL TASKS

Analysis of the educational system and subsystems shows the need for directing attention to instruction itself—the heart of the whole process. The talk-assign-test formula permits teachers to "mark" the students; that is, to sort the products into different boxes labeled A, B, C, D and E without being required to teach anybody much of anything. And many learn very little. A simple analysis reveals the direction that reforms might take.

When a school introduces the technological approach, a teacher will spend less time talking to the class, and more time in the role of manager, manipulating the input, the instruments of instruction, according to a purpose or design intended to produce the terminal behaviors sought. Hence, changes in the teacher's program are indicated, including familiarity with the newer methods and media.

An effective teacher has been defined[13] as one who "demonstrates ability to generate, test, modify and re-test where necessary, productive instructional hypotheses relevant to the instructional needs of the individual learner . . . (and is) capable of specifying instructional procedures which will prove effective in attaining the larger educational objectives." He must not only be able to specify them, but to perform them as well. Competence in these matters is the whole purpose of the program for preparing teachers for their job and, of course, are too extensive to be detailed here. A few more significant generalizations will be touched on briefly.

Manage. A teacher, as we have seen, should be able to manage the various tasks for which he is responsible. These include maintaining a good group climate and a reasonable degree of motivation, as well as developing skills, knowledge and understanding in relation to the subject matter content in which he has specialized. This involves selecting media, sequencing and content, providing for the effective use of instructional equipment and making such arrangements as are possible for external instructional support personnel; that is, having people other than trained teachers provide for some pupil needs—

mothers, fathers, civil servants, public officials, craftsmen, students in training, and others.

Adapt. A teacher should adapt his instruction to those who are being instructed, to his target audience. Failure to do this has been, in part, responsible for the condition in which the disadvantaged find themselves. Hence, he will seek to discover the nature of the influence of the community and of the peer group on school behavior, and adjust accordingly. He should adapt his teaching to the objectives and content.

There are three quite different teaching processes which are not always recognized—explaining, coaching and discussing.

Explaining is the most commonly used, and may involve visual and auditory presentations that will point to, show, display, illustrate or diagram what is seen or heard, to which pupils are to learn to respond in certain ways. Or it may require verbalization.

Coaching, with the emphasis on student response and teacher intervention, is what has been called monitoring in the language laboratory. A teacher may demonstrate or verbalize to show the learners how to improve their performance, but he often does not know what to say to bring about the desired improvement. He is supposed to be warm, friendly, rewarding, and so on; but just what does he say or do under various familiar circumstances to be considered warm and friendly, and to reward the improved responses of the student so that as a consequence the learner shows improvement in skill or understanding?

Discussing, or rather leading discussion, is the third type of teaching process and employs methods referred to variously as participant, democratic, pupil-centered, or heuristic. This is perhaps the most difficult of the three processes, for the discussion must be kept from being teacher-dominated at one extreme, and from being superficial and futile at the other, an occasion for the sharing of ignorance. Yet it provides the opportunity not only for learning how to take part in the quest for truth, but also for teaching desirable social attitudes, verbal skills and logical thinking.

Counseling and conferring are not usually thought of as teaching, perhaps because of the one-to-one relationship, or because immediate problems are of the main concern. Counseling techniques[14] are being taught to prospective school counselors and school psychologists more adequately than formerly, but many teachers spend a good deal of time in the individual counseling relationship with students, and in conferring with parents with a view to improving student behavior, so they could well be better trained for this responsibility. One young teacher I once knew was asked by the mother of one of his students why her son did not get along well in school. The young man had a ready answer: "He is a nice boy and tries hard enough," he said, "but he is just stupid, that's all." This may have been nothing but the truth, but it was the wrong answer. How many of our young graduates would have a better one?

Whereas at one time a whole lesson or series of lessons may follow one or another of the three teaching processes, at another time it may be best to shift the instruction quickly from one to another according to the nature of the content or to the student's needs. But few teachers are equally good in all areas, so some may be given extra training where needed, and others many come to specialize in one or another process as they do in counseling.

LEARNER TASKS

Methods are selected largely on the basis of the hoped-for terminal behavior, the content of the course; hence, an analysis of the components of the behavioral repertoire is appropriate. Usually the content is thought of as knowledge of the school subjects—math, science, social studies, languages, and so on. And this is all right as far as it goes if there is some reason for acquiring such knowledge, or if it is relevant—the popular word just now, though it is important that we ask, "Relevant to what?"

Besides subject matter knowledge, content may well include what his instruction enables a student to do with his hands and with his mind. Briefly stated, it is the problem of content vs. process, though there is no real conflict between the two except in competition for school time. One learns how to use his hands and his mind by practicing on the tasks referred to as content. It would be interesting to see what would happen if we employed the direct method and made a list of mental processes, such as perceiving, imagining, judging, reasoning, remembering, and so on, and selected the content accordingly. But for the present it is probably as well to use the familiar content as a means for developing the processes. Like the instructional tasks, they break down into three major categories: knowledge, social behavior and skill.

Social behavior, including attitudes and ethical conduct, has been, in part, a responsibility of the school, though the methods employed are generally archaic, depending as they do on the use of aversive stimuli—that is, on punishment of one sort or another. Psychiatrists and clinical psychologists have opposed this punitive form of control, but their efforts have been expended largely on the more disturbed cases to the number of which the system has contributed. Only a few sporadic efforts here and there have sought to teach good conduct by the use of recognized principles of learning, including monitoring and reinforcement.

The area has been called the "affective domain" by Krathwohl and others,[15] and in their taxonomy there are five major groupings: receiving (attending); responding (and finding satisfaction in response); valuing (preference and commitment); organization of a value system; and characterization (by a value complex or ethical code). Clearly, these provide a broad view of major stages and an excellent basis for implementation which has yet to be worked out.

Skill, both psychomotor and cognitive, is largely a matter of timing, as is evident not only in the grosser bodily movements of athletics, but also in the manual and vocal skills as in music and dramatics. The learner's practice attempts provide the feedback with their progressively closer approximation to his goal of perfect performance. He is aided, presumably, by the interventions of the coach or monitoring teacher and by the immediate reinforcement provided to shape his performance.

Thus the learner is actually a subsystem, and feedback consists of cycles of evaluation permitting prompt readjustment to be built into the system. It provides for regulation of the process based on evaluation of successive products or performances.

Knowledge or information belongs to what Bloom *et al.*[16] have called the "cognitive domain," of which there are six major groupings: knowledge, comprehension, application, analysis, synthesis and evaluation. These, as may be readily seen, can relate to any subject matter content; and various levels of mastery can be designated for each.

When the timing is slower, as in most vocational skills, what is learned is a process or series of unit skills that must be performed in a certain order, as in automobile repair, setting up apparatus, or cabinet-making. And the same is true of the cognitive skills such as reading, memorizing, translating, solving equations, or validating a test. These represent different aspects of what is called "chaining."[17] A chain is a form of behavior which involves a sequence of actions in which each action depends on the outcome of the preceding action.

In most psychomotor and cognitive skills or processes, the new knowledge is to be assimilated or made a part of the old, not just attached to or associated with it. When it is thus incorporated, it becomes a working part of the total process, in some cases even producing a certain style, and even a way of life.

16.
Behavioral Objectives in Education

Behavioral objectives should have first priority in the development of educational technology. Without them, all else is meaningless—curriculum, methods, media evaluations, and administrative procedures. The chief contribution of programming may very well turn out to be the emphasis it gave, and still gives, to this neglected phase of the instructional process.

OBJECTIVES, IMPLICIT OR EXPLICIT

The quest for objectives[1] seems to be a normal, rational, common-sense activity. Instead of taking traditional subject matter for granted and then trying to teach it, we merely ask a simple question: What do we expect pupils (students, learners) to be able to do as a consequence of receiving our instruction? Two possibilities follow from the question: (1) see that they are able to do it or, if they aren't, (2) modify our expectations. The third possibility now in current practice, to fail the student, seems neither intelligent nor profitable.

Actually, objectives have not been neglected in the history of educational theory and practice. Various groups have emphasized what they considered the most important values (Chapter 5), including knowledge, understanding, religion, vocational competence, service to man, health, enjoyment of life, moral virtue, all-round development, and so on.

Various value combinations have been assembled and elucidated by philosophers, committees of educators and others. Psychologists have enunciated wants, needs, interests, drives. Authors and publishers of textbooks, through selection of content, detail in exposition, pictures, diagrams and typography, have emphasized some things and not others. Assignments in the form of questions, exercises and "examples" provided by the teacher, or at chapter end, and in manuals and workbooks, have actually designated behavior changes sought while teachers, some with understandable qualms, have at times told their young hopefuls what would be on the next examination.

Some objectives seem to be implicit in the content, and students infer or guess at what they are expected to know and do. Others are more or less explicit. Only the assignments and the examinations can be called *behavioral* objectives and furnish more or less useful evidence of what learning has occurred. But they are likely to be too late, too restricted, or too sporadic, or to be ill-adapted to the pupils or to the instruction they have received. And there is little agreement. A more systematic procedure is urgently needed.

ADVANTAGES

Actually, every teacher teaches specific concepts and generalizations without raising the question of agreement or disagreement with every other teacher. Basic agreements on objectives could be used as a starter. Finer demarcations would be subject to modification based on further research. If instruction is to be effective, the statements of successive objectives should be much more specific than is customary, and should indicate just what at different stages the students will be expected to know and be able to do, e.g., to identify, differentiate, solve, construct, list, compare, contrast, etc.

A sequential statement of content objectives has many advantages, among them the following:

It clarifies for a teacher the successive competencies he should expect of a student in progress, and the goal or terminal behavior sought.

It clarifies for the student what is expected of him, and so reduces the strain of uncertainty about "what will be asked on the examination."

It places the emphasis on learning and teaching, where it belongs, and not on school marks.

It provides a succession of check points showing the progress made in the successive attainment of objectives, which for the student is rewarding, reinforcing and motivating and tends to reduce irrelevant conduct.

Thus the progress that each student makes is revealed by attaining the successive goals or objectives, which form a kind of checklist of his attainments—prospective and actual. Some of the items on the list would be subordinate to other more advanced or comprehensive objectives, the attainment of which would constitute criteria for certain awards, or for further experiences, whether others in the class are ahead or behind. There are many advantages accruing from such so-called criterion-referenced marking:

It gives each student an absolute rather than a relative measure of his achievement or performance, that does not depend on what others do.

It provides the opportunity for each student to compete with his own prior record. Over a period of time, a succession of measures reveals the progress that he is making.

It facilitates temporary groupings of students who have actually reached the same level for discussions, TV showings, field trips, etc.

It encourages arrangements by means of which students may proceed at their own rate: they do not have to be held back or pushed ahead.

It makes it easier to adapt instruction to those students who transfer from other schools, since grade standards vary so widely; and to help those who have been absent, since they can go on from the point where they left off.

It furnishes data for obtaining averages and deviations in proficiency for different age groups; and correlations may be found with whatever variables one may be interested in.

It forces attention on content objectives and individual differences in the progress of students. Hence, criterion-referenced marks would be useful now, and will be even more so in the future when needed for computer assisted instruction now being developed.

UTILIZATION

If behavioral objectives are to be provided, the matter of utilization is important. For instructional purposes, objectives are instruments, or tools; and, like all tools, they can be misused. To help avoid such misuse, the three maxims which follow may be helpful:

1. Students should *know* what they are supposed to be able to do. This should no longer be kept a secret, leaving them to guess the nature of the examination questions to be asked, or the criteria and weighting on the basis of which an essay or essay question will be marked.

2. Students should be *taught;* i.e., provided with the means by which they can learn what is expected, either in the course itself, or, if that is inappropriate, by referral. For example, biology students may be expected to be able to write a paragraph describing the habitat of the frog. After instruction, those who are found to be uninformed on this matter should have additional aid and time to acquire the information. Likewise, those who are unable to write a paragraph should be taught how, and not failed in biology for their inability in English.

3. The behavioral objectives sought should be *within the capacity of the learners.* Those who are too immature or otherwise incapable of describing a frog's habitat in the paragraph form called for by the objectives should not be required to do so and then marked down for their unsatisfactory performance. The practice of giving a low or failing mark to a student for not being able to do what he should have been taught (or what he is incapable of doing) has been an escape hatch for teachers for too long a time. Schools should no longer be permitted to evade their responsibility by recourse to the marking system.

These maxims for proper utilization—student knowledge of objectives, teaching required learnings, and demands not to exceed capabilities—provide directives for the formulator of objectives: specificity and selectivity.

The nature of specificity is clearly presented in Mager's highly valuable treatment.[2] It is to be hoped that he will bring out a revision that will be somewhat more comprehensive. Until he does, the taxonomies edited by Benjamin S. Bloom[3] and David R. Krathwohl[4] are stimulating sources of objectives.

By selectivity I mean that the teacher cannot expect the students to learn *everything*. Therefore, he or some other qualified person should select those objectives[5] [6] considered essential. It is readily conceded that no unanimity among experts is to be expected; but most would be willing to go along with any reasonable array. The effort to set up such a list would unquestionably produce results better than the present laissez-faire procedures.

At once it will be objected that to limit students to a minimal list would be undesirable, but such is not the intention. The problem is to satisfy the exploratory interests of students beyond the stated minimum, but at the same time to discourage them from trying to memorize facts and more facts merely to increase the probability of their doing as well as they wish on the examination. There should be a number of ways to accomplish this, such as for example, the two-part scheme for examinations described in Chapter 12. Part II, therefore (see Chapter 12) could well be made up of objective-type items, and no one would get a higher score for getting more than a certain fraction (say half) correct. Thus the time previously spent in cramming could be saved for sleep, exercise, or working on some exploratory project. Bizarre as this scheme may appear at first, it conforms to an intelligent adult approach to a field of learning: one wants to know something about a subject, but not everything; and one likes to put in his time on things that are of interest to him.

GETTING STARTED

But how will the teachers get started drawing up objectives, whether or not for programming? Perhaps it is not the teacher's job, any more than textbook writing or devising apparatus, though these activities may be engaged in, and profitably. In a sense, it is the job of the engineer or technologist operating in the area between the findings of science and the practical task. Some may prefer the analogy of the production of a script for film or TV.

Two columns on each page of an open notebook might be used for the construction of this enlarged lesson plan (see accompanying chart). The plan would take account of the maturity of the pupils, materials available, and procedures to be followed. Repetition of concepts previously covered and to be covered would improve mastery and facilitate retrieval.

Subject: Geography: *Topic* Arid Lands

Column I   *Column II*   *Column III*   *Column IV*

CONTENT   OBJECTIVES   MEDIA   METHODS

I. CONTENT
Location of arid lands; characteristics; rainfall (comparisons, reasons), temperatures; terrain; fauna, flora; products; culture and inhabitants (if any). Land utilization: none, mining, grazing, agriculture, national parks; possibilities of irrigation.

II. OBJECTIVES
1.   On pictures of arid regions, point to and name some of the characteristic features, including: terrain, animals, plants, irrigation.
2.   Name two factors causing land to be arid, and two results of its being arid.
3.   Construct a table showing the mean annual rainfall and the mean annual temperature in certain representative parts of the world (or U.S.). What conclusions can be drawn from these figures?
4.   Write a short essay (200 words ?) on either of the following subjects: Factors Causing Aridity, *or* Irrigation.

III. MEDIA
1.   Films and slides of desert lands, some showing ancient and modern methods of irrigation.
2.   Appropriate wall maps, charts, pictures.
3.   Atlases, outline maps, reference books, encyclopedia.
4.   Possibly some programmed material on basic concepts.

IV. METHODS
1.   Film lecture presentation of arid lands. Facts with explanations (list and preview available films.)
2.   Discussion-heuristic, suggestions of hypotheses, reasons, possible consequences, etc.
3.   Projects: student reports; projects, possibly as part of larger units, including displays of maps, charts, artifacts, products, etc.

Undoubtedly, this sample could be much improved; and some topics are easier to outline in this way than others. Once one has started on the task, it becomes increasingly interesting and absorbing.

In the sequence of topics or units constituting a course, a range of appropriate educational objectives should be included, tapping the different cognitive skills which the learners might be expected to develop. In the sample given, some are present, though they are not made explicit, as perhaps they should be. In psychological terms, they are such processes as observation (sensation, perception, discrimination), concept formation, imagination and creativity, hypothesis formation, induction, deduction, determination of factual relationships (temporal, causal, whole-part) and so on.

And the advantages: teachers and students will know where they are, where they are going, and when they get there.

17.

On Marks, Grades and Scores

Educationally, marking is what a teacher does to the (written) work of his students. He places marks on it, and these marks may be written suggestions, corrections, commendations, or perhaps caustic comments. On the other hand, as everyone who has been to school knows, they may be numbers or letters that follow a known code and symbolize the teacher's judgment as to excellence of the student's effort. Such judgments may be of no particular importance to some pupils, the good, average, or poor marks being about what they are used to. In other cases they may provide quite a surprise and mean the difference between passing and failing. In the middle of the term, they may be of little significance except as commendation or warning. But, on some papers, "failure" may mean that the student will no longer continue with his class, or that he will be "kicked out" of school or college.

Sometimes the marks are reduced to percentages, though it has not always been clear what the mark is a percentage of. Usually, the numbers or the first few letters of the alphabet, however, constitute a kind of indefinite rating scale, with 60 or E signifying failure and the points up to 100, or the letters back to A (or A+), varying degrees of excellence. The final marks are placed on what are called transcripts, which are fastened to a student like a ball and chain.

It is understandable that a commercial culture like our own would invent such a system, but it is incomprehensible, in view of its known weaknesses, that it should continue to be employed. We need only mention here a few of its weaknesses—the varying criteria employed by different teachers and in different subjects, the subjective nature of the value judgments made, the instability of the measures, the lack of equal intervals, the dependence on the level of the grade or class performance, and the evaluation of personal conduct that is often tied in with the marks given.

To overcome some of these objections, standardized achievement tests were developed which are *scored*, not marked. These tests have a computed reliability and validity, and hence are more accurate measures of test performance than marks. They are standardized on the basis of fairly large populations, with age and grade norms computed. These norms are often misinterpreted, but at best they represent the average scores for pupils of different ages or in different grades. The best tests are supposedly those for which there is a wide distribution of scores for each age or grade group.

This brings us to the "grade," a word which, as noun or verb, may mean the same as an evaluative "mark," but which also means a group of pupils of about the same age who have been in school about the same length of time, and who are therefore supposed to be at about the same stage of development, and are grouped together in the same rooms because they are supposedly ready to receive the same instruction.

But here is the anomaly. If they are ready for the same instruction, it would logically be expected that they are alike in their abilities, though they are assumed to be unlike on the basis of the marking system; and they must be widely different if their scores and the derived norms are to be depended on.

Accustomed as we are to our system of marks and grades, we see nothing odd in grouping pupils on the basis of equivalent ability, and at the same time assuming their abilities are so divergent that only a few will learn what they are presumably supposed to learn (those marked A or 90-100), and that all the rest will fall short of this, *some even failing entirely*.

With the advent of programmed lessons, whether used in a teaching machine or in book form, individualized instruction for the first time became practicable in mass education. It is hailed as the purveyor of the Socratic method and as the reincarnation of the tutor, who can now be provided for all instead of only for the rich or noble. And the claims are not without foundation, though the technology is in the process of development.

One of the results of the efforts to make good programs is the discovery of the need for sequence. Each frame should follow logically from the preceding, and be followed similarly by the next. The lessons proceed by short steps in a more or less linear form, without omissions, from the simple to the increasingly complex. This has always been good pedagogy, but often it has been neglected for various reasons, including the incompetence of teachers, the difficulty of arranging for such progression, the amount of class time, the variation in books used, and—most of all—the wide variation in the abilities of the students in any one grade.

Now that such progression is approaching a reality in programming, and since learners will more than ever before be allowed to proceed at their own rate instead of being directed by the clock and the calendar, the need for grades and for grade norms will disappear. And, by the same token, need arises for a different kind of test score—one that does not depend on the performance of others, whether in the same grade or even of the same age.

Let us compare two kinds of measures. The first can be illustrated by the usual achievement test. The procedure, considerably over-simplified, is somewhat as follows: A large number of items ranging from easy to difficult are assembled and tried out on a large number of pupils, scores are determined, and norms derived. If the children in Grade IV averaged 35 and those in Grade V averaged 46, these would be the norms for these grades. If a child in Grade VII scored 46, he would be said to have fifth-grade ability. But he would continue to be faced by seventh-grade tasks and be marked down and otherwise humiliated if he could not do them. How ridiculous can one get and not realize it!

But there is another angle. Two children in Grade V might both get the same score, say 35. They would both have fourth-grade ability, but they might have answered quite different questions. This would be an extreme case, but similar results might be expected if the test is a good one to the extent that it samples a wide range of abilities. Presumably it makes no difference what a pupil knows and what he does not, so long as he knows a certain number of things—enough to get a "passing" score.

Now, let us follow these two fifth-graders out onto the playground. One thing they do that day is to broad-jump. One jumps 10 feet, the other 12. No one figures out the grade norms; there is no need to. We know just how much better one is than the other. And the physical education teacher knows that the second is good enough to take part in the annual intramural track meet. He has in mind a more or less accurate criterion of competence for a particular purpose. Standard units of measurement, quite independent of what other fifth-graders do, or what other 11-year-olds do, make possible an objective measure of performance. Coaching will probably improve it. But anyone who can jump 12 feet can jump 12 feet, whatever grade he is in, or whether he is 11-years-old or 25 or 50.

It would seem more reasonable to have a measure of ability independent of age or grade entanglements, and then provide the instruction needed for a learner at that stage of development. Of course, this is what the grading system (both meanings), is intended to do; but it does it very badly.

From correspondence with some measurement experts, I learn that achievement tests could be devised on a scale of absolute performance from 0 to perhaps 1000, which would represent ideally perfect performance. It would be simpler to develop such instruments in subjects like mathematics, science and language, where there is a definable linear progression from simple to complex. It would be possible even in subjects like the social studies, if there could be some agreement on a series of progressively complex concepts. Fortunately, programming, to be successful, will demand just such sequences. Some subjects might require the measurement of more than one line of progress; language learning for example, in which pronunciation, vocabulary, etc., could be measured separately.

But the measurement men say they could not "sell it" to the teachers—that it has taken years to gain acceptance of the present norms and T-scores. They shudder at the thought of starting all over again. This pessimism I do not share. Present test scores, with their assumptions of variability within a grade, I believe, were hard to sell, not because of the difficulty of the statistics involved or the transition from the concepts of percentage to probability. I believe the cause was that the whole procedure is inherently ridiculous. But one can gradually get used to anything. And, once it is accepted, it is taken for granted, approved and then required; so that we find teachers trying to "mark" children in physical education even though objective absolute measures can be used. I have asked some physical education teachers what they use as the basis for the marks they are required to give, and am always answered by a wry smile.

The advantage of absolute measures relating directly to the degree of progress the student has made, once the grade concept is out of the way, would lie chiefly in the recognition it would give to the level of instruction needed, whatever "grade" it might be in—whether in elementary school, high school, or college. And the development of programs, tapes and films would make it possible to provide the instruction.

Once the tests are developed, ideas for interesting research studies immediately present themselves. Cutting points could be determined for different kinds of educational promotion and vocational employment. Methods of instruction could be more adequately compared than at present, as could the effects of withdrawal of instruction and the amount needed to maintain skills. Achievement at different age levels would be of interest when not contaminated by the system of annual promotions from grade to grade.

It should, perhaps, be added that probably there is still a place for the norm-based, content-sampling test. Such tests could be used to determine how much of a given content a student knows in cases where it is agreed that a knowledge of certain items, rather than others, is not necessary. In history, for example, certain concepts might be considered basic, but the particular facts used to illustrate these principles might be drawn from different periods or different countries. The same might be true of geography or the arts. It might be agreed that a student should know something about the culture of a country, for example, as a consequence of the study of its language. He would be given a wide range of items, with no expectation that anyone would know all of them, but rather that his choice of reading, the films he has seen, and so on, gave him an acquaintance with—and even considerable accurate information about—some of them.

Similarly, other kinds of tests would be needed if the purpose were to discover those students who were capable of original thought and creativity above the common run in solving problems in a given area and in devising new means to obtain their objectives, and even discovering new objectives. Further, there are some areas for which no known paper-and-pencil tests are adequate, and for which rating scales are therefore used. These matters are mentioned merely to emphasize some of the limitations of the proposal presented. It is to be hoped that those who have the "creativity" needed and who are skilled in test and scale construction, will get together with the scholars, the teachers and the programmers in various subject matter fields to see what can be done about the measurement of achievement directly, using an absolute score without reference to the learner's age or grade, to others in the same population, to the time he may have spent being instructed, or to the grades (or marks) his teachers give him.

18.
On Marks, Norms and Proficiency

I am not a school administrator, but if I were and saw the headline, PROFESSOR WOULD ABOLISH SCHOOL MARKS, I would emit the old "ho-hum" and go and watch television. Not that marks do not deserve to be abolished. Anyone who has not lived his life in the Ivory Tower, however, knows that trying to abolish them would be like trying to abolish money.

When a superintendent is daring enough to make the attempt, formerly ill-attended PTA meetings are crowded with protestors, news articles discuss competition as the American way of life, and teachers favoring the *status quo* explain that "he" is working for a degree at the university or trying to make a name for himself. Even some of the students, for whose benefit the move was undertaken, want to know where they stand in comparison with others in their classes.

USES FOR SCHOOL MARKS

Of course, marks do have their place, such as it is. They represent a teacher's evaluation of a student's performance on a limited academic task or on an extended series of such tasks, as compared with the others who happen to be in the same grade or class. But they comprise in reality a multiple-purpose system. Their general utility is revealed by even a partial list of their functions. They serve:

To inform teachers, students and parents of how well individual students are doing in comparison with the others in their grade or class; and at year's end to designate those destined for promotion and non-promotion.

To provide data for academic and vocational counseling and guidance.

To reward good performance—except for those who cannot do very well. (The rewards are not quite the same as reinforcement, and as a rule not efficiently manipulated.)

To punish poor performance, whether or not the student could do better. (If he could not, such action is at least ethically questionable.)

To motivate learning—but students are motivated to compete *for marks*, rather than to attain the more substantial values.

Although marks do serve useful purposes, the good and bad are almost hopelessly mixed in the traditional marking system, and the side-effects are mostly on the negative side. The superior are not challenged, but are often rewarded for a performance that for them is mediocre; they will "pass" anyway. The retarded are discouraged, as are the disadvantaged, for they are unfairly asked to do things they cannot do, and so get farther and farther behind ("cumulative ignorance") like Joyce (Chapter 6). There is no assurance that anyone, even those in the middle range of ability, are learning as well as they might.

In addition to the functions listed, marks serve as a basis for communicating with the home, for giving special attention to exceptional children, and for such tasks besides as promotions, award of prizes, and job recommendations. But even for these purposes, taken by themselves marks are dubious criteria for professional judgments.

For the time being, the solution seems to lie not in abolishing marks, but in reducing their unwholesome influence by also employing a different form of appraisal.

MARKS THAT DEPEND ON NORMS

Like achievement test scores, marks that depend on norms ("norm-referenced") are based on a comparison of the performance of each student with the others in his grade or class. If the student is in a bright class, he is liable to get a lower mark than he would if he were a member of a slow group.

Even the standardized tests are stacked against him; for they are designed to produce a normal curve, with hard questions included that a large proportion of the students cannot answer—and there may be no good reason why they should. It is uneconomical to spend time and money trying to teach pupils what it is known beforehand they will not learn. If there is any good reason to learn such items, they can and should be taught. But if they are taught, the whole class will be able to answer all (or nearly all) of the questions correctly, and "the curve" goes out the window. Or else the teachers would hold to it as an article of faith, and conclude either that the test on which everyone gets a good mark is not a good test, or that the students cheated.

The current marking system presents an anomalous situation, up with which we would not put, to paraphrase Winston Churchill's famous declaration, if we had not long assumed that it was the proper procedure. But this is not the end. Raw scores are practically meaningless, so they are transposed into the relative terms of age or grade norms. There is some paper convenience in this arrangement, but it tells us little or nothing of what a student actually *knows* or can *do*; and no one is likely to inquire. Instead, it only tells which students of the same age or in the same grade answered more or fewer questions correctly.

MARKS THAT DEPEND ON PROFICIENCY

What is needed is a way to measure student progress in school in absolute units as track and field skills are measured in units of time and distance. This is now possible, following programming procedures, by measuring student progress in completing different series of tasks that constitute the intermediate content objectives along some continuum. These tasks constitute the criteria of the "criterion-referenced" score, and their successive mastery moves the student along at his own rate whatever progress others are making. Criteria based on behavioral objectives, as noted elsewhere, are desirable but easier to draw up for motor skills, and even for mathematical and scientific content than, say, for social studies and art, where judgments are highly subjective.

When criterion-reference marking[1] is instituted, a number of advantages are gained, among which are the following:

Since students proceed at their own rate, it makes a basis for placement of school transfers.

It clarifies both for teachers and students the successive competencies and terminal behavior.

It takes the emphasis off working for marks and places it on developing proficiency.

It provides the student with a succession of check points revealing his progress, which is reinforcing and motivating.

It does not depend on competition with other students but tends to promote cooperation; any competition is with the student's own record or among those of comparable ability.

DUAL ASSESSMENT

Should the traditional norm-referenced marking system be continued? For the present, probably yes; partly because it would be more than one's life is worth to try to get rid of it, and partly because it provides a convenient comparison of the performance of pupils with that of others in the same grade or class, though proficiency scores would be more satisfactory for this purpose. It is quite possible that the old norm-referenced system will gradually wither away as the new criterion-referenced individual scores come into common use. The process of development can begin in a small way with the skills that are now measurable in absolute units; gradually we will move out to the other subject matter areas.

When a number of influential school administrators and teachers become aware of the possibilities and begin to apply pressure, the makers of standardized tests will become interested.

19.
Grades and Objectives
in Higher Education

When the numerical grading of college students with its percentage implications came to be replaced by the now familiar letter-grade system, there was a feeling of general satisfaction hardly justified by the consequences. It soon came to be realized that any one letter grade means different things in different colleges, and often within the same one. Yet so much often depends on it that student attitudes develop which are quite inconsistent with a love of learning.

So strong is the opposition that colleges abandon it intermittently and resort to a simple pass-fail system, particularly for courses of general interest, presumably on the theory that if little precision is good, less is better: If, for example, it is unnecessary to distinguish between a grade of 86 and one of 87, it is likewise unnecessary to distinguish between an *A* and a *B*, or an *A* and a *D*.

The two-way choice—yes or no, acceptance or rejection—is often appropriate or necessary, as when making a purchase, going on a vacation, judging a picture for an exhibition, awarding a prize, or considering an applicant for a job. If it is used, the disadvantages of the A-B-C system seem to disappear—such as the teachers' troublesome decision-making for borderline cases, and the students' anxiety and aggression.

The pass-fail system also has certain other advantages (if they may be called that) which are not usually argued in public. Professors do not have to read or score the examinations or papers; a quick glance is sufficient for most. And students do not have to study very hard. In fact, the abler students might not have to do any work at all, as it has been learned, at least in some cases that have been reported, for they can pass the final examinations before taking the courses. Even the poorer students would need to do very little work to obtain credit, because their work would not be in competition with the best efforts of the others. The persistent absentees might fail; and perhaps a few others who should not have been admitted to the course in the first place. These conditions would not become evident at once; it would take a little while—maybe two or three years—for all to realize their blessings.

For those future citizens who are most interested in the cash value of the degree, the pass-fail system is indeed an ideal solution, at least until conscientious professors begin slipping in plus and minus signs, and the faculty adds an "honors" or "with distinction." By that time, the old marking system will be back, but translated into a new set of symbols: H, P+, P, P-, and perhaps even F+ (high borderline), F, and possibly an F-!

FUNCTIONS OF THE MARKING SYSTEM

It might be supposed that in higher education, that is, in the colleges and universities, one would find a more sophisticated marking system in operation than in the elementary and secondary schools. But such is not the case. And, as a rule, there are fewer available supplementary scores and other records. And yet the system is called upon to serve all the functions of a better one.

It is used by administration as the basis for *selection* in admitting students to college, to graduate schools, and to professional schools as well as for letting them go (flunking them out!), and also for admission into a number of so-called honorary societies.

It is used by instructors as stick and carrot for the *motivation* of students in the courses in which they are enrolled, though the treatment often produces unfortunate side effects.

It is used by students for their own academic *guidance*; whether wisely or not, they tend to elect courses in departments where they get the best marks.

It is supposedly of some assistance in *instruction*, but actually has the reverse effect since it provides professors, as it does teachers in the lower schools, with an excuse for not teaching what the students are supposed to be learning.

The basic weakness of the marking system in higher education is that in spite of the individual help given by conscientious professors, it provides inadequate data to serve these four basic functions. Additional data can easily be made available—standardized test scores, ratings, and (less easily) evidences of what intellectual progress has been made. Possible sources are the family, the high school record, school and college testing services, and the student himself. For the latter, on a prepared form, students could rate their academic and vocational interests in different fields, and their instructors could rate their class behavior in most courses on a similar scale on such points as interests, participation, attitude, and personal judgment.

SPECIFYING OBJECTIVES

The chief requirements for adequate marking is that instructors specify the objectives of the courses they teach: What it is they expect their students to be able to do as a consequence of their instruction. Objectives in the usual form—to know, to understand, to appreciate, and so on—are commendable, but they are too vague. Instead, such directives as the following are more appropriate: define, differentiate, describe, explain, elaborate, draw, design, demonstrate, or write an outline, brief, paragraph, or essay. Students who cannot do what is prescribed for the subject they are studying should be taught how, either in that class or another, regular or special.

If fairly detailed statements of the objectives were available, it would be possible for professors and students to recommend and choose courses respectively that would be more appropriate for different students to elect. In any one student's record, there would be fewer unfortunate gaps and less duplication of content.

The specified objectives would relate intimately to the course content, so it is impossible in this brief space to indicate the variety of possibilities. There would likely be considerable agreement among instructors in the same course and at the same academic level; but there would be some justifiable differences, particularly of emphasis. In any one course, however, students should be informed as to what they will be expected to know, and must be prepared to deal with the facts, concepts, relationships, principles, problems, etc.

ORDER AND PROGRESS

Courses could, in some cases at least, be taken in a more rational sequence than is now customary. Similarly if the matter of emphasis were given more attention, students could be shown as they proceed, what content called for mastery—the essential knowledge and skills—and what might be viewed as a sampling of supplementary information.

Some subjects require that certain knowledge and skills be developed before others are undertaken—mathematics, for example, and foreign languages. Others may be taught in almost any order, though they are usually presented in some reasonably logical sequence (not always evident to students). Progress can thus be roughly outlined in such a way that students can at any time see their progress to date—a highly significant motivational factor.

Next, it is important to evaluate each student's work against the scale of proficiency, ranging from no ability at all, to the most skilled performance. The instructor indicates on this scale the criterion point that designates his objective in teaching, quite possibly differing for different students. While the exactness in measuring motor skills cannot be applied to academic subjects, a comparable attempt at precision is needed. It should not be necessary to refer to the accomplishments of other students who happen to be in the same class.

Competent students should not be downgraded because there happens to be a group of quiz kids taking the course at the same time. The task of the instructor, it should be remembered, is not to get a distribution of marks of a group of students, but to *teach* them—to arrange the environment in such a way that they will learn and will attain the objectives of the course. If many students do not, either the level of the instructor's aspiration should be lowered, or else there should be some better teaching.

20.
Leadership, the New Media and the Obsolescent Classroom

Do programmed instruction and educational television signal the dawn of a new day in education, or are they merely current fads soon to disappear over the horizon? Attitudes of educators of all varieties seem to hover between these two extremes of opinion, with a few still asserting that a heavier-than-air machine cannot fly, or that if you want to be sure to get there, get a horse!

Many manufacturers take the optimistic view, and the plans of some publishing houses envisage a future different from the past. Equipment is being manufactured; programs are being written; training courses instituted; companies are merging; and even in a few schools and colleges of education, seminars are being instituted to provide instruction in the use of the new media. Meanwhile, many who should be leaders in the profession still talk about *"the* teacher" and *"the* classroom" as if, like the laws of the Medes and Persians, they could never change.

CUSTOM AND TRADITION

Content with such clichés as "nothing can take the place of the teacher," they see "the book" as a sufficient means of adapting to the wide range of abilities in current classrooms, when it is quite obvious that the book alone does not do the teaching; otherwise there would be no need for teachers.

Now, if ever, is the time for rigorous intelligent leadership from within the profession. During the period of irresponsible attack on philosophy, curriculum and method, most educators "sat and tuck it." Will they continue in this role while the world moves ahead, and while their responsibilities for judgment and decision are gradually taken from them by outsiders? Or will they help to direct the change on the basis of their professional knowledge and experience? And if they do influence future trends, will they be in a forward direction, or will they circle around only to retreat to previously prepared positions?

Already there are a few ill-smelling straws floating in the wind. TV lessons are being prepared which are just another teacher with a blackboard, failing utterly to take advantage of the rich possibilities of this medium. Classes view the same TV showing whether the students are ready for it or not, or have already progressed beyond it, even though they are in what is supposedly the appropriate grade. Professionally trained teachers view the same TV lessons as their pupils, although such stand-by featherbedding has not been demanded by the union and, except where the teachers need the presentation, represents a definite misuse of public funds. Language laboratories chop up their offerings into hours and courses, and mark on the conventional basis, instead of moving at rates commensurate with the abilities of individual students and marking on the basis of proficiency.

Programmed courses still include formal grammar, without benefit of the newer linguistic modes. "Fourth-grade arithmetic" and "seventh-grade French" and the like, are constructed with apparently no realization on the part of the producer that grade norms are a fiction, and that step-by-step progression is essential, without regard to the obsolescent grade classification. Little or no effort is made to take advantage of the situation and determine just what children should learn. Instead, the good old method is employed of dishing it out and then measuring the amount the students soak up, whatever it is and whether or not it is important or necessary as a preparation for what comes next. Even worse than that, they still do not expect most students to learn what they are taught, as evidenced by the letters below A in a marking system based largely on a misuse of the probability curve, permitting teachers to rationalize their instructional failures.

FIRST STEPS

What is the role of those who profess to positions of leadership, whether at higher or lower levels? First, two "don'ts": Don't be so confused that you are led to think that one medium *replaces* another, like the college professor who wrote, and truly enough: "Because they cannot stop, . . . movies and radio (and TV) cannot replace the book or the study guide . . . for real learning." But they can *supplement*—each medium to do what it does best. And second: Don't buy a lot of expensive equipment that no one knows how to operate. Instead, use the present as the occasion to make some of the kinds of improvements that should have been made long ago. You will want to read up about it if you have not done so already. The following are some of the possibilities for any school or school system:

1. Make an appraisal of the extent, availability and use made of your present library and audiovisual materials and, perhaps with the help of outside specialists, develop a good instructional materials center.

2. Keep your present grades; only, for the present, don't call them grades—years or homerooms will do—because the word "grade" implies certain academic expectations. Put the homerooms in charge of psychologically-trained teachers. The students in them will be their case loads.

3. Bring along the teachers (though some of them may be ahead of you) by means of seminars at home, and courses and seminars at the neighboring university. If the university does not have any, ask why.

4. Start with the more enthusiastic teachers, but with short programs and with the present set-up of classes.

5. For those pupils who have learned to read, plan laboratories, conference rooms and larger classrooms, perhaps with team teaching, where they will meet for different purposes—primarily programmed learning, discussion and TV.

6. Make a study of each pupil to see how far along the line of development he is in each school subject, and provide programmed instruction for him, whatever room he is in, starting at his level.

7. Encourage students to request (not demand) innovations.

Don't worry if things don't go as well as you had hoped the first year or two; the students will learn as much as they usually do, and probably more. And remember that the schools are for learning, not necessarily for teaching, or at least some of the kinds we have been accustomed to. Teaching, like reading, is a means of promoting learning—and may take various forms, not necessarily that of *the* teacher in *the* classroom.

Now, for the first time, it is within the realm of possibility to make a dream come true—to provide individualized instruction in a group setting. Enthusiasm is high, financial support is available as never before. All the parts are actually in operation in many places; it is not "mere theory" that is here invoked. *These things are now going on.* The time is ripe. Let us not allow the old fogies, or the young ones either, to dim the vision of the future. Now is the time for leadership.

NEEDED–A BROAD VIEW

Since the invention of the teaching machine and programmed instruction, theorists have speculated about their usefulness, innovators have tried out various devices, and research workers have evaluated results. Unfortunately, however, much of the speculation, tryout and research have derived from relatively small units of instruction inserted into conventional school procedures—what has been referred to as innovation by intrusion. The process is analogous to one in which a farmer of an earlier day might have added a goat to his stable, or a business man a new file to his office, or a school principal a music teacher to his faculty. The new instructional medium thus employed is sometimes called an adjunct. By the same token, a textbook would also be an adjunct.

Too little attention has been given to the respective roles of all the adjuncts; that is, of the several media of instruction, and to the changes in organization and procedures which the introduction of a new medium makes possible and even desirable. The best uses to which each of the new media might be put have not been carefully studied, nor have the possible changes in traditional school procedures been adequately explored. In short, what has in industry gone by the name of systems research has been largely lacking in school systems.

It is here proposed to look into some of the implications of the new media in general, and of programmed learning in particular, so far as curriculum, personnel, method and evaluation are concerned. This is done on the assumption that the function of the schools is to promote learning, and not necessarily to maintain the *status quo.*

Curriculum

The curriculum can be viewed as an expression of accepted values in a series of learning activities in which the students are expected to engage. These activities are presumably selected on the basis of a set of nobly-phrased educational objectives, which may read somewhat as follows: to know and understand the world in which they live, to think clearly and rationally, to solve life's problems, to participate constructively as citizens in present society, to become what they are capable of becoming, and so on. But these tend gradually to be forgotten, and a single instructional objective takes their place—a knowledge of facts about a list of school subjects. There is an underlying, but very weak, assumption that if the students learn the facts about a subject, the nobler educational objectives will be met.

It is not contended that the purchase of a few teaching machines or programmed textbooks will necessarily produce the desired results. But one of the fundamental features of programming, as we have seen, is the insistence on specifically stated *objectives.* If facts are wanted, it can teach facts. But if transfer values are sought, it can either teach them or make clear that it cannot, and thus it throws the ball back to the school to find a way that will. Thus, hopefully, the effectiveness of the older methods and media will be put to the test, instead of being taken for granted.

Another aspect of the curriculum, in addition to its objectives, is its *selectivity.* Any one subject, or even part of a subject, requires a lifetime to approach true mastery. In schools, selection from a vast array of facts, relationships and operations is essential. But in spite of the similarities of the courses of study in each subject, there is little fundamental agreement among the experts as to what the students of different ages should know or be able to do. The curriculum, over the years, has been in a continuous process of change as new ideas come and go. Currently, modifications even of the relatively stable subjects of arithmetic and physics are being experimented with.

The traditional method of dealing with the problem of selection of course content is to include most everything, and leave it to the students as to what they will learn. There is little or no indication of just what is essential and what is not. Furthermore, as has been pointed out, there is no record of *what* each student knows, only *how much* (i.e., how many items on a multiple-choice test a student answers correctly) in relation to other students who happen to be in the same grade or class. The student receives a score or grade. Programmed instruction, on the other hand, requires a decision as to what students will know, what terminal behavior to expect. If any particular facts, principles, or applications are necessary, they can be taught. This presents a challenge to curriculum planners: do they know what is important for students to learn and what is not? The introduction of programmed instruction forces such a decision. If there are content areas in which it does not make much difference exactly what a student knows, so long as he knows *something,* the traditional sampling procedures may well be employed. For example, it would be difficult for authorities to agree on what facts a student should know about geography, history, art, or music. Certain priorities might be established; but, by and large, what the student is interested in or happens to remember is perhaps a fair enough determinant. He should not be an ignoramus in these areas, but considerable honest ignorance is expected, and much to be preferred to a knowledge of things that aren't so. The vast amount of misinformation that some students acquire is appalling. The situation is somewhat different, however, in mathematics and languages, for example, in which specific knowledge and skills are necessary at different levels of proficiency.

A third implication of programmed instruction for the curriculum, in addition to its objectives and the selection of content, is the *rate* of progress. Traditionally, the content is divided into annual chunks or segments—so much to be covered in a year by each grade or class. The teacher may actually be the only one who covers the course in the sense of attaining the objectives sought, because of the great differences of ability found in any one group or class. But, in any case, all pupils are expected to move at the same rate—the well-known "lockstep" in education—or, as it has also been called, "the convoy method" in which all must proceed at the speed of the slowest, so that all may be kept together. Many administrative techniques—grouping, individualized instruction, etc.—have been tried quite unsuccessfully to beat this system. Now, however, it is finally possible.

One of the chief characteristics of programmed instruction is that students can proceed at their own rate. If one can go twice as fast as another, all well and good. But the consequences are frightening to the traditionalist. What will the classroom teacher do with the students who finish a grade or subject by the time the course is only half over! Instead of doing the most natural thing, allowing such students to go on with the next program, or catch up on other subjects, some teachers, experimentally of course, have arbitrarily decided that so much of the program will be completed each day or each week. But they have found that this was too much for some students and too little for others. And so they were right back where they started. One would think that the plan of having *the* teacher in *the* classroom, whether self-contained or not, was derived from the laws of nature. But it seems clear that the grade system never served the purpose for which it was intended, and the sooner we get rid of it the better.

Teaching Personnel

It is often asserted somewhat belligerently that nothing can take the place of *the* teacher, while others more conciliatingly suggest that if the machine can handle some of the teachers' tasks expeditiously, conducting routine drill, for example, the teachers will be freed to do better what only they can do. But neither position takes sufficient advantage of the instructional designs that are now possible. Certainly there is no expectation of denuding the schools of instructional and other personnel, whether or not they are all called teachers. Already many innovations have become common practice. For the future, it is possible to distinguish two chief categories—staff specialists and subject matter specialists.

Individual testing and counseling with pupils, parents, and teachers is going on under a number of job titles, classifiable under *student personnel services.* These no doubt will be continued and developed under the *school psychologist,* who will direct the necessary examination and appraisal of student ability and achievement. In addition, *homeroom teachers* and *guidance personnel* will have more responsibility than at present. They must be well trained to provide for needed personal help, and to encourage group cohesiveness and *esprit de corps* in rooms which house children who are doing school work at different levels, according to their abilities. Continuing research on the effectiveness of the instructional procedures will also be necessary for purposes of student evaluation and development. In a different category, *technicians* will set up, service and repair machines and apparatus, and will range in skill from mechanics to electronics engineers.

At least six different categories of subject matter specialists may be expected. As learning materials centers are developed, librarians and audiovisualists, as *curators* and *consultants,* will advise staff members and students in the use of available materials. *Programmers* will select, revise and construct films, tapes and programs for specific local purposes. *Monitors* will be needed (they have already appeared in language laboratories), to run the several subject matter laboratories, to see that the different kinds of apparatus are operating satisfactorily, and to see that materials are properly distributed; but primarily to help elicit and reinforce correct responses. They can even serve as what might be called "climate-control officers" to help create a friendly, rewarding social atmosphere. And *demonstrators,* now called TV or studio teachers, will be those especially talented in presenting material via this medium.

Learning materials curators and consultants, programmers, monitors and demonstrators, whatever they may be called, are new specialized teaching positions required by the technological approach. Two other categories will carry over from the present, but their activities will be somewhat different as a consequence of the fact that many of the elementary aspects of the training they now give can be taken care of more effectively by the new media. One of these is the *discussion leader,* the teacher particularly competent in teacher-pupil planning, group projects, stimulating further reading, and in promoting discussion involving criticism, the calling out of original ideas, and providing occasions for creative solutions to problems. His work will be much more effective, whether in social studies, science, the use of foreign languages or any other subject when his student group is made up of those who have already arrived at a common level of competence. The other is what is called *director* in music and in dramatics, and *coach* in athletics. It is his responsibility to improve group coordination. Most individual skills can be taught in other ways, but a chorus, an ensemble, or team needs a unique form of skilled direction.

Thus, for the curriculum, there are at least three important implications of programmed instruction: a necessary firmer determination of course objectives; more rational selection of course content; and with the possibility of students proceeding at their own rate, the elimination of the grade system of school organization.

Method

Turning now to the implications of programmed instruction for method, it should be emphasized that method follows objectives and content. Whatever medium is most effective should be chosen. Here there is an embarrassment of riches. A great deal of investigation will be needed to determine how best to use books, workbooks, library resources, programmed instruction, teaching machines, television, other audiovisual materials and "the living teacher."

What forms will the new patterns of instruction take? The possibilities are both interesting and exciting. No one knows the answers yet, but the following directions seem to be indicated:

—TV, videotape, or sound track films for orientation to new topics, for perceptual experience and demonstrations of various kinds.

—Tape and recordings for music, literature, speech, and foreign language instruction.

—Programmed learning and teaching machines for concept formation, knowledge of facts and relationships and routine drill.

—Books for reference, practice in reading, enjoyment.

—Discussion groups of equivalent competence and/or preparation for reviews, planning, projects, application, and creative thinking.

—Direction (coaching) for acquiring motor skills and for group participation and team work in shop, sports, music and dramatics.

—Tests and conferences for adapting each student's program to his level of ability and assisting in personal and social adjustment.

There will be plenty of need for school personnel, even though *the* teacher in *the* classroom becomes gradually obsolescent. School rooms, of necessity, can no longer be thought of as equal-sized cells with *the* teacher as the queen bee in each; but rather as rooms of varying size including individual booths, small listening and discussion rooms, subject matter laboratories and large auditoriums.

Evaluation

Implications of programmed instruction for evaluation grow out of what has already been said. The emphasis is no longer on *the* teacher, his (usually "her") personality, and so on, but on learning. Programming provides for continuous progress from zero to high-level competence, from simple to increasingly complex performance. Measures of such progress in knowledge and skill therefore should represent points of proficiency along a linear scale, whatever the age or grade of the student and the abilities of his classmates may be.

If a linear scale of proficiency is used wherever possible as a basis for evaluation, instead of the curve or random sampling and grade norms, the student of whatever age can profit by a knowledge of his progress. And the estimates of competence based on sitting time in class become meaningless. Elementary grade norms, secondary Carnegie units, and collegiate credit hours become as obsolete as the sword and the mule in military establishments.

Thus the implications of programmed instruction for curriculum, personnel, method and evaluation are not to be taken lightly. We might even lose some of our sacred cows.

21.
Teacher and Television

"How can I use the new media of instruction in my teaching?" This question is continually forcing itself on teachers of all subjects in all kinds of educational and training institutions. In *Teacher and Technology,* I attempted to provide a few answers to this question. In this chapter, I am focusing on closed-circuit instructional television and its place among other available media, in an attempt to show its relation, on the one hand, to some of the learning processes and, on the other, to the on-going instructional activities.

The need for changes in educational procedures has been mentioned often enough in the literature, and many reasons have been cited: population growth, with the consequent shortage of able teachers; crowded classes and increasing costs; the mass of new knowledge from which selection must be made, with the consequent necessity of condensing or discarding some of the old; and the changing world, with its rapid technological developments, ultranationalism and race problems. Still another reason for change is the often unsatisfactory quality of present instruction and the increasing complexity, diversification and specialization in teaching roles.

ATTITUDES TOWARD CHANGE

In spite of its high potential, instructional television runs afoul of considerable opposition, partly because of the difficulties and complications it shares with other audiovisual materials. For example, equipment may not be available for use when it is needed. This is likely to be true, whether the items are being used somewhere else, are in the shop for repairs, or whether they are cameras, projectors, films, or videotapes.

Another difficulty is that the tapes or films, whether prepared on location or purchased elsewhere, may be of poor quality or not adapted to the needs of the target audience either in content or in level of difficulty. Then, too, there is the problem of keeping the class together, with little or no chance of adapting to individual differences or of allowing students to proceed at their own rate. And one may have the feeling that some other medium might do about as well and be far less troublesome; some always prefer to let well enough alone. And perhaps most important of all, it is one-way teaching; students are not usually called upon to respond; the audience is physically passive and quiescent.

In spite of these difficulties and complications, it is urged that instructional television has certain distinct advantages. The chief and unique advantage is that it can reach large numbers—not only in large groups, but also persons scattered in different rooms, different buildings, and even in different towns. Few seem to note the implications of this fact in connection with the problem of crowded classrooms and large concentrations of students in constricted geographical areas, and extension courses. It makes possible good instruction at a distance.

A second unique advantage is its immediacy—the capacity for presenting action *while it is happening.* Such first-hand experience can be provided, or if desired, video-taped for later use—court practice, classroom activities and surgical operations are a few such activities that have been piped directly into classrooms.

A third advantage, one that television has over the motion picture film, is videotaping, providing an electronically-recorded playback that can be used immediately, or for later broadcasts. After the initial equipment is provided, videotapes can be produced at a fraction of the expense of photography with sound track on film. Thus the expensive discarding in editing is no longer necessary. Various processes, including kinescope recording, can be employed if the convenience of motion picture projection is sought. The film so produced can be used directly with a 16 mm projector, or it may be broadcast as a whole or in part as an insert in a television production. Still further reduction in costs may be expected with the commercialization of 8 mm film.

A final advantage is that television instruction is very likely to be improved instruction—providing the television teacher is wisely chosen, properly trained, adequately paid, and given time and funds to prepare good broadcasts. With a little ingenuity a production can be made much more effective by the use of pictorial inserts, artifacts, specimens, and so on. Experts in different enterprises can be invited to appear on programs, thus adding interest, information and authenticity. But neither specimens nor personnel can be brought in to every class each time a certain content is to be taught. And as the need is revealed, successive revisions can be made.

WHO DECIDES?

Some schools have no television equipment, others are experimenting with it, while still others have already adopted it as an integral part of their instructional program. The reasons for this divergence are not far to seek. Many teachers are fairly well satisfied with the routines they have developed (whether or not they should be), and are merely uninterested in any change. They point to possible disadvantages, and doubt the value of any innovations.

If there is to be change in an institution, it will come about as a result of a combination of internal and external pressures. Common external pressures may be expected from one or more of the following: state and federal legislatures in passing laws and providing (or withholding) funds; private foundations through grants to various projects; professional organizations in making studies and recommendations; publishers and equipment manufacturers in pushing sales; and citizens as individuals, parents, or representatives of various social and civic organizations.

The internal determiners of change are the boards of education; the school administration, i.e., the superintendent (probably the most influential) and principals, supervisors, curriculum directors, staff psychologists, guidance personnel and teachers; and, lastly, the instructed, the students, whose opinions and whose failures and successes are constantly being researched. Variations in the force of the pressures account for the differences found in the extent to which such innovations as instructional television are adopted.

There is no need here to go into the various techniques of the change agent. He will, of course, be met with all the stock arguments ("no demonstrable need," "the time is not ripe," "I am not convinced," "no funds," and so on). And little can be done if the top man—be he superintendent, principal, president, dean, comptroller, manager, or commanding officer—is opposed or lukewarm in his support. A logical argument may be less effective than the desire to keep up with the Joneses—the bandwagon technique. Even top-level support may be ineffective if it is suspected that it is influenced by hope of promotion, a better position, or even a thesis subject at the university; or unless it is clear that staff members will profit in some way by the adoption and the innovating practices. Any argument, however, is likely to be effective if supported by a substantial grant. Continuing pressure, probably over a number of years, will be necessary before a school system is properly equipped for television instruction, though small beginnings are possible earlier. Industry and the armed forces, in general, are more fortunate.

Probably the best support for developing an instructional television program is to be found in customer satisfaction. For this, the first essential is good equipment and adequate servicing. The second is good programs. Too many that have been tried merely reproduce mediocre teaching; and there is little advantage in presenting on ITV just the familiar talking face. Off-the-cuff production is not likely to be effective. It is said that as much as a whole day is given to taping a one-minute television commercial—and this does not include preparing the script.

A third essential is adaptation of the lesson content and presentation to audience needs, chiefly in terms of density and redundancy. Density refers to the speed with which the ideas go by, which may be too fast for some and too slow for others. Redundancy refers to the amount of enlargement and repetition provided to make the content comprehensible. A fourth essential is good utilization—the way in which the material is presented and the follow-up provided. These and other considerations emphasize the fact that educational psychology has perhaps been overly preoccupied with learning theory at the expense of theories of teaching.[1]

LEARNERS—THE TARGET AUDIENCE

While attention here is directed chiefly to the elementary and secondary schools, much of what is said applies to instructing adults as well as children and young people, and refers to any location where instruction is carried on—special institutions, trade schools, professional schools, the armed forces, industry, church, and fraternal and other social groups, to say nothing of the people in underdeveloped nations. For all these, instructional television has an important part to play, particularly if it is adapted, as it can be, to the groups involved. Whatever the audience, chief among the factors of concern to the producers are age or maturity level, general and special aptitudes, personality differences, physical handicaps, and social and cultural background.

It is important that showings take into account the readiness of the learners for the instruction provided. Are they mature enough to attain the proficiency expected? Is their previous training and education adequate? Are they sufficiently motivated to give the needed attention? There are several attention-getting devices that help in this matter: close-ups, zooms, camera angles, sound effects, stopping the motion, alternating voices, slow and emphatic narration, and changes in the shape, color, sound, intensity, pitch, or quality.

OBJECTIVES OF INSTRUCTION

In deciding on method and media for ITV presentation, or any instruction for that matter, perhaps the most important question applies directly to the parts of the school subjects (or training skills) being taught; that is, to the objectives of instruction. There are three chief categories of objectives; the acquisition of sensory-motor skills, of knowledge and of attitudes—what have been termed the psychomotor, cognitive and affective domains.

Skill, Knowledge and Attitudes. Television can be most useful in the psychomotor domain by demonstrating, and hence revealing, the correct model ("This is what you should do.") and in providing feedback to the learner on his own performance so that he can make the necessary corrections. Physical education and sports, industrial skills and processes, and the use of instruments and apparatus yield themselves to this approach, serving to "shape" the performance.

Attitudes—the Affective Domain. Attitudes are of three kinds— those that tend to move an individual toward another object or situation (acceptance), away from it (escape), and against it (aggression). With the best of intentions, much school work tends to produce negative attitudes (escape and aggression) toward its own activities and toward the people responsible for them, as well as toward what are sometimes referred to as the finer things of life.

At the start, *interest* in the content may be sufficient to induce attention, or it may be low or virtually non-existent. In either case, for a particular showing, *attention* is necessary and is favored by the medium, unless the signal is of low quality or has to compete with too much "noise," that is, with distractions of various sorts. With enough, but not too many attention-getting devices, students may be expected to attend—and even show a little interest—if only of a passive sort.

Motivation to learn, however, is a different matter, and may be expected only if utilization—as well as production factors—are properly dealt with. If, before showing, a teacher can preview a planned presentation, he may be able in various ways to arouse expectations and anticipation and even at times to provide a little suspense. He can indicate what to look for and can supply questions which the showing may be expected to answer. He may even announce a test. He can be assured that most of the audience is "ready" for the presentation, and in the future it may perhaps be expected that commercial producers will validate their offerings by reporting the results of pre-release tryouts on previous similar audiences.

After showing, the students can try to answer the questions previously asked and carry on a discussion of the theme, and can be encouraged to read relevant assignments, look up reference materials, or develop related projects, whichever is most appropriate.

Television and sound motion pictures probably provide the most adequate media for developing *value* choices, including attitudes toward the arts and toward varieties of human conduct. Students are constantly making choices which lead inevitably to later choices, until the pattern of life is well established and change is unlikely. In the early stages, if positive attitudes are developed, as TV could help to develop them, toward rationality, group participation and good citizenship generally, the elusive goal of self-fulfillment and the good life may be more often reached than it now is.

Knowledge—the Cognitive Domain. Acquiring knowledge, which was indicated as one of the content objectives above, can be more explicitly described than the intangible and more elusive objectives of the affective domain. And terminal behavior sought can be made more explicit than it usually is. The cognitive objectives can be conveniently described under the following heads: percept and concept formation, thinking and problem solving, and retention and transfer. Bruner[2] has classified representation in the field of knowledge in three categories: enactive ("a set of actions appropriate for achieving a certain result"), iconic ("a set of summary images of graphics that stand for a concept"), and symbolic ("a set of symbolic or logical propositions . . . governed by rules or laws for forming and transforming propositions"). It is evident that television is most effective for the realism of enactive representation, somewhat less so for iconic, and for symbolic. Likewise, it is most effective for developing percepts and also concepts, and less so for promoting thinking and problem solving, and memory and transfer.

Built-in features and techniques have been described as promoting attention and motivation; they may also aid in developing percepts by *pointing* ("ostensive definitions") in one way or another to the objects or cues needed to identify the objects, movements, characteristics, and the like, some of which may be crucial. Among the built-in features are pointers, moving arrows, numerical labels (pop-ins), verbal labels (dissolves), close-ups and colors. Among the utilization techniques, a teacher can identify significant parts that will appear on the screen, or present symbolic diagrams, pictorial charts or cut-aways; and for sound he can quote short passages or play motifs on the piano. Irrelevant cues can be passed over unless they are likely to cause confusion.

Perception involves learning what things are, their names, and how they look and sound under varying circumstances and in varying combinations. It involves learning significant or identifying cues from the world at large, and also from the feedback from one's own performance, his knowledge of results or consequences as one gradually builds up the correct or more nearly correct responses.

Percepts are perceived particulars; *concepts* involve multiple discrimination. A concept is any class or category of objects, events, or relations having one or more common properties; it can be identified by a label (name) or a definition. For example, one may perceive this tree, but he has a concept, tree, that applies to this one and to others because of their common properties. Television is admirably suited for instruction in percepts and concepts, representing, as it can, both visual and auditory phenomena enactively, iconically and even symbolically.

Similarly, *thinking* can be aided by presenting data that lead *to* a principle (induction), and also what follows *from* a principle (deduction or application). It makes possible what is loosely called "understanding," but which may be more sharply defined as a knowledge or relationships—what will happen when different objects or conditions, or people, are brought together under given circumstances. To follow Guilford, thinking may be convergent, arriving at the single correct solution; or it may be divergent (creative), arriving at new, original, and unique solutions.

Problem solving, a particular kind of thinking, involves making hypotheses and considering consequences of possible action; and requires more in the way of student response than television instruction usually provides. However, demonstrations can be followed by questions or problems for students to answer or solve while the television is shut off to allow them time to do this. If this technique is employed, it is essential that enough time be provided, or frustration and confusion are likely to result.

Retention, or overcoming forgetting ("storage and retrieval"), can be aided by repeating the showing, perhaps without the sound track (sometimes provided by the students from memory), by the use of questions and outlines (mimeographed) or in a workbook for review, and more particularly, by building up a sequentially or otherwise logically interrelated cognitive structure that is something more than a memorized list of separate items.

Learning tasks have been categorized as reproductive and productive. The former are, as a rule, easier to test, and in the case of manual and vocal tasks are all-important. They include memorizing (nomenclature and operations as well as prose and poetry) and skilled acts of a vocational or pictorial nature. Productive tasks include recognizing concepts or events when stated differently (transformation), writing in one's own words, explaining, giving examples, solving problems, and translating a foreign language. At his own cognitive level, one must learn, observe (look, listen, read, study), recite (answer questions orally and on written tests), and confirm, correct and reinforce.

Looking to the future, more people will have to engage in scientific thinking; achieve competence in the use of language; become acquainted with the operation of man-machine systems and with systems theory; and also, let us hope, maintain contact with the ends for which most of these things are but means, i.e., be cognizant of life values. Clearly all this requires a multi-media approach, but television can provide much of the basic experience needed that is not now to be found in the schools, either in slums or suburbs.

UTILIZATION OF ITV

It has no doubt become apparent that the selection of content, and the way that content is utilized, can easily make the difference between success and failure of a television program. Also, it is not difficult to see why the results obtained from research aimed to determine whether TV or "regular" instruction is better show disappointing results. It is some consolation, perhaps, to find no statistically reliable differences, which is the usual outcome. But one can hardly expect more from a research design that does not accurately describe the nature of each pattern of instruction used, as well as the subjects and the measuring instruments.

It might be advantageous to consider some of the conditions under which ITV should *not* be used—when it would be unnecessary or ineffective—though some enthusiasts would doubtless take exception to such generalizations.

But it is also hazardous to describe in general the occasions when television instruction is most likely to be effective. Suggestions have appeared from time to time in this chapter, and it may be that the following generalizations will be helpful. If the signal is clear and the programs are well constructed and presented, ITV may be expected to make a distinct contribution:

1. When perceiving and discriminating cues and developing concepts are important educational objectives.

2. When knowledge of small, close-up, distant, past, unusual, or live events is needed.

3. When an orientation or lecture-demonstration or other appropriate unit is used to support regular instruction.

4. When immediate playback is desired.

5. When no competent instruction is available, as in a small isolated community.

6. When it is desired to teach large numbers together, or an audience widely scattered geographically.

7. When the object is to provide training for novices in industry (supervisors, workers), or in the professions when the learner must become acquainted with new environments and processes.

TELEVISION AND TEACHER PREPARATION

One place where vigorous development of instruction by television might be expected is in the institutions for teacher education, both because of instructional improvements that might be introduced and the familiarity it might give to those who later may be expected to use it. But with a few notable exceptions, the opposite is the case. This may be the consequence of the basic conservatism of higher education—for teachers are, of course, prepared in other departments as well as in the schools and colleges of education.

But in the latter, among the possibilities, most of which remain unrealized, are the following:

1. Orientation to acquaint the students with different kinds of schools and teaching situations and variations in practice, or at the beginning of new units of instruction for what Ausubel has termed "advance organizers."

2. Observation of pupils and of teaching, which has become almost impossible to provide for adequately in view of the increasing numbers of trainees.

3. Study of the teaching process—the ways in which different teachers successfully (or unsuccessfully) handle different instructional or behavioral problems.

4. Case reports, preferably longitudinal, of growth processes, handicapping conditions and their treatment.

5. Samples of different instructional and noninstructional teacher roles.

6. Playback of student counseling and of practice teaching with the ensuing conference with the supervisor.

All these relate primarily to preservice education. Similar materials can well be prepared by the schools for assisting in the supervision of new teachers and other inexperienced school personnel. There seems to be no doubt that teacher preparation could be much more effective if more of these possibilities were realized, but recent news items suggest that proposed expenditures to these ends are among the first to be struck from the list.

As to the future, the crystal ball is still cloudy, but the possibilities are exciting—and, in the electronics industry, well nigh endless. Computer assisted instruction (CAI) is already here on an experimental basis. But the computer, like its maker, requires compromises, and there is a question as to how much education can be sacrificed to efficiency. For the present, however, instructional programs need to be prepared in quantity and revised on the basis of tryouts on selected groups of students of all ages in all content and training areas. And the criterion should not be whether the students stayed awake, or even whether they liked it, but *what did they learn?*

NEW DIRECTIONS

Because this chapter is focused on instructional television, it should not be concluded that other media and other educational innovations are considered of lesser importance. The direction of change seems to be toward greater flexibility. The basic considerations are two: better adaptation of instruction to learner differences and needs; and greater precision in defining and attaining instructional objectives. Greater flexibility is called for:

1. In methods and media, including different kinds of programmed instruction.

2. In class size, ranging from independent study and small classes to large classes with team teaching.

3. In scheduling, with shorter periods (15 to 20 minutes) or "modules" in various combinations.

4. In plant design, including small and large rooms, laboratories, and resource centers.

With the developments in the electronics field proceeding at such a rapid rate, still further changes may be expected. Computers have already made the individual television screen a reality, placed in the student's carrel for individual study along with other pieces of apparatus. It will not be necessary much longer to get a group together for an ITV showing; instead it will be switched on by each student when he comes to the point where it should be fitted in. Computer assisted instruction adapted to individual student needs is already visualized at three levels: drill and practice systems, tutorial systems, and dialog systems. But the computer's behavior depends on the data fed into it. What data on a student are needed, and what information and experience should be provided, and in what form, are still unanswered questions. There is much to be done, and the sooner a start is made, the better.

Part V
Technology and Educational Reform

22. SOME BASIC PSYCHOLOGICAL ISSUES IN AUTOMATED TEACHING

Outside pressures may help reduce the fifty-year lag between innovation and acceptance.

23. PSYCHOLOGY AND THE BEHAVIORAL SCIENCES IN THE SCHOOLS

Psychology could be more advantageously taught in the schools as parts of general sciences and the social studies, or as area study, than as a separate course.

24. THE FUTURE OF SCHOOL PSYCHOLOGY

The sources of present-day psychology suggest its possible functions in education for the present and future.

25. AN EDUCATIONAL MODEL FOR SOCIAL LEARNING

The medical and educational models should be supplanted, with the emphasis not on treatment or punishment, but on teaching and learning.

26. FIRST THINGS FIRST—EDUCATIONAL RENOVATION

Procedures in schools should first be renovated and brought up to the level of better schools.

27. PSYCHOLOGY AND EDUCATIONAL INNOVATION

School psychologists and educational technologists have a responsibility for introducing and promoting reform measures.

28. IN SUMMARY—REFORM FROM WITHIN

Four postulates and six theses for educational reform.

22.

Some Basic Psychological Issues
in Automated Teaching

Never before have there been so many new ideas in the educator's waiting room, clamoring to be admitted to full standing in the school organization. A possible exception was the period following World War I, when the Thorndike-Woodworth experiments demonstrated the untenability of the doctrine of formal discipline; when the psychologies of Pavlov, Freud and the Gestalt school began to affect educational practice; when Dewey's theory, referred to as "learning by doing," was being translated into the problem-project method; when the kindergarten and junior high school were gaining general acceptance; and when, as a consequence of the work of Binet, Terman and others, psychological testing moved from the Army into the nation's schools. Those were the great days. And what were then innovations have now found their accepted places in the educational process.

Occasional dissident voices are still heard, however; and some schools are still operating as if these things had never happened, bearing out the oft-stated conclusion concerning innovations, that decades elapse between the discovery that past practice is indefensible and the capacity of an institution to respond to its role in society and to new insights concerning its techniques of operation—usually about fifty years. The process of diffusion is slow at first, then quite rapid, then slows down again for various reasons, including costs and the influence of the apathetic or the recalcitrant. The process is speeded up if there are pressures from the outside.

Sputnik was one such pressure, following which it has looked as if American schools have been trying to beat the Russian schools into the twentieth century. And the population pressures, coupled with multi-million dollar grants and even some high-powered advertising, have served as additional outside pressures. Now we have not only radio, slide and film projectors and disc and tape recorders, but also open- and closed-circuit television, lectures by telephone and public address systems, teaching machines and programmed textbooks, to say nothing of team teaching and lay helpers, with high-speed computers moving in over the horizon. Unlike the earlier innovations, which were primarily psychological, those today seem to be largely mechanical, although they have important psychological implications. In addition, there is the new content that must be sifted and organized for curricular purposes, and there is the increasing number of people, young and old, here and abroad, who are looking to the schools for education and training.

One characteristic of innovations is that they are introduced as small, separate changes, often without any realization at the time either that they are parts of a larger movement, or that other institutional systems will be affected. Those who bought a Ford in 1905 could not know that it was the beginning of a new phase of the industrial revolution—from manufacture to transportation. Nor could they know the effect this revolution would later have on highways, railroads, agriculture, urban development and even international relations. Similarly, those school administrators who approved the purchase of a slide projector in the 1920's could not recognize it as a part of what was to be called automation, nor could they foresee the later effects on class scheduling, teaching roles, testing and promotion, school architecture, textbook publication, psychological research, the use of computers, and no telling what else.

But the current educational innovations may be thought of as a part of something other than automated dollar efficiency. Whereas the schools of the past offered to all pupils the *opportunity to learn,* even though many were incapable of profiting by it, today this is not enough. Innovations are introduced because of an as yet barely recognized feeling of *responsibility* for seeing to it that *all children learn.* It is from this point of view that four psychological issues are discussed here, as they relate to educational automation through the use of the new media of instruction. We shall not be concerned with the details of program planning or the technicalities of television, but rather with more fundamental issues relating to attitudes, individual differences, motivation and the teaching-learning process.

ATTITUDES–THE STEREOTYPE

First, the attitudes toward the new techniques in teaching are important, whether favorable or unfavorable, and whether they are based on knowledge, ignorance, prejudice, or anxiety. Some people and some communities are rather rigidly opposed to change, while others are more flexible, more ready to try out what is new. The stereotype of *the* teacher in *the* classroom (presumably a self-contained classroom) tends to produce rigidity, since it suggests that the traditional set-up is *necessary*. This gives support to a false dichotomy: the *status quo* is good; change is bad. Illustrations are found in many of the silly pronouncements concerning the new media: "No machine can take the place of a gifted teacher," or "Children are not automobiles on an assembly line," and others.

Then, too, some teachers are comfortable in their present roles, and they do not wish to be disturbed, while others fear that they will be replaced by machines. What is likely to occur is that some will be *dis*placed, that there will be a further differentiation of roles, as has been suggested, e.g., giving lecture-demonstrations on television, producing films, constructing programs, and monitoring, as in the language laboratory. More careful attention will be given to specialization in such current techniques as directing discussion and student participation, guidance and counseling, coaching and directing teams and ensembles as in athletics, music and dramatics, and providing for direct experience through field trips and cooperative training. Team teaching, too, suggests possible changes in "staff utilization," as the phrase is. Few teachers are really good at *all* teaching skills, and there is no reason why there should not be some further division of labor to take advantage of special talents and predilections. The proposed innovations will, in reality, make the teachers' work no harder, but it will be more satisfying than formerly—because it will be more effective. If we are to assume the responsibility of having pupils actually learn, instead of being content merely to give them the opportunity, we cannot remain content with the less effective ways of the past.

INDIVIDUAL DIFFERENCES
AND PROGRAMMED INSTRUCTION

Since the days when personal tutors taught the sons of the titled and wealthy, it has been assumed that individual tutoring is the ideal form of teaching. Whether it has been worthy of the confidence placed in it or not, research has not yet revealed. However, mass education has taken over the practice. As the tutor talked to his pupil, so the teacher talks to his class. But with numbers came a difference. And the difference has presented problems which, though recognized, have never been solved. Various kinds of grouping have been employed to adapt instruction to the abilities and needs of individual pupils in grades and classes, but they have not been successful. Now we have the auto-instructional devices by means of which pupils can move ahead at their own rate, and there is the further possibility of programs that cover the same content but which differ in difficulty. Here, if anywhere, would seem to lie the answer to the educator's prayer.

But there are further difficulties. If pupils proceed at their own rates, one of the main reasons for programming, some students jump way ahead, while others fall far behind. The class supposedly has to be kept together if TV lecture-demonstrations or films are used. Thus the teacher who wishes to employ programmed instruction and audio-visual aids is in a quandary. Actually, it is a familiar situation, since the pupils in a grade or class never are really together, though they may *seem to be* because they are at the same place in the book. Fortunately, the program-film quandary is an easy one to get out of, for reruns can be used with any sized group as often as needed.

Students proceeding at their own rate present yet another and more serious problem. Some will not have completed a course when the term is over, while others will have finished it some time earlier. This is virtually what happens now, but it is masked by daily assignments spread out over the year, is rationalized by means of the marking system, and corrected to some extent by belated remedial instruction. What is a teacher to do when a half dozen students have finished the program, and there is still a month to go before the end of the term? Or when the school year is over, and another half dozen still have several hundred frames to go!

The obvious solution of the difficulty is the ungraded school, in which students, when they have finished a program, either get caught up on another one or go on to the one that comes next. This takes a little organizing; and high-speed computers are not yet needed for the purpose, although they have already been employed for flexible scheduling involving variations in class time. Actually, the greatest roadblock is the present paucity of continuous programs. But, even now, students could be given credit, not for time spent in class, but for what they know and can do. They could move at their own rate, and when they have attained the proficiency set as the course objective, go on to the next more advanced course. Those who have not attained this goal by the end of the term will keep on until they do. What "classroom" they are in is immaterial, since they will be working on programs individually, and will meet with students who are making progress similar to theirs in each of the different subjects.

We are already beginning to accommodate the extremes of the distribution—from the mentally handicapped to the academically talented. But the "normal curve" for achievement is not segmented, and good programming is beginning to provide for finer discriminations than are implied in the common phrase, "ability grouping." Furthermore, as we know, students are not always fast or slow in all subjects, but may be advanced in one and retarded in another.

Any student's growth is normal for him. He is good or poor, fast or slow, passing or failing, only in comparison with other students with whom the school system forces him to compete. He himself is developing at the rate determined by his biological constitution and the circumstances of his home and school experiences, neither of which he controls. Psychological studies have not yet done justice to the effect that continuing failure, and the expectation of failure, has on growing children. Those who have been through college have not had the experience of never making a "good" recitation, never receiving a "good" mark, never being honestly complimented for a task well done. To force children into such a situation year after year is not competition—it is cruelty. There is much they can learn, and content and method can be so employed that, although they do not always succeed, all will have the experience of success. If we are to be responsible for pupil learning, we must provide for the continuous progress of each student, instead of merely presenting the *opportunity to learn* in wholesale fashion, an opportunity of which, like Joyce (Chapter 8), many will not be able to take advantage because they will never catch up.

MOTIVATION

The new media can be adapted to individual differences; in some areas they can also provide better teaching than was formerly possible. Carefully prepared programs and visual and auditory devices help students to understand concepts and meanings and perform the tasks of which they are potentially capable. When instruction is individualized, and its form improved, students are less likely to be frustrated by the too-difficult task—or bored by the too-easy one. They are thus much more likely to be motivated, especially since the older media and methods are likewise available—books, group discussions and activities. And competition can be what it should be—the individual student competing with his past record or with his equals. However, if programs, films and tapes only copy the old content, or merely supplement it here and there, using the same amount of time for all, the new motivational advantages are not likely to accrue.

Even as it is, students sometimes report that they are bored by the programs. This may be because some that are in use are too easy for the brighter ones—the "small steps" are *too* small. Or they may be too difficult for the slower students—the small steps are too large. Some students reported that a certain program was just plain dull and tiresome. This complaint has two answers. One is that students are coerced by a program into working continuously instead of being able, as in class or in the library, to escape occasionally into inattention and daydreaming. It is possible that brief relaxation periods would improve motivation. Certainly, the school day should be broken up into a number of different kinds of experiences. The other answer is that perhaps the program really is dull. Efforts to brighten it up with a little humor, some pupils report, make it more fun, while others say they don't like the "wise cracks." You can't win! But with the variety now possible, with programs adapted to pupil differences, and with greater skill in program construction and use, a high level of motivation is possible, and is in fact usually found, as it is apt to be when learners see that they are making definite progress toward their goals.

THE TEACHING-LEARNING PROCESS

An interesting consequence of the use of teaching machines and programs, and of educational television, is that it has occasioned an inquiry into the effectiveness not only of these innovations, but of traditional procedures as well, and particularly into the nature of the teaching-learning process. It has again raised the question with which Rice perplexed the educators of his day, the doubtful relation of teaching time to the amount learned. And it has pinpointed the significance of what is referred to as *entering* and of *terminal* behavior, and the relation of the latter to instructional objectives. Anyone who has made a study of programming will never again be content (if he ever was) with such a definition of teaching as the transmission of the cultural heritage, which in translation means little more than dishing it out and trying to get it back on the examination.

Essentially, teaching involves four phases in a process of controlling and manipulating the learner's environment:

1. presenting stimuli (lectures, explanations, pictures, demonstrations, directions, questions) calling for learner responses;
2. providing for feedback to the learner concerning his responses (knowledge of results, further directions);
3. reinforcing the learner's good responses so that they are habituated or improved; and
4. providing new situations in which the good or improved responses are emitted appropriately, either in the same form (retention), or modified (transfer, application, problem-solving).

B. F. Skinner has referred to this total process as the "shaping" of responses, and has pointed out that the usual teaching is likely to fall short at one or another of these phases. For example, lectures and audio-visual methods are likely to stop at Phase 1, since they are devices for listening and watching; and since the learner's responses are not overt, no one knows what they are, or what, if anything, he has really learned. A preliminary set, subsequent discussion, and supplementary reading and practice are needed and frequently provided.

For the remaining three phases, with a group of learners, a teacher cannot give the individual attention to each that is necessary, whether the learning task is the forehand drive, speaking a foreign language, historical causality, or problems in science or mathematics. Learners therefore habituate wrong responses because the teacher cannot give the needed time to each, or because corrected papers are necessarily returned too late to have the desired effect. Programming, however, whether by machine or textbook, can handle each step, for at least a part of every subject. But it needs to be supplemented by other media—by films and recordings for orientation and for clarification of percepts and concepts; by monitoring for feedback and reinforcement; by reading for enrichment; and by group discussion, which, when it follows a programmed unit that provides common knowledge and understanding, is no longer an experience in sharing ignorance, but becomes instead one of cooperative problem-solving and creativity.

Stimuli presented by the teacher may be written, printed, taped, filmed, televised, telephoned, role-played, may be a mock-up, or a natural situation. A call for different kinds of responses may be verbally, visually, or aurally presented. When stimuli are non-verbal (signals or perceptual patterns of things), as in the arts and sciences, calling for identification and discrimination, still or motion projection is indicated. When the stimuli are social (people in action), the notoriously ineffective current methods can be supplemented by the sound track for perceptual tasks, programs for cognitive experience, and role-playing and other forms of simulation for practice in teaching responses to social situations.

Retention, transfer and application (Phase 4) tend to be neglected by new methods, as well as by the old. Here, too, simulation can provide for training, on the basis of the formula: when you see this, do that. And in situations in which stimulus or response generalization is necessary, and in which choices must be made and problems solved, the formula would be: in this situation, consider what would be the most adequate response. The student must learn to solve problems, whether the process is called thinking or creativity, and whether the solutions lie within or outside the boundaries of any one discipline.

Now is the time to set ourselves to the task of determining what kind of behavior is sought as a consequence of instruction and then to set about obtaining it. The variety of possibilities requires a clear formulation of specific educational objectives in all parts of all school subjects. Cold-blooded professional judgments are required, and a willingness to foresake old ways that work, but that do not work well enough. New ways will be tried, modified and tried again and again, if we are not only to provide students with the opportunity to learn, but also be responsible for their learning. As one stops to think about it, it seems a little foolish to spend quite so much time and energy as we do in trying to teach students what they *don't learn.*

23.
Psychology and the Behavioral Sciences in the Schools

Although introductory psychology has commonly been taught as a freshman or sophomore subject in college, special textbooks and courses in the field have been designed for use in high schools. As a rule, the fare has been somewhat lacking in protein, and has tended to concentrate on "how to study" or on personality adjustments. No doubt, the diet has been helpful to some students. But in view of the recent developments in psychology, the time seems to be appropriate for the well-known "hard look" at the situation, with a view to recommendations for major changes.

ASSUMPTIONS

The recommendations here presented carry with them the following assumptions, which are listed without elaboration:

1. Psychology should be taught at the pre-college levels.

2. The psychology courses now taught at these levels are inadequate both in content and in the number of students reached.

3. Psychology, broadly defined, together with the related behavioral sciences, is rich in valuable content that could well be included in the curriculum of the schools.

4. Instruction in "how to study," except when tied in with specific content, has proved of little or no value.

5. Psychological content should be adapted to the interests and needs of those who go on to college, and also of those who do not.

A COURSE IN PSYCHOLOGY

The simplest plan for improving the position of psychology in the curriculum would be to survey the field and include the content thought to be desirable in a single course. This plan would follow that of curriculum reform in some of the other disciplines, notably mathematics and physics, in which obsolescent material has been thrown out, and newer techniques and findings have been inserted.

A number of considerations, however, seem to make this plan inadvisable. One is the problem of placement: at what point in the school program would it best be offered? Should it be in the ninth year—to catch the largest number of students before they begin to drop out—or the eleventh or twelfth, when they are more mature? Another consideration relates to the diversification of content: a single course would be likely to duplicate much of the introductory college course. Furthermore, it would place even a one-term course in psychology in competition with the well-established courses in an already-crowded curriculum. It would necessarily be elective, and hence only a relatively few students would be able to benefit from it.

More important than the questions of placement, duplication and competition with other courses, however, is that of the goals or objectives sought. What is it desired that the high school course will accomplish? Is it that students will know something about psychology, as presumably they do about the other sciences? If so, should what they are to know about be basic principles or applications, say, to business and industry, the arts, education and medicine? And would the concern be the development of the self or the psychology of "the other one"?

A COURSE IN PSYCHOLOGICAL ADJUSTMENT

A second possibility would be to set up a scheduled course for formal instruction in conduct. It might be called by any one of a number of names—ethics, morals, social learning, life problems, or life adjustment. In a way, it is surprising that what is perhaps the most important kind of learning, a kind that is sorely needed if the prevailing maladjustments—delinquency and crime—are any criterion of need, has no place of its own in the curriculum; instead, it is taught incidentally, if at all.

Such a course could be partly didactic, with practice (laboratory), as one might teach language or etiquette, and partly on a problem-discussion basis, with role-playing, audio-visual aids and little or no formal course organization. While similar efforts, like "home and family living," have not been crowned with unmitigated success, and have suffered the adverse criticisms of certain of the self-appointed custodians of science and scholarship, there is something to be said for continued effort. Unacceptable behavior in school has traditionally been inconvenient behavior. A thoroughgoing analysis, together with a study of conditions which produce it, *and* research on the effectiveness of different means of shaping socially acceptable behavior, are badly needed. A direct attack on the problem might or might not teach young people *about* psychology, but presumably they would learn to use it.

A variation of such a course might be considered that would involve adjustment, but with a more positive orientation and with the emphasis on developing human values. A number of such courses[1] are being tried out experimentally here and there that have been designated as "humanistic education," an unfortunate title because of likely confusion with classical and with religious humanism and even with humanitarianism.

Some of these courses appear to relate to current student questions about "setting goals, clarifying values, forming identity, increasing a sense of personal efficacy, and having more satisfying relationships with others." The varied objectives of those who labor in this vineyard are revealed by still other humanistic education courses which "include training in: achievement motivation, awareness and excitement, creative thinking, interpersonal sensitivity, affiliation motivation, joy, self reliance, self esteem, self assessment, self renewal, self actualization, self understanding, strength training, development of moral reasoning, value clarification, body awareness, meditative processes, and other aspects of ideal adult functioning."

In spite of this diversity, most of these courses are seen as showing four general goals in addition to their special emphases: developing imagination, improving non-verbal communication skills, developing emotional responses (since "how people feel is considered more important than what they think about things"), and living fully and intensely. How many people need this kind of training just now, is, of course, a question even if the schools were able to provide it. Possibly substituting a learning approach for the traditional punitive pattern of school management might attain many of the goals sought without being exposed to the charge of anti-intellectualism.

A CORE PROGRAM

Certain advantages would accrue from a combination of the first and second possibilities in the form of a core program in which English, or biology, is combined with social studies. If English, the humanities would not be neglected; if biology, the behavioral sciences would be more adequately covered. The possibility of a sequence of such courses could be explored, with the result that different combinations could be used in successive years. Perhaps the chief advantage of this scheme over the other two would be that these subjects are already in the curriculum.

Some would consider it a disadvantage not to have psychology represented by name. The chief disadvantage, however, would be the uncertain place of core in educational theory. It has provided opportunities for integration of content that have not been fully exploited, and it has been characterized by a rather thoroughgoing use of democratic methods, particularly teacher-pupil planning, and by the use of heuristic methods, which are again coming to the fore. While all these methods have many advantages, there is nothing in the core idea which demands that they be used exclusively. True, pupil participation is rather necessary, if the two-hour period is to be employed; but modules could well be substituted so long as the main purposes—group participation and the integration of content—are achieved. A didactic approach is often quite as effective and less time-consuming for certain kinds of subject matter, particularly if combined with the use of programmed instruction and of audio-visual aids. These and team teaching fit quite nicely into the core structure, and would contribute to the objective of adapting to individual differences. The dual purpose of better instruction in the behavioral sciences and provision for individual and social development could be well served by this plan.

PSYCHOLOGY BY INCORPORATION

Another plan is to incorporate psychological content in the regular courses in the natural sciences (chiefly general science and biology) which would include neurological and health factors, and in social studies, which would deal with ecological and personal relationships in the space and time dimensions of geography and history. These could advantageously be combined, when social studies experts see the advantages of the area study pattern.[2] While in one sense this is a variation of the core plan, it is yet very different, since it does not call for any specific kind of reorganization of class procedure. According to either plan, the psychology included would be taught in the wider context of related concepts, even leaving room for an introduction to the normative disciplines—logic, ethics, and esthetics. It would there-fore provide a richer background for interpreting life experiences and for later college work than would a separate course.

The chief disadvantage of the plan lies in the present chaotic condition of these related courses, particularly the social studies. But these are being improved, and consideration of psychological factors might tend to promote desirable changes. The work would have to be done by competent committees made up of psychologists and curriculum specialists, and also teachers. The chief advantage would be that psychological material could be inserted all along the line, beginning in the elementary school, wherever it is appropriate, and adapted to the level of development of the students concerned.

24.
The Future of School Psychology

There are always difficulties in implementing reforms, which may succeed or fail according to the competence of the personnel selected for the varied new tasks and responsibilities. Important contributions can well be expected not only from teachers and administrators, but also from those with psychological training, particularly along the technological lines recommended in these pages. Yet there is considerable uncertainty on the part of school people and others as to what may properly be expected of school psychologists. Defined as psychologists working in an educational setting, they have been gradually added to the staff in American elementary and secondary schools, but their function varies from school to school, and the profession is judged largely from the work of psychologists one happens to know.

One approach to an answer to the question of the proper role of the school psychologist is to consider what tasks other than teaching need to be done in the schools. Clearly janitorial and secretarial are now outside the bailiwick of teachers, as well as psychologists. The remainder are performed by what are often referred to as student personnel workers, and derive from various sources—from the ranks of attendance officers, social workers, health and physical education teachers and coaches, academic advisors, vocational guidance people and homeroom teachers, while regular teachers are expected to enforce discipline and administrative officials are generally held responsible. It is not a system; it is a form of chaos—the natural product of successive attempts to satisfy needs, but guided largely by penuriousness and expediency.

190

If, instead of trying to decide what should be done, we ask what is likely to happen, if we assume the continuity of professional interests and project the lines of development of the past into the future (not the immediate future, but say the next turn of the century), what will such an extrapolation show? What will be the division of labor among the psychological personnel of the schools?

At present, psychological knowledge and skills are employed in schools to serve in five major areas: *psychometric, clinical, ecological, medical,* and *instructional.* There is considerable overlapping, and the services vary in competence. However, improvements along the lines of developing technology are imperative if the educational reforms we seek are to find a place in the schools of the future.

THE PSYCHOMETRIC AREA

The first psychologists were employed in American schools to administer the Stanford Revision of the Binet Intelligence Examination. In the latter part of the nineteenth century, Alfred Binet had been assigned the task of developing a scheme for selecting feebleminded children in the Parisian schools so that they could be given special treatment. In collaboration with the work of Th. Simon, Binet's construction of the first mental test and his invention of the mental age as a unit of measurement constituted a real break-through. The test was translated and adapted for use in England, Germany and in other countries, while in America, the revision of Lewis M. Terman of Stanford was followed by others, that of Wechsler being widely used at present. Adapted for group administration, the Army Alpha, and Beta for illiterates, were administered to recruits in World War I, the first psychological tests to be so used. After the war further adaptations were made to school use of both group and individual tests. The ratio of mental to chronological age, called the intelligence quotient (IQ) became an indicator of native intelligence.

The need the Parisians felt for the measure continues, and school diagnosticians or examiners are expected to administer these and other individual tests in order to differentiate pupils as not trainable, trainable but not educable, and educable, and recommend whatever treatment seems indicated. In some cases, special help or special classes are recommended, which sometimes cannot be provided, and in fact the "treatment" is the weak part of the whole procedure. And it has become more so since a number of American psychologists have come to reject the hereditary factor as the cause and instead, favor the view the Russians have long held, that the differences in intelligence are environmental in origin. They have contended that the tests are "culture bound," though there is a high correlation with the results on the supposedly "culture-free" tests that have been devised.

A similar pattern was followed for standardized tests of school achievement, which are not intended to make any predictions for the future but only record the student's level of performance in comparison with others of his age, or in his grade or class, on what has supposedly been taught. These have been standardized as group tests and are often administered by teachers but under the direction of someone who has been psychologically trained.

The development of probability statistics, originally from the odds of the race track, has made it possible to employ research methods to interpret the scores obtained under varying circumstances, e.g., the appraisal of the quality of instruction. The work in measurement should and no doubt will be further expanded in ways that will permit *all* children to be taught on the basis of their individual abilities and needs. The title, *psychometrist*, can advantageously continue for those whose competence lies in this area.

THE CLINICAL AREA

Probably an equally well-known psychological role in the schools is that of guidance and counseling, or what is referred to as clinical psychology. It is employed with students of all ages (often with their parents) in dealing with the maladjustments of those who are variously referred to as disturbed, problem children, and children with problems.

Counseling got its start as vocational guidance during the early part of the century when the schools were flooded with the children of immigrants who had come to supply manpower for America's burgeoning industries; and it included "academic advisement," needed in the new comprehensive high schools. But it acquired depth, as well as academic status, from the labors of Sigmund Freud, the Viennese physician, who never practiced medicine, but who had studied French psychiatry and British associationism, and brought the two together with his technique of free association which he developed to deal with neurotic behavior. But on the principle that everybody is at least slightly neurotic, his doctrines became widely used to interpret the behavior of supposedly normal people.

Something more than a superficial knowledge of child nature is necessary to deal with emotionally disturbed children. The non-directive therapy of Carl Rogers has made it possible for school psychologists, who as a rule are not Freudians, to avoid the more drastic and time-consuming analyses of the Master and of his disciplines; so *guidance counselors, mental hygienists* and *clinical psychologists* are endeavoring to fill this need. Some employ the so-called projective tests, of which the Rorschach ink-blots are perhaps the most well known; this and Murry's Thematic Apperception Test (TAT) and later variations in which a person is asked to tell a story about a number of pictures, which provide opportunities for subjects to interpret what they see in such a way as to reveal attitudes which may be at the root of some of their difficulties. But more than skilled counseling will be necessary to teach acceptable behavior. The "treatment" will need to include drastic changes in school procedures along the lines indicated in this volume.

THE PHYSIOLOGICAL AREA

Tangential to the clinical area is the work of those who are concerned chiefly with physiological factors, with the structure of living organisms, the human in particular. Growing chiefly out of Herbert Spencer's contributions to the applications of evolutionary theory, they developed what was formerly referred to as genetic psychology, with an interest in heredity and growth. One phase was the early child-study movement followed later by researches on child development and maturation. Data on the nervous system and the endocrine glands have tended to become more medical than psychological, though Cannon's theory of homeostasis is basic cybernetics. More recently, the work on the effects of drugs has come to the fore, and experiments on starvation may revolutionize theories of intelligence. Space travel has dramatized the need for special training in medical psychology, some of the findings of which will undoubtedly be of interest to education. No doubt *medical psychologists* will have a more important place than at present.

THE ECOLOGICAL AREA

Other equally disparate investigators and practitioners are less concerned with physiological matters than they are with sociological. They are dedicated environmentalists—as all educators must be up to a point. Sociologists and anthropologists have long made a study of interpersonal relations and institutions and their place in the culture as a whole. The licensed practitioners in this area are the school social workers (sometimes called visiting teachers), who combine counseling techniques with sociological knowledge, and who work in cooperation with the various social agencies in the community.

The sociologists have been influenced not a little by the Gestalt psychologists, who have argued the importance of the environmental structure even as a native determiner of perception, and chiefly by Lewin, whose concept of life-space is purportedly of greater influence than instinctive drives in influencing behavior.

The term "ecology," which came to the fore with the expanded public concern about pollution, was originally a biological term signifying the mutual relations of an organism with its environment. "Ecological" is more specific than the general purpose term "social" and may well be appropriated by psychologists and educators referring to the social as well as to the natural environment.

In the past, educators who might be placed in such a category, beginning with the report of Rousseau on his brain child, *Emile,* and on down to the present have sought to change the environment of children and youth. Pestalozzi replaced punishment with love; Froebel, the founder of the kindergarten, encouraged child play and natural growth. And those today who start schools of their own in the "ghettos" and elsewhere seek to replace the domineering authoritarianism usually found with a freer type of control and decision making. They are the dreamers, the empiricists with a message and a knack of getting along happily with children. They should be listened to, for most of their criticisms are valid, and their solutions seem to work, at least when they employ them.

We might hope, and even expect that a *school ecologist* might take shape whose responsibilities would not only be to ferret out and correct if possible the evil home influences of the maladjusted, but also to have a hand in determining the play of social forces in school and community that might be arranged to provide the "treatment" that counseling cannot give, and at the same time reduce the numbers who need it.

THE INSTRUCTIONAL AREA

Psychological doctrine directly influencing school learning has derived primarily from three sources: the British philosophers, who took their cue from Aristotle and developed the principles of association—similarity and contrast, contiguity in space and time, and recency, frequency, and intensity; the experimentalists, whose god-father, Wilhelm Wundt founded the first psychological laboratory of Leipzig in 1879; and the physiologist, I.P. Pavlov of St. Petersburg, whose experiments demonstrated the conditioned reflex.

At first concerned with the introspective study of mental states (structuralists) and then with mental processes (functionalists), they gradually embraced objective experimentation under the influence of John B. Watson, the founder of Behaviorism.

Parallel with this development, and actually a little ahead of it, was E.L. Thorndike of Columbia, whose Teachers College affiliation slowed down his acceptance by the Bourbons in the departments of psychology. Prolific experimenter that he was, he drew many of his hypotheses from the British associationists. His firsts are without equal: animal learning experimentation (the maze and puzzle box); the psychology of school subjects; the adaptation of statistics to educational psychology; word counts (for the study of difficulties in learning to read); tests and scales for measuring abilities in school subjects; measurements of the goodness of a city; and pioneer research in heredity and in the transfer of learning.

However, what has been learned is slow in being utilized in spite of the continuing efforts of successive generations of investigators. In the future, those whom we may perhaps call *educational psychologists* will need to be experts in learning and instruction. As a consequence of current interests and the influence of educational technology it may be that they will begin to select more significant problems to investigate and will give attention to the all important matter of application.

Thus, for the complete student personnel set-up of school psychological services, there would be the following officials: psychometrist, mental hygienist, ecologist, medical psychologist, and educational psychologist. For each there would be two possible levels of training and responsibility. Referrals would be made by the *chief school psychologist,* who would be a specialist in one or more of these areas but well versed in all; so that, like the medical doctor, he could make proper referrals to specialists and interpretations of data collected. He would be in charge of the whole effort.

Of course, in many school sytems, an individual would wear more than one hat, while in the larger systems each function would be performed by a large staff. These tasks seem to be the continuation of the lines of modern psychological development, which began over one hundred years ago. It may be that all that is necessary is to allow evolution to take its course; but being such a slow process, perhaps the thing to do is to make plans along the extrapolated lines.

25.
An Educational Model
for Social Learning

It has long been taken for granted that for what we may call general learning (in the process of obtaining a general or liberal education), that is, the acquisition of cognitive and also esthetic and motor skills, knowledge and attitudes, an *instructional* approach is employed. So, in all cultures, teachers have been provided for this purpose. The traditional model, followed more or less effectively, seems to be

assign—test—mark,

in place of which the model here recommended is

assess—teach—evaluate.

But for acquiring socio-ethical knowledge, skills and attitudes, that is, *social learning,* either for motivation, adjustment , or as an end in itself, quite a different procedure has generally been followed. Instead of teaching and instruction, a "nature is wrong" policy, characterized as *discipline,* is supposedly needed, involving rules and regulations, and punishment for infractions. This model seems to be

apprehend—accuse—prove guilt (sometimes)—punish.

The approach to the problem of illness, that is of developing and regaining health, has been different still, the model being the *medical* one,

refer—diagnose—treat.

A fourth approach might also be mentioned, a laissez-faire "nature-is-right" policy that often makes the headlines. Children are

expected to *develop* by being permitted to follow their own interests and inclinations, in the belief that the usual educational objectives are attained in this fashion and that creativity and decision-making are thereby enhanced. The model for this approach might be
provide—permit—pace.

Adherents have advocated and elaborated their several doctrines and the techniques that supposedly produce the most satisfactory outcomes. One may teach, punish, treat, or permit; but too little thought has been given to such questions as when and how to use which on whom! It seems futile to discuss such matters, for example, as programs for teacher training until someone knows what teachers should be doing in the process of teaching, and until more of them learn to avoid the alternative traditional formula, assign—test—mark (or grade). It is, unfortunately, probable that what many are doing is quite ineffective; and even that it actually creates the very maladjustments the psychologists, visiting teachers, diagnosticians and counselors are trying to correct.

The schools are set up to employ all the different models. That they have not been successful is clearly evidenced by the errors both of omission and of commission among the juveniles in the schools and the adults who have passed through them: the ignorant, gullible, functionally illiterate, vocationally unskilled, the vandals, swindlers, delinquents, criminals, the physically and mentally pathological, and currently the anti-establishmentarian protestors and half-baked revolutionists.

The schools need more money, true enough, but money is not the solution if it just gives us more of the same. This is just what we will have, however, unless some keen intellects that are not hag-ridden by tradition are prepared to make the needed educational changes. My contention here is that the failures of our educational system are the consequence of applying the wrong approaches or models in specific situations, or of applying them unskillfully, whether in inner city, suburbs, or rural areas. Specifically, the disciplinary and even the medical model, as commonly employed, are inappropriate and ineffective for social learning, that is, for developing social knowledge, skills and attitudes. Instead, an *educational model* should be employed—but not the archaic "assign, test, mark," which should be abolished even for cognitive learning. The effort should be made to create a learning atmosphere with the emphasis not on punishment *or* treatment, but on *teaching.*

I have discussed some of these matters in preceding chapters and in Chapter 26, where the distinction is made between educational *renovation* and *innovation.* Renovation is viewed as the process of bringing a school into the twentieth century, particularly in matters of plant and equipment, morale or climate, and curriculum, while innovation calls for changes in grading and marking, teaching roles, methods and media, and the clear delineation of objectives. If these matters were properly taken care of, instruction could be more nearly what it is supposed to be, and the other false approaches would tend to fade away.

For social learning, the medical and disciplinary models are quite inadequate; and here, as in cognitive learning, there must be a new emphasis on *teaching.* The schools have visibly assumed responsibility for punitive behavior, with their arsenal of punishments for misconduct as has been noted: traditionally the birch rod and hickory stick; and later, the ruler, rubber hose, scolding and reprimand, staying after school, lowered marks, sending to the principal's office, isolation, suspension and expulsion.

The negative attitudes developed under a punitive system have led some to the other extreme of permissiveness, but fortunately the psychoanalytic, psychiatric and mental hygiene movements gradually became influential; and psychologists developed measuring and counseling techniques which have replaced some of the barbarities. For medical cases, the refer—diagnose—treat is an improvement; but as now widely used, it has two chief weaknesses.

One of these is that the diagnosis is inadequate, as the review of a sampling of psychologists' reports will clearly show: mention of a few of the client's more obvious physical characteristics, a "Binet" and/or "Wechsler" test score, indication of test-item successes and failures, a judgment of probable academic competence, a guess as to the possible factors responsible for the referral behavior, and a vague recommendation for treatment that may be quite impossible to carry out.

If the psychological diagnosis is inadequate, the final step of the model—treatment—is usually futile. In medicine, this is not the case; diagnosis is followed by medication, hospitalization and sometimes surgery and a period of prescribed convalescence. In schools, however, the diagnosis, such as it is, is likely to be followed by little more than a room transfer, or a little counseling, following the psychoanalytic use of the medical model. But medical practitioners are aware that cure does not take place on the couch. Counseling is valuable, but it is not enough. What is important is the living environment.

If parents and teachers are still governed by the traditional assign—test—mark procedures, the psychologically oriented and the increasing number of educational technologists in our midst should be able to by-pass the medical refer—diagnose—treat formula (reserving it for definitely medical conditions), to the educational assess—teach—evaluate.

Renovations and innovations affecting all the pupils would be undertaken, including the substitution for the barbaric marking system of criterion-referenced instead of norm-referenced marks. The similarly-barbaric grading system would be replaced by an ungraded school, with curriculum and instruction adapted to individual pupil needs. These steps would cut down the supply of referrals.

Assessment, therefore, would be the process of determining pupil needs. *Teaching* would be modified in harmony with the findings, and teachers would have to be experts in the three quite different kinds of teaching that all now are called upon to perform—i.e., demonstration and explanation, coaching ("progressive approximation") and group discussion. *Evaluation* would be intended to discover how well the school, not the pupil, had done; whether the teaching has brought about the desirable behavioral changes; and to provide a factual basis for continuing or changing it. All this would apply to cognitive learning, but it should also apply to social learning. Appropriate educational techniques should be employed to teach children in groups or individually the desired social behavior, whether in regular classes or in remediation sessions. The computer is being played with in such programs, but we do not know yet what should be fed into the computer or what to do about its answers. Once the idea of giving instruction in desired social behavior, instead of punishing the undesired, is fully grasped, all sorts of possibilities are opened up,[1] minimizing aversive stimulation and accenting any number of positive reinforcements. At first, it will not be necessary to bother about intrinsic or extrinsic motivation. Nothing is more extrinsic than the sanctions that produce the kinds of social behavior we find all about us.

If such procedures are employed, not only the counselor, but also the teacher, becomes a partner with the child in helping him to improve; someone who is "on his side," instead of someone who is out to *get* him. Of course, it should not be expected that learning will be instantaneous in this area any more than it is in the cognitive sphere, or in the motor skills, or the arts. But the scheme provides a program of teaching, and it is this for which the schools presumably were established.

26.
First Things First –
Educational Renovation

I visited a new suburban high school in Cincinnati some forty-five years ago, and was shown around the building by the principal. I had called on him at his office, where he was engaged with three young men—students in his school—who had been up to some kind of mischief. As we left, he told me a little about the difficulty and ended by saying something I have never forgotten: "We can't blame them," he said. "The real trouble is that we just haven't got anything here for them."

Schools now have more than they had forty-five years ago. Much has been done to correct the situation. But as we look about us on the troubled academic scene, it is quite clear that what we have done is not enough. After pondering the problem on and off during the intervening years while working at what I was paid for, now, nearly half a century later, I am trying to do something about it.

One thing that neither the principal nor I realized at the time was that these three obstreperous young men were in all probability not the only ones the school was not adequately serving, which would no doubt have been revealed by a head count of dropouts. Now the dropouts are being asked to speak for themselves, and what they have to say is by no means gratifying. "School as Perceived by the Dropout" is the title of an article by George H. Weber and Annabelle B. Motz in the *Journal of Negro Education,* and reported in the June 30, 1968 issue of *Educational Technology*:

"School dropouts see themselves as fugitives from the captivity of boring, uninspiring and threatening teachers 'whose positions in the educational structure enable them to be authoritarian and puni- tive.' . . . They see the school personnel as a team–counselors, teachers, principals–united in their opposition to the students."

With all our efforts–our researches, evaluations, surveys, our journals, national and state societies, conferences, our degrees, certifi- cates, accreditations and the rest of the top-heavy superstructure– although we have unquestionably developed the best educational system that has ever existed, we have begun to realize that we cannot rest on our laurels. We cannot continue to run traditional schools and try to fit children and young people into them. The fact is now being brought violently to our attention. Not only students, but teachers also, are protesting–and in many places are in active revolt. But, like the earlier educational critics, the protests and revolts are often against the wrong things, and take the form of the irrational behavior of frustrated persons striking out against what they see as the enemy: the salary scale, the system, the establishment, the petty prohibitions that limit freedom of choice–often conditions seemingly rendered necessary by the sheer number of people per square mile who also want higher pay and more freedom of choice.

One dissident spokesman recently stated that, if it were possible, he would tear down the whole educational structure and build a new one to replace it. But, as J. B. Priestly says in his fantastic parable, *Saturn over the Water,* "I do not believe you can make a better world by making a bad one worse . . . I believe anything created by people who start by doing wrong will itself be all wrong." Then, too, this spokesman is too young and inexperienced to see beyond the wrong and the right to the ingrained past and to the future consequences, and to realize that many others would not wish to build what he wants, or that the new structure would be the work of the same kind of fallible human beings responsible for the old, or that he and his ilk often deny or override the rights that already exist. And he is painfully ignorant of the careful thought and effort which over the years have been devoted to planning and developing what we now have; and which, thanks to other contributing factors, have produced the amazing results we see on every hand in this country.

But *what has been done is not enough.* Remarkable accomplishments have been counterbalanced not only by sad deficiencies, but also by grave injustices. While we can be proud of the great numbers of children who are able to profit from attending our schools, we know that there would be many more dropouts if the legal age were lowered, and that there are still far too many emotionally disturbed and delinquent children, and adults, in our population—people who are a burden both to others and to themselves. We know that the rich and well-to-do generally send their children to private, not public, schools, and that many of the children of the poor, whether black or white, Indian, Mexican, or Puerto Rican, have meager opportunities to learn, especially if they are crowded together in cities, or if they are shunted off into narrowly vocational courses. We know that the bright children are forced to slow their pace to the prisoners' lockstep and left to find other things to do that may be more troublesome than educational. And as for the dull—the slow growers—we know that the more they are promoted, the farther behind they get.

One is reminded of the drunk who found his way to the top of the third flight of stairs in a cheap apartment house, where he got into an altercation with a roomer, who kicked him down one flight of stairs. On the landing, another roomer saw what was going on, though he didn't know what it was all about, and kicked the drunk down the next flight, where another roomer, entering into the spirit of the occasion, kicked the intruder down the next flight. At the bottom, he picked himself up, looked up the stairwell in admiration, and exclaimed, "My God, is this a system!" One is sometimes moved to emit the same exclamation when he sees the efficiency with which some children are deprived of an education.

AN AGE OF PROTEST

Educationally, the last half century, handicapped as it was by two world wars and a severe depression, can well be characterized as an age of protest.

Industrialists protested the old, uniform classical curriculum inherited largely from the Renaissance and Reformation; and so vocational and technical education were expanded, along with vocational guidance, in order to help the children of those who had come to our shores to man our rapidly expanding industries.

Progressives protested the rigid sterility of the resultant efforts, and pressed for greater flexibility, utility and individual self-expression.

Essentialists insisted on not being sidetracked from the fundamentals of education. While they differed as to what the fundamentals are, most of them were willing to settle for the three R's and "learning to think."

More recently, self-styled scholars and scientists and a few journalists engaged in what has been called "the great debate," insisting on "the disciplines" and rigorous examinations for all, with splinter parties arguing for the great books, spiritual values and the new knowledge.

Now the desegregationists are protesting discrimination, and are demanding courses in Afro-American history. Many will be surprised when they learn that slaves were not always black, and that slaveholders were not always white.

Meanwhile, educational experimentalists have been trying out new methods of instruction, new media, and the new technology, including cybernetic systems and computer assisted instruction.

There is no question of the legitimacy of each of these protests and recommendations, unfortunately often called "demands," nor of their value, up to a point. But each was promoted like a bottle of patent medicine for snake-bite, chilblains and heartburn, to cure the unpleasant symptoms if not the fundamental malady.

Two well-established Ivy League scholars once considered collaborating on a book, but they had to give up the idea: their names were, respectively, Patch and Tinker. They might well have been the authors of many of the educational reforms advocated over the last half-century. Many of them were patch and tinker jobs, to be done in the same old mills and factories with the same old machinery of traditional education, and all doomed, if not to fail, at least to be less effective than they could be with modern buildings and equipment. Real modernization is what should have priority. This is where reforms are most needed. They are the first things that should come first in our efforts to improve the situation. And if they are properly attended to, many of the difficulties that are so disturbing will of necessity gradually fade away. It is never too soon to start eliminating what is bad and replacing it with the best that can be found in modern practice.

CONDITIONS IN SUCCESSFUL SCHOOLS

Let us first consider three factors that research and practice agree are favorable to learning which are now found in the better schools throughout the country, and which should be found everywhere: *high morale, adaptation of instruction to the learner* and *good teaching.*

High Morale: There can be a school atmosphere or climate that is encouraging, challenging and helpful, not discouraging, frustrating and punitive. The older terms, morale and *esprit de corps,* should not be forgotten. In schools where the morale is good, there is no visible discipline, and it all seems so easy. But this ease is deceptive. It is like observing an accomplished actor who seems to be so "natural," but whose success is the result of talent and hard work. The good school climate is not to be modeled after the ultra-permissive clinic. Though there can be considerable freedom, there must be well-established limits to behavior that is destructive, disruptive, or merely futile, and appropriate sanctions invoked. These must be in the form of established penalties for certain acts, not punishments of the individual who, as a person, is not rejected, but accepted, encouraged and helped to learn.

The school climate should rather be modeled after the studio or workshop, or the *atelier* of Renaissance times, where ideas found formal expression, and apprentices were guided and inspired by the work of master craftsmen. Of course, there will be some frustrations, but they should be of the sort that stimulate effort, not evasion, anxiety, alienation and hostility.

The finest example of group morale I know—a really happy ship—was the Houghton Elementary School in Detroit, back when slums were familiar but no one knew about inner cities. It had a small dirt playground without a tree on it. The old building, even in 1930, was surrounded on all sides by factories, garages and filling stations, and other old buildings; and the parents of the children who attended came from a dozen different foreign countries. But as soon as a visitor entered the building, he recognized that something was different. It was clean, well kept and tastefully decorated. One of the pupils would soon appear and ask if he could be of help. Children in hallways were smiling; even the teachers were smiling. I was told by one of them that when she was caught in a jam, other teachers offered to do some of her work to help her out, saying merely that maybe she could do the same for them sometime; whereas in the school where she had previously taught, nobody would do anything for anybody.

I attended a third-grade council meeting, which was faced with the problem of what to do about the paper towels on the floor by the washbowl. More unusual was the problem of the girls' rest room, which was admittedly a mess, complete with writing on the walls. The fact that some of this writing was in Greek baffled the teachers, who could not be sure that it was some obscenity and not a quotation from the Greek classics! A conference was called of all the girls in the upper grades of the school, gripes were aired, suggestions were called for, which included redecoration. They asked if they could plan the decorations. They could. Would their plans be carried out? They would be. A committee was appointed, its recommendations were approved— blue star-studded ceiling, purple and red-striped walls, gilded fixtures. Specifications were followed, and after that, woe to any girl who messed up "our rest room."

Pupils had freedom, but they learned respect for its limits. They were taught how to behave, and were given opportunities for practice. Tea parties were featured, since many of the mothers were accomplished cooks in different nationalities and cultures, and cakes and cookies of different countries were popular. Children from the same grade in nearby schools were sometimes invited to the tea party, and then there was a return invitation. One neighboring school where invitations were exchanged was nearly all Negro. "They look different," one little girl said, "but they act just like us."

Funds from a character education project permitted a small gift to the school. The children could decide what it would be. They decided they wanted a tree in their school yard. Thereafter visitors were always asked if they would like to see "our tree."

Esther Braude, the assistant principal, was the miracle worker. She was not a dynamic go-getter, but a quiet, modest woman, doing a job. She has now retired, and Houghton School and its tree are gone, since they were in the path of a super-highway. But I confidently believe that the spirit of Esther Braude permeates the lives and hearts of the hundreds of children who passed through the portals of Houghton School, to say nothing of the teachers who contributed their share to its success.

Adaptation of Instruction to the Learner: There can be content adapted to each learner's abilities, interests and needs—not too difficult, nor yet too easy, dull, or irrelevant. Schools have long sought to adapt to pupil abilities by various grouping devices, but without any marked success. With the new technology, that goal is well within our reach. Relevance seems to be the current word for individual and social need satisfaction. Additional and continuing effort is now necessary if this condition is to be met.

Good Teaching: There can be a method that results in learning that is successful, continuous and rewarded or reinforced; not one that results in expected failure, lack of progress and punishment in the form of low marks, threats, scoldings and other aversive stimuli.

The good conditions can prevail for all students, though with the present structure of the school it is most difficult to maintain them. One reason is semantic—the connotation of the terms used practically forces one to remain mentally within the old framework. This may be illustrated in various ways. For example, if one reads that in the evening the room was well lighted, he would take it for granted that the electric lights were turned on. But, in a historical novel, the sentence might refer to candles, oil lamps, or gas lights. Similarly when discussing educational needs, such terms as the teacher, the classroom, report card, grade and credit are used; and the traditional stereotypes almost compel the discussants to think in terms analogous to candles, oil and gas. Modern educational technology—not machines but *systematic organization and procedure*—is making it possible to break the old mold, if only competent and influential people understand what the argument is all about and are willing to work for the needed changes.

FIRST THINGS IN NEED OF CHANGE

Let us now consider some of the conditions that should be given attention in many existing schools. They have been discussed in previous chapters, but can advantageously be repeated here.

The Plant. If you happen to have seen the newly reprinted 19th century McGuffey Readers, you were probably somewhat surprised to note that they were not "graded." The children who used them, mostly in one-room schools, read the stories suitable to their level of reading ability. As the numbers of pupils increased, more rooms were added, and those of different ages were separated. School architecture has left its visible record in many communities. Certainly there have been many improvements in appearance, heating, lighting and furnishings, but the old pattern tends to persist—multiple units, the so-called egg-crate pattern. Educators who should know better still talk of the need for a certain number of classrooms, as if they were identical units of measurement, even though some buildings have already been constructed that follow quite a different plan.

The Teacher. Teachers have too many things to do, to do them all well. They are, at present, necessarily generalists because of community expectations. I drew up the following list a short time ago. (See *Teacher and Technology—New Designs for Learning*, pp. 45-46.) The teacher is expected to be custodian, clerk, foster parent, disciplinarian, examiner, audiovisualist and technician, librarian, student adviser, therapist, recreation leader and responsible citizen. But this list includes no teaching. So I had to add the following:

> Communicate with pupils having a wide range of mental ability;
>
> Plan and prepare lessons and develop instructional materials;
>
> Assess readiness for instruction and provide it at the proper level of individual development;
>
> Demonstrate equipment, skills and processes;
>
> Give out information;
>
> Explain facts and their interrelationships, leading to the development of concepts and generalizations;
>
> Provide educational feedback, reinforce and motivate student efforts;
>
> Lead discussions so as to arouse questions and develop original thinking and creativity;
>
> Keep up with the professional and content literature, attend educational meetings, and conduct research.

Strictly speaking, the last is not teaching, but it is closely related.

Both new and experienced teachers are called on to do any or all of these things, for some of which no professional preparation is needed, while for others considerable training and practice are necessary. The need for a revised concept of the teacher is evident.

The Grade. The grading system as we now know it, took shape as recently as the middle or later 1800's. Children can be grouped; but for better or for worse they cannot, like milk or olives, be graded. It is a well-known fact that children who are put in the same grade because they are all supposedly ready for the instruction given there, actually differ in general ability and achievement as much as six years. And the special abilities of any one child likewise vary over a wide range. Because of these facts, efforts to classify children in high, medium and low groups have been unsuccessful, and the idea of homogeneous grouping has proved to be a will-o-the-wisp. Yet the old efforts continue.

The Mark. Procrustes was the legendary Greek host who followed the plan of fitting his visitors to the bed in his guest room by chopping off a section if they were too long, and stretching them a bit if they were too short. The schools have been more humane, providing as they do, a dozen or so beds of different sizes, so that much less chopping and stretching is necessary. Promotion policies vary in different schools. Although slow growers seem to learn more when they are promoted than they do when they are compelled to repeat a grade, they don't learn much, for they are given a bed that is too long; so they need more stretching, which they get in the form of prodding, scolding, and insult.

Examinations are so constructed that teachers know before administering them that a goodly number will receive low or failing marks. In fact, they can predict the results with considerable accuracy, and are surprised at an unexpected high or low score. It would be interesting as an experiment to discover what would have happened in the lives and personalities of the teachers and administrators who perpetuate this absurd system if for ten years of their lives, or one year—or six months—they had been compelled by law to compete in a system in which *they would never succeed.*

The system of marking (also called grading), is unjust primarily because it is norm-referenced instead of being criterion-referenced. It employs grade norms, as do standardized tests, based on the seeming necessity of getting a spread of distribution of scores, which means including questions that it is known many of the students will be unable to answer. But there is a further injustice. Scores are based on standardized, short-answer-type questions, which are fairly reliable, though the test as a whole may not be valid; but marks are based on these *and* on other, much more elusive, data. Teachers differ on the marking of a single paper, judgments are subjective, and criteria vary—and sometimes even include classroom conduct.

I would not have dared to press this point, had it not been for the following "letter to the editor" from a junior high school student, which appeared in the *Ann Arbor News* of May 10, 1968:

"Since the point of going to school is learning, it seems only reasonable that grades [i.e., marks] should measure the amount the student learns and how well he applies the knowledge.

"If this is true, why do teachers continously threaten to 'lower our grade' or 'give us an E' if we don't stop talking or misbehaving. Teachers tell us that grades are unimportant; it's what we learn that counts. Five minutes later the same teacher is informing us that she has lowered our grade one fourth. . . .

"The majority of teachers who use grades to punish say, 'I hate to threaten with grades, but if you don't shut up, you'll all get E's.' Actually this is saying, 'I realize this is wrong, but I'm too lazy to use a more effective means of punishment.' " One might add—and of instruction.

The Method. Measures of the proportion of class time that teachers talk vary. Two thirds to three fourths is about par for most courses including not only explanations and directions, but also orders, threats and scoldings. The telling (lecture) method is often economical and sometimes essential, as in the case of demonstrations and providing feedback and suggestions. But the satisfaction that teachers, and professors too, obtain from "telling them" often seems greater than the students' gain.

One teacher was well pleased with the attention a kindergarten child was giving while she was telling him where to get off. But she began to doubt the efficiency of her method when she had finished, for, with the delightful smile of discovery on his face, he exclaimed, "Did you know your upper jaw doesn't wiggle when you talk!"

The familiar phrase, "How many times do I have to tell you!" suggests that there might just possibly be better methods of instruction, at least if children are expected to remember what they have learned. In this respect, even the AV aids, valuable as they are in helping to clarify concepts, are of doubtful value with symbolic learning. I remember a lecture by an authority on various insurance schemes. The slides he had prepared were excellent; it was practically a perfect job. But, by the time he had finished, I was more confused than ever about premiums, options, hospital care, out-patient treatment, privileges of the surviving spouse, etc., etc.

The Objectives. General educational objectives have been formulated and enunciated for years, but they often bear little relation to what goes on in classrooms. The specific objectives of a course or subject constitute one of the best-kept secrets in the school. The children are not told, much less taught, what they are supposed to learn; otherwise they might defy expectations and answer the questions correctly on the examination—and so destroy the balance of the resulting curve. But the chief reason that the secret is so well kept is that the teachers, as a rule, *do not know it themselves.* Once in a while a teacher, desiring to teach the little brats *something*, will say, "Now I am going to hold you for that on the examination." But this is supposed to be bad pedagogy because it is teaching the examination and not the subject and because it makes it practically unnecessary for the pupils to know anything else, or even to remember it after the examination is over. But at least it is a step in the right direction.

If you object to my statement that the teacher does not know what the objectives are, ask one sometime what he expects the children to be able to do as a consequence of the instruction he is providing. Most of those who teach motor skills (physical education and applied music) can answer fairly accurately; cognitive skills (symbol manipulation) will come a little harder; and social skills (personality and character development) will probably not figure, since these are nobody's business; yet, many teachers spend a good deal of time on them.

THE OUTLOOK

The germ of protest has fortunately always remained alive in these United States, and educational theory and practice are not immune. Today, it seems to be appearing in a rather more virulent form than in the past, not because conditions are worse than heretofore, for they are not, but more probably because of the widespread unrest of the times. In any case, we would be guilty of misfeasance and malfeasance if we did not take the protest seriously. We need not accept the cures proposed for final answers, though we should probably bring some of the protestors into the discussions and broaden the base of the decision-making process. We are well aware of the real weaknesses and of the difficulties in finding solutions for the problems they raise. But in most cases we need little or no new knowledge to solve them.

SUMMARY

If we survey successful schools, we find that at least three characteristic conditions exist: there is high morale; instruction is well adapted to the students' needs; and teaching is competent, with learning appropriately rewarded or reinforced.

Before taking steps to insure that these conditions exist in other schools, however, it is essential that the usual concepts of certain school practices be sharply revised and clarified—concepts of the teachers' roles, of grading and marking systems, of methods employed, and of the nature and use of educational objectives. What specific changes should be made, and the part psychologists should play in bringing them about—that is another story.

27.
Psychology and Educational Innovation

In view of various criticisms of educational practices and of the present academic turmoil, we might well ask who are the ones responsible for improvement, and consider the possible role of the psychologically trained. Many things are wrong with the schools that higher salaries, desegregation, decentralization and even a diffusion of decision-making will not cure. School psychologists know what many of the unsatisfactory conditions are, and they have, or could acquire, the knowledge and skills to remedy them.

It is now time for some of them to be less preoccupied with their testing kits and report blanks and, as educational technologists, to begin to take a leading role in determining educational policy, in restructuring educational organization, and in improving the pattern of instruction. Obsolescent educational procedures cannot be allowed to continue to produce more and more disturbed cases that must be diagnosed and treated. Tradition and vested interests tend to maintain the *status quo.*

For the past fifty years, the plan has been to try to help teachers and administrators to operate psychologically, largely by means of courses given by educational psychologists in teacher-training institutions. But it is now evident that the abundant psychological facts and principles have not been adequately translated into educational practices: prospective teachers who take the formal courses in educational psychology find little relationship to their methods courses, and are unable to apply much of what they have studied to their practice teaching or to their work on the job.

More recently, a second plan has been developed, i.e., to prepare psychologists for practice in educational institutions,[1] usually either as psychometrists or as counselors, but primarily on the technician level. Thus far we have been applying cosmetics to patients who need antibiotics, or even a major operation. Or, to shift the figure, we have been using bows and arrows when we should have been building up a powerful task force for a vigorous offensive against the powers of darkness—ignorance and prejudice. What is required now is that the psychological training of teachers and the educational training of psychologists be continued and improved; but, in addition, that the psychologists add a competence in school learning to their professional equipment, so as to enable them to plan and participate in educational reform.

The main task of the educational psychologists or technologists in the schools will have to be to facilitate pupil learning by improving instruction in the cognitive, motor and social skills—directly for the latter, and indirectly for all three, through a skillful collaboration of teachers and administrators. The means by which this will be brought about may well include suggesting, reminding, recommending, cajoling, pressuring and bludgeoning if necessary; and selling administration on enabling policies, and teachers on conferences and workshops for training in improved instructional methods.

If those who are psychologically trained are to take the lead, as I believe they must, it will be necessary to recruit competent candidates and insure high standards of training, to which the educationally oriented divisions of the American Psychological Association and the state associations might well give their attention. The aid of certain psychologically receptive educational organizations could also well be solicited, such as the Society of Professors of Education, the American Association of Colleges for Teacher Education, and the American Educational Research Association.

For the medical model, *refer-diagnose-treat,* an educational model must be substituted with the formula *assess-teach-evaluate,* as noted earlier. To assess is to discover the educational status and needs of individual students; to teach is to provide a learning environment adapted to the status and needs; and to evaluate is to determine the effectiveness of the teaching (rather than of the student), and make the needed changes in it. The psychological services will thus have a function from which not just the disturbed, but *all* children, will benefit.

RENOVATION

Educational reform may advantageously be classified as *renovation* and *innovation*. Under renovation as discussed in the preceding chapter, we can consider the changes which may be needed in some schools to bring them up to the level of present-day good educational practice—to get them into the twentieth century. This is the task that Conant seemingly set himself. Schools requiring renovation may be in the inner city, in the backward rural areas, or even in smaller cities and some suburbs. Renovation will have to be undertaken in at least four areas: plant and equipment, morale, curriculum, and teaching.

Plant and Equipment. Whether a new building is to be built or an old one remodeled, those trained in psychology should be sufficiently well informed to be influential members of building committees and know what is meant by *function* in school architecture, for they will recognize the analogy with the laboratory apparatus, i.e., an environmental structure designed to affect the behavior of those within the environment.

Morale. A good learning climate or atmosphere, in view of present student protests and disturbances, is even more important than formerly, and more difficult to come by. It requires "relevant" tasks adapted to the student's developmental level, appropriate rewards, shared decision-making, a nice balance between freedom and control, and warm, friendly attitudes transferring to students from administration and staff members.

Curriculum. Content is, of course, primarily the responsibility of the culture operating through the subject-matter specialists—the teachers who depend on textbooks and on what their major professors taught them. Psychologists here will have a two-fold responsibility, however: first, to see that content is adapted to the students' interests and abilities—to their respective stages of development—and, second, to their intellectual, social and vocational needs. These cannot be entirely separated from the needs of the smaller and the larger society in which they live.

Teaching. The psychologist's chief concern, however, should be with learning. He should be able to help teachers employ their instructional skills effectively, and encourage children not only to be original and creative, but also to be critical and exact. In colleges, educational psychologists can help by developing certification courses that are truly functional, remembering that they are in a professional school where, in pre-certification and in inservice training, the emphasis should be placed on *doing* as well as *knowing*. We owe it to the children in the institutions with obsolete buildings and equipment, low morale, outdated curricula, and mediocre teaching—we owe it to these children—to do much better by them in the future than we have done in the past.

INNOVATION

Some of the schools that need renovation will probably not be ready for any innovations much before the year 2000. But many others are ready now, and some have already incorporated newer practices in their ongoing programs.[2] In fact, nothing here recommended has not been tried, and with at least as satisfactory an outcome as obtained under the old regime, and often with results that are much more gratifying.

One of the reasons that the efforts have not been even more successful is that the installation may not be a true example of what it is supposed to be, as has been found to be the case, for example, in some so-called non-graded schools. An innovation may not be properly set up or administered, or it is an intrusion rather than an intervention, and so it does not harmonize with the traditional procedures, but is rather hampered by them in its operation.

The chief innovations are to be found in grades and marks, teaching roles, methods and media, and educational objectives. At this point these items call for only brief elaboration.

Grades and Marks. The school grading and marking systems in current use have been emphasized because they are at the center of the domineering, punitive system of control which produces so many evil effects, and because, like the identical egg-crate classrooms, their necessity is largely taken for granted. The individualizing of instruction now possible has rendered a graded grouping system obsolete; and the distinction between normative and criterion scoring has done the same for the emotion-packed marking system. A mastery of the main-line continuity of the instructional program to be followed at the student's preferred rate would still permit a sampling of branch-line endeavors following the student's interests.

Teaching Roles. If the evils of grading and marking are eliminated, teaching roles change for the better. Instead of attempting the impossible task of keeping a heterogeneous group of people together, teachers will primarily employ the techniques in the practice of which they are most talented, whether explaining, coaching, or promoting discussion, and using the media that are most effective in instructing the students, each at his own level of development. Thought can be given to the prime task of determining specifically what words and actions to use in different situations. Just what might one *say* or *do* to invoke the desired responses? Haim Ginott[3] has recorded a number of useful expressions to help parents make their children more likely to emit desirable social behavior. The technological term *instructional strategies* can be taken seriously, and real improvements may be expected.

Explaining is familiar as the process of pointing, telling, presenting, showing how—the lecture or demonstration. The teacher may ask questions (which can be arranged for on TV) that are intended to clarify rather than confuse; and students are encouraged to ask questions, but these are misleading since they may or may not be typical of student difficulties. And who should answer the questions? If the students are called on, progress is slow because of the time consumed in making corrections. And yet this is the way they presumably will learn. If the teacher answers them, not all the students will understand the explanation. But some will, and they can amuse themselves while the teacher is going through the explanation again for the benefit of some of the others. Some, of course, never will get it. Surely improvements in this archaic procedure are possible. Perhaps programming will help.

Coaching is what is usually needed when one wishes to improve a skill. The coach observes a learner's performance and intervenes at appropriate times, listening in on the student's circuit in the language laboratory, suggesting a change in stance or movement on the field or track, and correcting written work. These are illustrations of coaching—monitoring in the broader use of the term—as are coaching athletic teams and directing dramatic and musical productions. It is perhaps the essence of teaching, and yet relatively little attention in the literature or in practice teaching is given to revealing to the future teacher what he can most advantageously *say* and *do* under different circumstances.

Discussing may be profitable or not. It may include teacher-pupil planning, but it may include much more. Aside from the group plans that may be made, discussions provide opportunities not only for students to test out their ideas among their peers, but also further to acquire a modicum of practice in the area of logical discourse, including a knowledge of the nature of myths, beliefs, assumptions, presuppositions, bias, evidence, and proof, and the more persistent logical fallacies. The bull-in-the-china-shop kind of behavior that recently became popular, featuring "non-negotiable demands," suggests that schools may have been neglectful of their responsibilities in this area of oral discourse.

Methods and Media. So much attention recently has been directed to the instructional media, both old and new, that the question of method has suffered relative neglect. Over the years enthusiasms for one or another method of teaching have waxed and waned. But Herbart's inductive method, lecture, questioning, recitation, and demonstration methods, the problem and project methods, and now the revived heuristic method are all still good if a teacher knows how and when to use them.

Educational Objectives. The final set of innovations have to do with the matter of educational objectives. What is done about them depends on the ideas of those in charge as to what the school is for, what its purposes are, i.e., on the objectives of instruction. It is said that when Columbus set out, he didn't know where he was going; when he got there, he didn't know where he was; and when he got back, he didn't know where he had been. This seems to describe equally well the situation in education. But we cannot count on such serendipity.

Programming has taught us the value of detailed behavioral objectives and has demonstrated ways in which they may be constructed so that students can know what they are supposed to know and be able to do. Psychologists can be expected to collaborate with teachers in drawing up behavioral criteria in the several school subjects in acquiring cognitive, motor, and social skills—the latter on the assumption that the new educational model has been substituted for the medical.

It is sometimes objected that while a collaboration of psychologists and teachers might work in cognitive and motor skills, social skills involving social attitudes seem to be in a different category. But even here, experiments providing reinforcement contingencies have been found to produce the behavior sought. It seems indicated that school psychologists will operate at two levels, and will continue with their present tasks. But it is not too much to expect them also to be the stimulators or catalyzers for desirable changes, whether renovative or innovative.

The time is short. A one-sided control is possible, either half-way, partially effective educational procedures, or some that may be efficient but educationally dubious, promoted by business and industrial combines on a contractual basis. I believe that psychologically trained educational technologists can and will unite their efforts with educational theorists and practitioners, and launch a task force that will actually do the renovating and innovating that need to be done in order to provide the kind of education to which our children and young people are entitled.

28.
In Summary –
Reform from Within

While it is generally agreed that present-day American education is remarkably good, it is still not good enough. Critics, both lay and professional, intuitive and empirical, have pointed out its many shortcomings, and have prescribed their favorite remedies. But most of the criticisms are based on an individual's value judgments of some one aspect of education, and hence the recommendations for reform are similarly biased. Even reform measures based on research studies follow the law of the single variable: compare resultant change in, say, student performance or attitude, with that found in what is considered to be the "regular" school program.

Thus, whether the reform involves programming, team teaching, television, modules, or computer assisted instruction, the results are often discouraging, since, as should have been expected, *all the other traditional environmental variables continue as before.* The innovation has little chance against their combined influence, especially since it may itself be operated none too expertly. We should waste no more time on this stupid procedure. What now seems obvious is the need for a change in the *total pattern* of instruction, so that each of the innovating variables will be operating in relation to the others. And to attain this end, reforms must be initiated and carried forward by persons inside the educational organization. To be workable, they must bear the professional stamp. There must be active cooperation between education professors, authorities in subject-matter fields, teachers and school administrators.

In advocating multi-variable innovation, I shall present a series of four postulates, followed by a series of six theses. At this stage, any elaboration of the postulates is unnecessary, though for the theses some clarification will be needed. If the postulates are accepted, the theses could well be incorporated as projects in one or more selected schools for trial runs. This should not be attempted, however, until careful plans are laid and the participants have undergone a period of instruction and special training. But first, the postulates:

POSTULATES FOR EDUCATIONAL REFORM

1. Teacher education is primarily professional and, secondarily, general or liberal.

2. As a professional enterprise, its function (or role) is to improve educational practices. This is done (through publications and in other ways) by improving (a) the preparation of teachers and other practitioners and (b) educational procedures in the schools.

3. At present, both functions are less effectively performed than they might be. The reason for this lies in such external conditions as social and technological change and in such internal factors as disinterest, tradition, formalization and multiplication of courses, and satisfaction with patchwork innovations.

4. A thoroughgoing educational reorganization is now needed. The form this organization should take is a matter of opinion. I support a coordinated multi-media approach as outlined in the following six theses, which I hereby tack on the doors of the Cathedral of Learning:

THESES FOR EDUCATIONAL REFORM

1. Specification by teachers of the performance objectives of whatever content they teach.

2. Skillful use of appropriate methods and media fitted into the development and utilization of modern educational technology.

3. Differentiation of instructional roles.

4. Adaptation of content and method to the individual differences of the students—physical, intellectual and cultural.

5. Modification of educational evaluation and student classification procedures.

6. Sequence and continuity in the instructional program.

Instruction *might* be improved if only one or two of these theses were followed, especially the first; but the operation of all six in a system is the minimum we should expect. Furthermore, they relate to programs of teacher training, as well as to instruction in the schools. We cannot continue to employ old-fashioned procedures in preparing teachers for the schools of today and tomorrow, nor can we fail to use our influence to help bring about the needed reforms. By way of clarification, some of the implications of the six theses are here indicated:

1. *Specification by teachers of the performance objectives of whatever content they teach.* On the surface, it seems reasonable that students should know what it is they will be expected to be able to do as a consequence of taking a course or "subject," and, further, that they be taught to do it. Yet this information is very difficult to obtain, in part because it is usually couched in terms of generalized values such as "to know," "to understand," or "to appreciate," or "the ability to" apply, generalize, deduce, and the like. Furthermore, examination items are kept secret, on the assumption that if the students know what it is they are expected to learn, they would indeed learn it.

Instead, the objectives should be specific and clearly stated, the directions being couched in such behavioral terms as discriminate, describe, demonstrate, construct, draw, list, etc.—always assuming that the students are to be *taught* to do these things, not merely to be *examined* on them. As in motor skills, they might be stated in temporal or spatial units or in the ability to handle progressively complex concepts and their relationships. The behavior expected is what serves as an indicator of the presence of the more generalized values. Naturally, other than cognitive goals are to be considered—attitudes, for example. The means employed to attain them can be carefully charted, and the evidence of their attainment sought.

2. *Skillful use of appropriate methods and media fitted into the development and utilization of modern educational technology.* It is no doubt an enlightening experience for a teacher to program a unit of instruction, or to bring in a motion picture film where none had been used before, or for a school to acquire a language laboratory or a TV

set, or hire a couple of teachers and call them a team. But this is not educational reform, which must be much more thoroughgoing. As a start, objectives must be established and hypotheses must be set up as to the best methods and media for the attainment of those objectives for different parts of each course in the curriculum. There is no need for three teachers, however, when one, or a videotape, will do the job. On the other hand, more should not be demanded of a medium than it can produce. Teachers need training in the selection of the most effective methods and media for different purposes and for their utilization.

3. *Differentiation of instructional roles.* One of the fruitless educational quests over the years has been for a description of "the good teacher" and "the poor teacher." Whether the description is couched in qualitative or behavioral terms, there are too many ways to be good or poor. Instead, it would be better to find where an individual teacher's talent lies, develop his skills there, and relieve him of responsibilities in areas where he is less successful. By tradition a teacher is a generalist, not a specialist, but some specialization has crept in, largely by way of self-selection, particularly in subject-matter departmentalization, and also in grade level; but more is needed.

As has often been pointed out, many of the routine and housekeeping tasks required of teachers can be performed just as well, or even better, by non-professional personnel. But in addition to this, of the three main teaching jobs—explaining, coaching and discussion— few teachers can do more than one well; yet all teachers are expected to do all three. *Explaining* is lecture-demonstration, which can often be done best on film or tape, since details can be carefully worked out and the voice can be supplemented by well-chosen displays. A teacher with this talent is a great improvement over the sad, but all too familiar, efforts of those without it to "explain things," motivate students, and arouse their interest. *Coaching* is monitoring, directing, improving the learners' skill in the performance of some task, and employing Skinner's principle of progressive approximation through pacing and reinforcement. *Discussing,* that is, leading discussion, may take the form of teacher-pupil planning, or may be an effective means for heuristic learning, instead of a technique for sharing ignorance. If successfully handled, it includes developing skill in debate, conference, and committee work, as well as some instruction in the logic of argument and its fallacies.

4. *Adaptation of instruction to individual differences—physical, intellectual and cultural.* Efforts to individualize instruction, of which the most effective were probably the Winnetka and Dalton plans, have never been particularly successful because of the lack of materials and adequate techniques. So, instead, children are still graded by chronological age or in other ways, and the consequent evils are taken for granted and even projected onto the pupils themselves. The situation looked hopeless, in part because of the changes in IQ, and in part because of the wide differences in educational opportunity. Now, with the discovery of the disadvantaged youth—especially of the inner city—the problem has become more acute. We are paying for our neglect of the concept of readiness, and frantic but sporadic efforts are being made to do what should have been done years ago, namely, to conduct diagnostic placement testing and to provide the kind of experiences, direct and other (pictorial, verbal, numerical), which are needed to attain the educational objectives sought.

Fortunately, films, videotapes and programmed instruction, with and without teaching machines, are now availabe to take care of special sectors of learning that do not call for group interaction or are not well adapted to group instruction. Their use, if made routine procedure, would eliminate many current difficulties.

5. *Modification of educational evaluation and of student classification procedures.* Present practice employs extremely coarse methods of screening in its grade-placement system, sometimes modifying it by different forms of grouping. As a consequence, one of the basic tenets of teaching has been disregarded, i.e., beginning instruction where the student is. Instead, the system of grade placement forces the child into a blind machine-like operation: the grade (or subject or course) a child is in, instead of the student's abilities and previously acquired competencies, determines what the school will try to teach him. The vague criteria for promotion, coupled with the marking system, has *got to go.* It is stupid and unjust to continue placing young people in situations where they are bound to fail on tasks to which they are thus arbitrarily assigned—or where they could acquire the required skills and abilities in half or three-quarters of the time assigned to them. Much of the undesirable and troublesome pupil behavior is the direct consequence of this malpractice.

There is no reason that children should not continue in the same homeroom for years, but only if they meet individually, or in groups or classes made up of those who are at the same level of development in a particular content area, with curriculum and assignments adapted to that level. The ungraded school must be developed to take the place of the present barbaric system of grading and marking. The changes can be brought about, however, only if sequential behavioral objectives are definitely specified, and students are marked not in comparison with what others do, so as to get a distribution, but according to the progress that each makes individually in attaining the sequential objectives, i.e., criterion-referenced rather than norm-referenced marking.

6. *Sequence and continuity in the instructional program.* The chopped-up instructional program likewise needs to be overhauled. The differentiated curriculum and the elective system succeeded in breaking the stranglehold of the rigid classical curriculum, but the present system of interchangeable parts, in which one credit (or credit hour) can be replaced by almost any other, carries things too far. It is an impressive monument to administrative convenience. A student may go on taking a pinch of this and a spoonful of that for a number of years, and then all that is needed to make him a graduate is an adding machine! For special job or promotion requirements, all he needs to do is to show that he has "had" so many credits of this or that, whether he knows anything about them or not.

Instead, some rational continuity of content in line with the specified educational objectives can and should be mapped out. (If desired, a distinction can be made between required *mastery* of certain necessary skills and abilities at different levels of proficiency and a sampling of content directed by the students' individual interests.) Thus, with criterion marking the student can see his own progress during a course or a year, and will be ready for the next that follows it sequentially.

The art of teaching is in about the same state as was the art of war in the 15th century, when the Roman legion had been supplemented by the English longbow, the cross bow and the innovative gunpowder. Educationally, we now have other instruments—the equivalent of the tank and the airplane—which we try out now and then, but we put our trust in the old weapons and an occasional cavalry charge!

It is high time in the war on ignorance that we throw out the archaic and the obsolete and train our soldiers—the teachers—in the use of modern equipment. And it is high time we banished the futile laissez-faire procedures of the past, using whatever instrument appeals to us in a succession of scattered raids. Instead, we must develop a coordinated attack on all fronts. The war on ignorance is no petty quarrel between rival principalities; it is a struggle for survival.

References

CHAPTER 2

1. Quoted by E.P. Cubberley. *Public Education in the United States,* p. 58.

2. From *New England's First Fruits.* London, 1643. Quoted by E.P. Cubberley in *Readings in History of Education,* p. 292.

3. From the admission requirements drawn up in 1745. Cited by E.P. Cubberley in *Public Education in the United States,* p. 30.

4. Thomas Jefferson. Notes on the State of Virginia, pp. 243-249. See E.P. Cubberley. *Readings in the History of Education,* pp. 427-428.

5. *The Works of the Late Dr. Benjamin Franklin.* New York: E. Dyekinck, 1807, pp. 266-267.

6. John Locke. *Some Thoughts Concerning Education.* Quoted by E.P. Cubberley. *Readings in the History of Education,* pp. 364-365.

7. Herbert Spencer. *Education: Intellectual, Moral, and Physical.* New York: D. Appleton and Co., 1859.

CHAPTER 3

1. Ernest Horn. "Language and Meaning." In *The Psychology of Learning.* 41st Yearbook of the National Society for the Study of Education, Part II, 1942, p. 392. Professor Horn cites other interesting illustrations of children's confusions.

2. From the Lewis and Clark journals, quoted by Ralph Gray. "Following the Trail of Lewis and Clark," *National Geographic Magazine,* June 1953, *301,* pp. 714, 731. Quoted by permission.

3. As told by Stephen Corey.

CHAPTER 4

1. Pleasant Roscoe Hightower. *Biblical Information in Relation to Character and Conduct.* University of Iowa Studies in Character, Vol. III, No. 2. Iowa City: University of Iowa, 1930.

2. Negley K. Teeters. "The Role of Religious Education in Delinquency and Crime," *The Arbitrator,* July-August 1943. Quoted in V.T. Thayer. *Religion in Public Education.* New York: Viking Press, 1947, pp. 109-110.

3. Hugh Hartshorne & Mark A. May. *Studies in Deceit.* Studies in the Nature of Character, I. New York: Macmillan Co., 1928, pp. 356-375, 240-241, 181-189.

4. Edward L. Thorndike. *Man and His Works.* Cambridge, Mass.: Harvard University Press, 1943, pp. 183-205.

5. Edward L. Thorndike. *Your City.* New York: Harcourt, Brace & Co., 1939, pp. 96-100.

6. John A. Bath. "A Study of Selected Participants and Non-participants in a Program Directed toward the Development of Initiative and Good Citizenship," *Journal of Experimental Education,* March 1948, *16,* pp. 161-175.

7. Hartshorne & May, *Loc. Cit.*

8. Hugh Hartshorne, Mark A. May & Frank K. Shuttleworth. *Studies in the Organization of Character.* Studies in the Nature of Character, III. New York: Macmillan Co., 1930.

9. Ernest R. Groves. "Let's Face the Problem of Cheating," *National Parent-Teacher,* October 1936, *31,* pp. 6-7, 24.

10. Jean W. MacFarlane. "The Relationship of Environmental Pressures to the Development of a Child Personality and Habit Patterns," *Journal of Pediatrics,* July 1939, *15,* pp. 142-154.

11. Jean D. Cummings. "The Incidence of Emotional Symptoms in School Children," *British Journal of Educational Psychology,* November 1944, *14* (3), pp. 151-161.

12. Vernon Jones. *Character and Citizenship Training in the Public School.* Chicago: University of Chicago Press, 1936.

13. Vernon Jones. "Child Development: XIII. Moral Concepts and Conduct," in Walter S. Monroe (Ed.) *Encyclopedia of Educational Research.* New York: Macmillan Co., 1941, pp. 168-171.

14. Hartshorne & May, *Loc. Cit.*

15. Ronald Lippitt. "An Experimental Study of the Effect of Democratic and Authoritarian Group Atmospheres," *Studies in Topological and Vector Psychology,* I, pp. 45-195. Studies in Child Welfare, Vol. SVI, No. 3. Iowa City: University of Iowa Press, 1940.

16. Hartshorne & May, *Loc. Cit.*

17. Lewis M. Terman. *Mental and Physical Traits of a Thousand Gifted Children.* Genetic Studies of Genius, Vol. I. Stanford, California: Stanford University Press, 1925, p. 638.

18. Cyril Burt. *The Young Delinquent.* New York: D. Appleton & Co., 1925.

19. William Healy & Augusta F. Bronner. *Delinquents and Criminals.* New York: Macmillan Co., 1926.

20. Willard C. Olson. *Child Development.* Boston: D.C. Heath & Co., 1949, pp. 233-238.

CHAPTER 5

1. Herbert Fiegel. "The Difference between Knowledge and Evaluation," *Journal of Social Issues,* 1950, *6* (4), pp. 39-44.

2. Wolfgang Köhler. *The Place of Value in a World of Facts.* New York: Liveright Publishing Corp., 1938; Clarence I. Lewis. *An Analysis of Knowledge and Valuation.* LaSalle: Open Court Publishing Co., 1946; "Symposium," in *Personality,* April 1950, pp.1-74.

3. John Dewey, "Theory of Valuation," *International Encyclopedia of Unified Science.* Chicago: University of Chicago Press, 1939, Vol. 2, 67 p. Also, see Lepley, *op. cit.*

4. George Geiger *et al.* "Values and Social Sciences," *Journal of Social Issues,* 1950, *6* (4), pp. 1-79.

5. Franz Alexander. "Values and Science," *Journal of Social Issues,* 1950, *6* (4), pp. 28-32.

6. Clyde Kluckhohn. *Mirror for Man.* New York: Whittelsy House, 1949.

7. E.L. Thorndike. *Selected Writings from a Connectionist's Psychology.* New York: Appleton-Century-Crofts, Inc., 1949, Chapter 21.

8. Educational Policies Commission. *Moral and Spiritual Values in the Public Schools.* Washington: National Education Association, 1951.

9. William Clark Trow. "The Public School a Scapegoat?" The University of Michigan School of Education *Bulletin,* November 23, 1951, pp. 17-22; "Professional Education and the Disciplines: an Open Letter to Professor Bestor," *Scientific Monthly,* March 1953, *76,* pp. 149-152.

10. Max Hutt & Daniel R. Miller. "Value Interiorization and Democratic Education," *Journal of Social Issues,* 1949, *5* (4), pp. 31-43; Daniel R. Miller & Max Hutt. "Value Interiorization and Personality Development," *Journal of Social Issues,* 1949, *5* (4), pp. 2-30.

11. National Education Association, Commission on the Reorganization of Secondary Education, *Cardinal Principles of Secondary Education.* Washington: Department of the Interior, Bureau of Education, Government Printing Office, No. 34, 1918.

12. Ray Lepley (Ed.) *Value: A Cooperative Inquiry.* New York: Columbia University Press, 1949.

13. Talcott Parsons & Edward A. Shils (Eds.) *Toward a General Theory of Action.* Cambridge: Harvard University Press, 1952.

14. Charles Morris. *Signs, Language, and Behavior.* New York: Prentice-Hall, 1946.

15. *Ibid.*

16. R.K. White. "Value Analysis: a Quantitative Method for Describing Qualitative Data," *Journal of Social Psychology,* 1944, *19,* pp. 351-358.

17. A. Bavelas. "A Method for Investigating Individual and Group Ideology," *Sociometry,* 1942, *5,* pp. 371-377.

18. C.L. Hull. "Moral Values, Behaviorism, and World Crisis," *Transactions of the*

New York Academy of Science, 1945, 7, pp. 90-94.

19. J.B. Maller & E.M. Glasser. *Interest Values Inventory.* New York: Bureau of Publications, Teachers College, Columbia University, 1939, 1943.

20. G.W. Allport & P.E. Vernon. "A Study for Personal Values," *Journal of Abnormal and Social Psychology,* 1931, *26,* pp. 231-248; and Gardner Lindzay (Ed.) *A Study of Values: Manual of Directions.* revised ed., Boston: Houghton Mifflin, 1931, 1960.

21. Eduard Spranger. *Types of Men: The Psychology and Ethics of Personality.* Halle: Max Niemeyer Verlag, 1928.

CHAPTER 6

1. Stanley Elam & William P. McLure (Eds.) *Educational Requirements for the 1970's.* Bloomington, Indiana: International Headquarters, Phi Delta Kappa, 1967.

CHAPTER 8

1. N.L. Gage. "An Analytical Approach to Research on Instructional Methods," *Phi Delta Kappan,* June 1968.

2. William Clark Trow. *Teacher and Technology—New Designs for Learning.* New York: Appleton-Century-Crofts, 1963; Also, "Teacher and Television," Chapter 21, this volume.

3. Robert Mager. *Preparing Objectives for Programmed Instruction.* San Francisco: Fearon Publishers, 1962; Benjamin S. Bloom *et al. Taxonomy of Educational Objectives—The Classification of Educational Goals. Handbook I: Cognitive Domain.* New York: Longmans, Green and Co., 1956; Wm. Clark Trow. "Behavioral Objectives in Education," *Educational Technology,* December 30, 1967.

4. William Clark Trow. "The Credentials Mill in a Technological Age," Chapter 14, and "Grades and Objectives in Higher Education," Chapter 19, this volume.

5. Benjamin S. Bloom. "Learning for Mastery," *Evaluation and Comment.* University of California at Los Angeles, Center for the Study of Evaluation of Instructional Programs, May 1968.

6. Robert Glaser. "Psychology and Educational Technology." *Educational Technology,* May 15, 1966; also, W. James Popham, Robert Glaser *et al. Criterion Referenced Measurement.* Englewood Cliffs, N.J.: Educational Technology Publications, 1971.

CHAPTER 9

1. J.D. Koerner. *The Miseducation of American Teachers.* Boston: Houghton-Mifflin, 1963.

2. James B. Conant. *The Education of American Teachers.* New York: McGraw-Hill, 1963.

3. J.V. Marani. A Symposium on James Bryant Conant's *The Education of American Teachers. Journal of Teacher Education,* 1964, pp. 15, 36.

4. G. Gallup. *The Miracle Ahead.* New York: Harper & Row, 1964.

5. Joseph W. Krutch. *Human Nature and the Human Condition.* New York: Random House, 1959.

6. Herbert Spencer. *Education: Intellectual, Moral, and Physical.* New York: D. Appleton & Co., 1861.

7. George S. Counts. *Dare the School Build a New Social Order?* New York: John Day, 1932.

CHAPTER 10

1. Stanley Elam. "The Age of Accountability Dawns in Texarkana," *Phi Delta Kappan,* June 1970, *51,* pp. 509-514. The story of one seemingly successful experiment reported in detail. Notes from others.

CHAPTER 11

1. Fred N. Kerlinger. "The Ed.D. and the Ph.D." *Teachers College Record,* February 1965, *66,* pp. 434-439.

2. James B. Conant. *The Education of American Teachers.* New York: Mc-Graw-Hill Book Company Inc., 1963.

3. Stanley Elam (Ed.) *Improving Teacher Education in the United States.* Bloomington, Indiana: International Headquarters, Phi Delta Kappa, 1967.

CHAPTER 12

1. B.T. Lee Calvin (Ed.) *Improving College Teaching.* Washington, D.C.: American Council of Education, 1967.

2. Robert F. Mager. *Preparing Objectives for Programmed Instruction.* San Francisco: Fearon Publishers, 1962; and Benjamin S. Bloom *et al. Taxonomy of Educational Objectives–The Classification of Educational Goals. Handbook I: Cognitive Domain.* New York: Longmans, Green and Co., 1956.

3. William Clark Trow. *Teacher and Technology–New Designs for Learning.* New York: Appleton-Century-Crofts, 1963; Robert Glaser (Ed.) *Teaching Machines and Programmed Learning II.* Washington, D.C.: Department of Audio-Visual Instruction, National Education Association, 1965.

CHAPTER 14

1. Robert F. Mager. *Preparing Objectives for Programmed Instruction.* San Francisco: Fearon Publishers, 1962.

2. Benjamin S. Bloom *et al. Taxonomy of Educational Objectives–The Classification of Educational Goals. Handbook I: Cognitive Domain.* New York: Longmans, Green and Co., 1956.

3. J.P. Guilford. "Three Faces of Intellect," *American Psychologist* 1959, *14,* pp. 469-479.

CHAPTER 15

1. Norburt Wiener. *Cybernetics.* Cambridge, Mass: The MIT Press, 1948; revised ed., New York: John Wiley and Sons, Inc., 1961.

2. Walter B. Cannon. *Bodily Changes in Pain, Hunger, Fear, and Rage.* New York: D. Appleton and Co., 1915, 1929.

3. B.F. Skinner. "Teaching Science in High School—What is Wrong?" *Science,* 1968, pp. 704-710. Quoted by Albert H. Yee. "Teacher Education: Rube Goldberg or Systems Management?" *Educational Technology,* September 1969, *9,* p. 39.

4. T. Antoinette Ryan. "Systems Techniques for Programs of Counseling and Counselor Education," *Educational Technology,* June 1969, *9,* pp. 7-8.

5. Stephen Yelon. "Toward the Application of Systems Analysis to Counselor Education," *Educational Technology,* March 1969, *9,* p. 55.

6. T. Antoinette Ryan. *op. cit.*

7. Robert M. Gagne (Ed.) *Psychological Principles in System Development.* New York: Holt, Rinehart & Winston, 1962.

8. William Clark Trow. *Teacher and Technology—New Designs for Learning.* New York: Appleton-Century-Crofts, 1963.

9. B.F. Skinner. "Reflections on a Decade of Teaching Machines." In Robert Glaser (Ed.) *Teaching Machines and Programmed Learning II: Data and Directions.* Department of Audio-Visual Instruction, The National Education Association, 1965, Chapter 1.

10. Susan M. Markle. *Good Frames and Bad—A Grammar of Frame Writing.* New York: John Wiley and Sons, Inc., 1964; and Phil C. Lange (Ed.) *Programmed Instruction.* The Sixty-sixth Yearbook of the National Society for the Study of Education, Part II. Chicago: The University of Chicago Press, 1967.

11. Susan M. Markle. "Empirical Testing of Programs." In Phil C. Lange (Ed.) *Programmed Instruction.* The Sixty-sixth Yearbook of the National Society for the Study of Education, Part II, Chicago: The University of Chicago Press, 1967, Chapter 5.

12. Robert F. Mager. *Preparing Objectives for Programmed Instruction.* San Francisco: Fearon Publishers, Inc., 1962; also, "Search for the Simple," *Illinois Journal of Education* (in press); the film, "Programming Is a Process," by Markle and Tiemann (Chicago: Office of Instructional Resources, University of Illinois at Chicago Circle, 1967) is enlightening as is the one by Mager and Rahmlow, "Goofing Off With Educational Objectives" (Mager Associates, 13245 Rhoda Drive, Los Altos Hills, California).

13. J. William Moore. "Instructional Design: After Behavioral Objectives What?" *Educational Technology,* September 1969, *9,* p. 45.

14. "Counseling Technology," *Educational Technology,* March 1969, *9.*

15. David Krathwohl *et al. Taxonomy of Educational Objectives. Handbook II: Affective Domain.* New York: David McKay, 1964.

16. Benjamin S. Bloom *et al. Taxonomy of Educational Objectives–The Classification of Educational Goals. Handbook I: Cognitive Domain.* New York: Longmans, Green and Co., 1956.

17. Francis Mechner. "Science Education and Behavioral Technology." In Robert Glaser (Ed.) *Teaching Machines and Programmed Learning II: Data and Directions.* Department of Audio-Visual Instruction. The National Education Association, 1965, p. 464; see also F. Mechner. "Behavioral Analysis and Instructional Sequencing." In Phil C. Lange (Ed.) The Sixty-sixth Yearbook of the National Society for the Study of Education, Part II, 1967, Chapter 4; and Robert Glaser (Ed.) *Training Research and Education.* Pittsburgh: University of Pittsburgh Press, 1962.

CHAPTER 16

1. Raymond Bernabei (Ed.) *Behavior Objectives, An Annotated Resource File.* Harrisburg, Pa.: Department of Public Instruction, 1969.

2. Robert F. Mager. *Preparing Instructional Objectives.* San Francisco: Fearon Publishers, 1961.

3. Benjamin S. Bloom *et al. Taxonomy of Educational Objectives–The Classification of Educational Goals. Handbook I: Cognitive Domain.* New York: Longmans, Green and Company, 1956.

4. David R. Krathwohl *et al. Taxonomy of Educational Objectives, Handbook II: The Affective Domain.* New York: David McKay Company, Inc. 1964.

5. C.M. Lindvall (Ed.) *Defining Educational Objectives.* Pittsburgh: University of Pittsburgh Press, 1964.

6. Robert M. Gagne. "The Analysis of Instructional Objectives for the Design of Instruction." In Robert Glaser (Ed.) *Teaching Machines and Programmed Learning,* Vol. II, Washington, D.C.: National Education Association, 1965.

CHAPTER 18

1. Robert Glaser. "Psychology and Educational Technology," *Educational Technology,* May 15, 1966, 6, pp. 1-14; Robert Glaser & Richard C. Cox.

"Criterion-Referenced Testing for Measurement of Educational Outcomes." In Robert A. Weisgerber (Ed.) *Instructional Process and Media Innovation.* Chicago: Rand McNally, 1968, pp. 545-550; Robert Glaser & Anthony J. Nitko. "Measurement in Learning and Instruction." In Robert L. Thorndike (Ed.) *Educational Measurement* (in press); see also mimeographed and other articles from the Learning Research and Development Center at the University of Pittsburgh and the Oakleaf Project by C.M. Lindvall, Richard Cox, Glenn T. Graham, and others. See also note 6, Chapter 8.

CHAPTER 21

1.   Eugene E. Haddan. *Evolving Instruction.* New York: The Macmillan Company, 1970.

2.   J.S. Bruner. *Toward a Theory of Instruction.* Cambridge, Mass.: Belknap Press of Harvard University Press, 1966.

CHAPTER 23

1.   Alfred S. Alschuler. "Humanistic Education," *Educational Technology Magazine,* May 1970, *10;* also, *Educational Opportunities Forum, New Directions in Psychological Education.* Albany, N.Y.: State Education Department, January 1970, entire issue.

2.   William Clark Trow. "An Area Study Social Studies Curriculum," *Social Education,* 1965, *29,* pp. 142-146.

CHAPTER 25

1.   W.C. Becker, C.H. Madsen, Jr., R. Arnold & D.R. Thomas. "The Contingent Use of Teacher Attention and Praise in Reducing Classroom Behavior Problems," *Journal of Special Education,* 1967, *1,* pp. 287-307; D.R. Thomas, W.C. Becker & M. Armstrong. "Production and Elimination of Disruptive Classroom Behavior by Systematically Varying Teacher's Behavior," *Journal of Applied Behavior Analysis,* 1968, *1,* pp. 35-45; G.R. Patterson. "An Application of Conditioning Techniques to the Control of a Hyperactive Child." In L. Ullman and L. Krasner (Eds.) *Case Studies in Behavior Modification.* New York: Holt, Rinehart and Winston, Inc., 1966, pp. 370-375.

CHAPTER 27

1. David M. Aspy. "Educational Psychology: Challenged or Challenging?" *Journal of Teacher Education,* Spring 1970, *21,* pp. 5-13; also, John C. Flanagan. "The Functions of Educational Psychologists," *Educational Psychologist,* February 1970, *7,* pp. 1, 9-10.

2. Berlie J. Fallon. *Fifty States Innovate to Improve Their Schools.* Bloomington, Indiana: International Headquarters of Phi Delta Kappa, 1967.

3. Haim Ginott. *Between Parent and Child.* New York: The Macmillan Co., 1965; and *Between Parent and Teenager.* New York: The Macmillan Co., 1969.